ITALIAN POLITICS

Previously published:
Italian Politics: The Return of Politics, edited by David Hine and Salvatore Vassallo

ITALIAN POLITICS
The Faltering Transition

Edited by
Mark Gilbert and Gianfranco Pasquino

A Publication of the Istituto Cattaneo

Berghahn Books
New York • Oxford

Italian Politics: A Review, Volume 15

First published in 2000 by
Berghahn Books

Editorial Offices:
604 West 115th Street, New York, NY 10025 USA,
3, NewTec Place, Magdalen Road, Oxford OX4 1RE, UK
www.berghahnbooks.com

© 2000 Berghahn Books

ISBN 1-57181-840-5 (hardback)
ISSN 1086-4946

CONTENTS

Acronyms of political parties   vii

Glossary of other acronyms and terms used in the text   ix

Chronology of Italian Political Events, 1999   1

1.   Introduction: The Faltering Transition   21
   Mark Gilbert and Gianfranco Pasquino

2.   Forced Ally? Italy and 'Operation Allied Force'   33
   Osvaldo Croci

3.   The End of Italy's Referendum Anomaly?   51
   Mark Donovan

4.   The Municipal Elections of 1999 and the 'Defeat' of the   67
   Left in Bologna
   Gianfranco Baldini and Guido Legnante

5.   The 1999 Elections to the European Parliament   87
   Philip Daniels

6.   The Election of Carlo Azeglio Ciampi to the Presidency   107
   of the Republic
   Gianfranco Pasquino

7.   History in the Courts: Andreotti's Two Acquittals   123
   Jean-Louis Briquet

8.   The Funding of Political Parties and Control of the Media: 139
   Another Italian Anomaly
   Véronique Pujas

9.   Transformations in Italian Capitalism: an Analysis of   153
     Olivetti's Takeover of Telecom Italia
     Dwayne Woods

10. Italy's December 1998 'Social Pact for Development and   169
     Employment': Towards a New Political Economy for a
     'Normal Country'?
     Michael Contarino

11. The New South in the New Europe: the Case of   185
     Sviluppo Italia
     Vincent Della Sala

Documentary Appendix   203
Compiled by Davide Martelli

About the Editors and Contributors   270

Index   272

Acronyms of political parties used in the text

Listed below are the main acronyms used in this text. The extreme fluidity of the Italian party system in the 1990s makes it difficult to provide an up-to-date list of acronyms. Some labels have been used only in some areas, and for some elections.

AN	Alleanza nazionale
CCD	Centro cristiano democratico
CDL	Cristiani democratici per le libertà
CDR	Centro democratico per la repubblica
CDU	Cristiani Democratici Uniti
DC	Democrazia cristiana
DS	Democratici di sinistra
FI	Forza italia
LN	Lega nord
MS-FT	Movimento sociale - fiamma tricolore
MSI	Movimento sociale italiano
PCI	Partito comunista italiano
PDCI	Partito dei comunisti italiani
PDS	Partito democratico della sinistra
PLI	Partito liberale italiano
PPE	Partito popolare europeo
PPI	Partito popolare italiano
PR	Partito radicale
PRC or RC	Partito della rifondazione comunista; Rifondazione comunista

PRI	Partito repubblicano italiano
PS	Partito socialista
PSDI	Partito socialista democratico italiano
PSI	Partito socialista italiano
RI	Rinnovamento italiano-Lista Dini
SDI	Socialisti democratici italiani
SI	Socialisti italiani
SVP	Südtiroler Volkspartei
UDR	Unione democratica per la Repubblica
UDEUR	Unione dei democratici europei
UPE	Unione popolare europea

Glossary of other acronyms and terms used in the text

For the help of students and non-specialists, this brief list is intended to give short definitions in English of certain technical acronyms, words and abbreviations used in the text.

ACLI	Catholic workers' association.
Bicamerale	A joint committee on constitutional reform of the two chambers of parliament
CGIL	General Confederation of Italian Workers (ex-communist trade union)
CISL	Italian Confederation of Labour Unions (Catholic trade union)
CIPE	Interministerial committee for economic planning
CNEL	Constitutional council for the economy and labour
Comunione e liberazione	an evangelical organisation of young Catholics
Confindustria	The national association of industrialists
Consob	The stock exchange watchdog
Dpef	Annual White Paper on public finances
DPSC	Treasury department specialising in development policy
ENEL	A recently privatised electricity company
ENI	A formerly state-owned oil company
FINAGRA	Merchant bank specialising in agricultural investment
IG	Young Entrepreneurs' association

INSUD	A promotional agency for southern business initiatives
IPI	Institute for the promotion of industry
IRI	The holding company managing the nationalised industries
IRPEF	A form of income tax
ISTAT	The national statistical agency
Pentiti	Informants collaborating with the judicial authorities
Polo delle libertà	The right-wing coalition based upon FI and AN (Liberty Pole)
Quirinale	the presidential palace
RAI	The national broadcasting service
RIBS	An agency specialising in investment in the agriculture sector
Scala mobile	index-linked pay agreement
Sviluppo Italia	The Italian Development Agency
SPI	Agency specialising in the development and promotion of entrepreneurship
STET	The pre-privatisation name of Telecom Italia
Tangentopoli	The corruption scandal in the early 1990s
TIM	Telecom Italia's mobile phone division
Trifoglio (Clover leaf)	a coalition of parties briefly headed in 1999 by former President Cossiga
UIL	Union of Italian Workers (The 'lay' trade union)
Ulivo (Olive Tree coalition)	The centre-left coalition launched by Romano Prodi in 1996

The Istituto Cattaneo's Internet Site

http://www.cattaneo.org

At this web address one may visit the Istituto Cattaneo's Internet site. It consists of many pages, two of which deserve special attention:

Archives

In this page the Istituto Cattaneo provides free access to documentary archives regarding various characteristics of the Italian social and political system: a chronology of the main political and social events from 1990; book reviews of studies and empirical research published over the last three years; background data on Italian society; election results; party membership (since 1945); government and institutional posts of the republican era.

Data

Through this web page citizen and the scientific community may access data which reflect the Istituto Cattaneo's statutory pledge to promote empirical knowledge on Italian society. The data are located in two distinct archives which are periodically updated: the first contains detailed Italian election results (ADELE: "Archivo dati elettorali"), the second offers sample survey data (DICA: 'Dati inchieste campionarie").

The "Archivio dati elettorali" (ADELE) contains data concerning the national elections for the Chamber of Deputies from 1948 to 1966; the data is organized at the municipal level (over 8000 ecological units). For each national election (1948, 1953, 1958, 1963, 1968, 1972, 1976, 1979, 1983, 1987, 1992, 1994, and 1996) one may access the number of those having the right to vote, actual voters, valid votes and party list votes. The archive also contains the results of the elections held June 2nd, 1946, which gave birth to the Italian Republic (institutional referendum and election of the Constitutional Assembly).

The "Dati inchieste campionarie" (DICA) archive currently offers data regarding two major research programs: itanes (Italian National Election Studies: 1990–1996); political participation and social situation in Bologna (1984–1994). The user who accesses this archive can engage in interactive statistical analysis of the results of any single survey, generating, for example, frequency distributions, contingency tables, and selected statistics.

CHRONOLOGY OF ITALIAN POLITICAL EVENTS, 1999

January

2 Italy greets the launching of the Euro with satisfaction. The presidential message is interpreted as announcing Scalfaro's candidature for a second term.

3 Cossiga fields Amato as a candidate to run against Prodi for the presidency of the European Commission.

4 The Euro takes off, the Milan stock exchange is bullish. In 1998 the public sector borrowing requirement was 6,000 billion lire.

5 The Euro falters. D'Alema announces that the government will propose Prodi as a candidate for the presidency of the European Commission.

6 Discussion begins on a bill presented by Amato to introduce a dual ballot electoral system. Prodi declares his unwillingness to exchange leadership of the Ulivo (Olive Tree Coalition) for the presidency of the EU.

8 The first post-communist Prime Minister visits the Pope in the Vatican. The centre-left reaches a 'shared orientation' on the electoral reform bill, which Amato will now propose to the *Polo delle libertà* (Liberty Pole). Satisfaction expressed by the Greens and the PPI; the DS is doubtful.

9 Cossiga announces that he will support Prodi as an 'independent' candidate for the presidency of the European Commission if he abandons the 'carrion' of the Olive Tree, and he proposes Marini as a candidate for the presidency of the Republic if he

remains 'immaculate', i.e., untainted by the Ulivo. A wave of petty crime hits Milan and Naples.

11 During his Monday press conference, the Prime Minister declares that a great deal has already been done to combat crime and reassures all present.

13 Prodi announces that he will field a list for the European elections together with Di Pietro's 'Italy of Values' movement and the 'Hundred Cities' mayors, amid the indignation of the PPI and the criticisms of the DS.

15 The leadership of the PPI is unable to sort out its tangled relations with Prodi and rejects any alliance with Di Pietro.

16 The mayors ask the Constitutional Court to declare the electoral referendum inadmissible. In Milan, tens of thousands of people led by the Liberty Pole demonstrate against crime. After two months in Italy as an unwelcome guest, the Kurdish leader Ocalan leaves the country.

19 The Constitutional Court declares the electoral referendum admissible. A meeting of the members of the Olive Tree coalition reaffirms the validity of the arrangement. Cossiga threatens to withdraw the UDR ministers from the government.

20 After frenetic consultations, the UDR ministers stay in the D'Alema government, but Cossiga announces his resignation as chairman of the party.

21 Prodi and Marini clash during a televised debate on the future of the Ulivo.

22 Veltroni urges Prodi not to present a list jointly with Di Pietro and the mayors for the European elections.

24 Prodi announces that he cannot 'miss a round' and that the Olive Tree's project for a majoritarian and bipolar democracy requires continuity of political action.

26 During a speech at Bocconi University, D'Alema calls for greater flexibility in work organisation, provoking strong criticisms from unions and parties.

27 D'Alema explains that flexibility means job creation not job losses and invites employers to invest their profits. The debate on Amato's proposal for electoral reform resumes.

28 The Chamber votes on a fast-track procedure for yet another law on funding the political parties.The AN, Forza Italia and Di Pietro's 'Italy of Values' movement vote against the proposal.

29 A rattled D'Alema and Prodi squabble over the paternity of the Ulivo. The split between Prodi and Marini widens.

30 Favour comes out in favour of work flexibility and political stability. Cofferati reiterates that the 'workers' rights are not for sale'.

31 Veltroni offers a olive branch to Prodi and to the 'Hundred Cities' mayors: they are not, he says, enemies. Casini proposes a technocrat Liberty Pole candidate for prime minister, instead of Berlusconi.

February

1 Amato is severely critical of the splits within the Ulivo, talking of a 'hundred irons in the fire'. His name continues to circulate as a possible candidate for the presidency of the European Commission and also of the Republic.

2 Veltroni proposes a single list ranging from the UDR to the PDCI for the administrative elections. The response is cool.

3 During stormy exchanges in the Chamber on artificial insemination, the Catholic parties are supported by AN and, to a large extent, by Forza Italia.
The European Commission announces that Italy's public accounts are unsatisfactory. D'Alema says that he has no intention of introducing a mini-budget.

5 Prodi launches the *Democratici per l' Ulivo* (Democrats) list for the European elections jointly with Di Pietro and the 'Hundred Cities' mayors, provoking consternation and criticism from the PPI and Veltroni. Cossiga once again proposes Amato for presidency of the European Commission.

6 Prodi replies to his critics that 'competition is competition'. Veltroni floats the idea that the Olive Tree coalition should hold primaries to select its candidate for prime minister.

8 Europe announces that Italy's accounts pass muster but asks for more rapid privatisation and reform of the pensions system.

9 The government issues a further amnesty for 250,000 immigrants.

12 The parliamentary majority reaches agreement on a proposal for electoral reform – a dual-ballot constituency system with limited proportional representation – followed by an unusual statement of personal support from the Prime Minister. The proposal will later become a government bill.

13 The Prodi group, the Di Pietro group and the 'Hundred Cities' mayors press ahead with the merger of their respective movements. In Milan, the trade unions organise a street demonstration calling for tolerance towards immigrants.

15 The chairman of the regional council of Emilia-Romagna, Antonio La Forgia, resigns his post and leaves the DS to join Prodi's Democrats. Conflict erupts over the Amato-D'Alema proposal

for electoral reform. An institutional log-jam is feared: electoral referendum, presidential election, European and administrative elections. There is talk of an early end to Scalfaro's mandate and of D'Alema's candidature for the presidency.

17 Berlusconi announces obstructionism against Amato's electoral proposal. D'Alema says that Prodi's movement is a 'hangover from the First Republic'.

18 Cossiga leaves the UDR and joins the mixed group in the Senate. Marini repeats that he does not want to die a Social Democrat.

19 The Council of Ministers schedules the electoral referendum for 18 April. D'Alema accuses Prodi of creating a 'taxi-party'. Olivetti launches a 100,000 billion takeover bid for Telecom Italia.

20 The 'Italy of Values' joins Prodi's movement, of which Di Pietro recognises Prodi as leader.

22 Consob, the financial market-place watchdog, declares that Olivetti's takeover bid for Telecom is technically 'inadmissible'.

23 The president of Confindustria asks the government to remain neutral between Telecom and Olivetti. Pressure is applied to Prodi to withdraw as a candidate for presidency of the European Commission. D'Alema proposes him once again, but Spanish premier Aznar reacts coolly.

24 The UDR splits after a clash between chairman Buttiglione and secretary Mastella. The Chamber votes in favour of surrogate motherhood, provoking a violent editorial in the *Osservatore Romano*.

25 Bernabé, the managing director of Telecom, goes on the counter-attack. The chairman of Consob, Spaventa, calls on D'Alema in Palazzo Chigi. The results of a public opinion poll suggest that the electoral referendum will not achieve a quorum.

26 The PPI decide to campaign on their own for the European elections.

26 The Democrats choose a prancing donkey as their symbol. Consob gives the go-ahead for Olivetti's takeover bid for Telecom.

28 D'Alema suggests that Scalfaro should remain in office for two further years, until the reforms have been completed.

March

1 Reactions to D'Alema's proposal are hostile; even among the PPI, who want Scalfaro to serve a full term. Boselli's attempt to rehabilitate Craxi at the Congress of the European Socialist Parties fails utterly. Prodi's candidacy for the presidency of the

European Commission forges ahead, and it is now also supported by the British prime minister, Tony Blair.

3 Amato relaunches federalism. Prodi speaks out in the Chamber against the public funding of parties and sues the PPI to obtain his share of their electoral reimbursement.

4 Fierce clashes erupt in the Chamber between the centre-right and centre-left on party funding. Achille Occhetto with the Ulivo and a number of members of the PPI set up the 'Associazione 14 giugno' to reorganise the centre-left. Veltroni declares that there is no need for any more 'wreckers'. There is angry reaction to the sentence by the American court martial acquitting the pilot allegedly responsible for the Cermis tragedy.

5 Fazio sounds the alarm over Italy's public accounts, but Ciampi contradicts him. The Radicals begin their assembly 'for the liberal revolution and the United States of Europe'. A committee proposes Emma Bonino as a candidate for the Quirinale.

6 Emma Bonino agrees to be a candidate for the presidency of the Republic, to the surprise of the parties, which propose alternative candidates.

8 The government, the employers and the trade unions clash over the state of (non-) implementation of the 'Social Pact'.

9 The government relaunches the idea of federalism and announces a constitutional change to restore parity of representation between the sexes. The Palermo prosecutors' office asks the Chamber for authorisation to arrest the Forza Italia deputy Marcello Dell'Utri, who is already on trial, for tampering with evidence.

11 The law on electoral reimbursements is approved by the Chamber on its first reading. D'Alema delivers a scathing attack on Prodi's party, accusing it of being devoid of European roots.

12 Veltroni lists the seven features of his ideal presidential candidate: Carlo Azeglio Ciampi.

13 The delegates at the Greens' Congress decide that they will remain in the government coalition as long as they can, assessing their position after the European elections. Scalfaro announces his willingness to step down before the end of his mandate. The under-secretary Giarda rules out the possibility of an emergency financial manoeuvre.

14 Scalfaro's announcement of his early resignation is applauded. The PPI criticise Veltroni for proposing Ciampi as a candidate without prior consultation. Manconi is re-elected spokesperson for the Greens.

16 The parties, except for the PRC and the Greens, welcome Scalfaro's early resignation. Prodi's chances of appointment as

president of the European Commission improve. Berlusconi attacks the left and the magistrates.

17 Francesco Saverio Borrelli is appointed general prosecutor of Milan and leaves the *Mani Pulite* team.

18 Bertinotti opens the PRC congress.

19 D'Alema asks the industrialists not to lose faith. Prodi says that he is available for the presidency of the European Commission if the appointment is 'not temporary, not provisional, not conditioned'.

21 On his re-election as secretary of the PRC, Bertinotti threatens to precipitate a political crisis if the government does not oppose NATO's intervention in Kosovo. The Italian banking system tries to reorganise itself with a proposed merger between Unicredit and Comit and between San Paolo-Imi and Banca di Roma.

24 The European Council of Ministers appoints Prodi to the presidency of the European Commission. NATO begins its attacks on Milosevic's Serbia.

25 To the consternation of Italy's allies, D'Alema asks NATO to halt its action in Serbia and calls for a 'return to politics'.

26 With some dissent in the majority coalition, the Chamber and the Senate approve a government motion that 'immediate negotiations' should be held with Milosevic. Scalfaro announces that he may not step down early.

27 Demonstrations against NATO and against the government, with an attempted assault by demonstrators on the DS headquarters. A convention is held to launch Prodi's Democrats in Europe.

28 Marini declares that the PPI has both the right man and the right woman for the Quirinale.

29 The committee campaigning for a 'no' vote in the electoral referendum suggests that abstention, too, is a form of voting.

30 Caselli announces that he will leave the Palermo prosecutors' office on conclusion of the Andreotti trial. During a televised address D'Alema reaffirms Italy's support for NATO's action against Serbia.

April

1 The Italian Communists and the Greens urge the government to halt the NATO bombing of Serbia during Easter. Cossutta threatens that his ministers will resign. A split opens up in the ranks of the DS. The committee for a 'yes' vote in the referendum announces that it will step up its campaign.

3 The Italian Communists and the Greens decide to stay in the government coalition in order to 'maintain vigilance'.

6 Bossi invites voters not to turn out for the electoral referendum.

7 The bickering continues, and the Greens and the Italian Communists continue to keep their distance from the government. Cossutta finally goes to Moscow.

8 In Palermo, the prosecutors ask for a fifteen-year prison sentence to be passed on Andreotti. The Consent to Prosecute Committee of the Chamber of Deputies saves Dell'Utri, with the deciding vote being cast by the PPI. Berlusconi refrains from taking a position on the electoral referendum.

9 Cossutta has a two-hour meeting with Milosevic, who concedes nothing. Berlusconi abandons the committee for the 'yes' vote in the referendum. Dini outlines his own foreign policy to flank that of the government.

10 The assembly of the Telecom shareholders convened to decide on Olivetti's takeover bid fails to reach a quorum. The Radicals announce that they will promote twenty new referendums.

13 Prodi announces to the European Parliament that he will not be a candidate in the European elections.

15 Prodi declares that anyone who votes 'no' in the electoral referendum is not part of the Ulivo.

17 Rumours spread of a deal between Telecom and Deutsche Telekom. The Italian government appears to be in favour.

18 The electoral referendum fails to achieve a quorum by fewer than 200,000 votes. Only 49.6 percent of voters turn out at the polls.

19 D'Alema delivers a fierce attack on Senator Di Pietro. The proportionalist campaign regains its impetus. Marini backs Scalfaro for the presidency.

20 Wrangling over the Quirinale continues. Veltroni is ready to support Scalfaro's re-election; Marini declares that his candidate is Mancino. Fini distances himself from Berlusconi.

21 Veltroni is opposed to any inclusion of Berlusconi in the government coalition, as suggested by Marini. The government gives a cautious go-ahead for the Telecom-Deutsche Telekom deal.

22 Prodi refuses to let the PPI and the DS use the Ulivo symbol for the European elections. AN opts for shared lists with Segni's movement for the European elections. 170 parliamentarians belonging to the majority parties declare their opposition to any land invasion of Serbia.

24 Prodi asks the Ulivo for a joint effort in Italy and Europe, but reactions are hostile, especially from the PPI.

26 The lists standing for the European elections present their symbols; none of them is the Ulivo symbol.

28 Veltroni rejects the Polo's request for a shortlist of names for the Quirinale and asks the centre-left to agree on just one candidate.

29 The Euro falls to its lowest-ever level. Business booms on Wall Street.
30 The Perugia prosecutor asks for Andreotti to be given a life sentence for his supposed role in commissioning the Pecorelli murder.

May

 2 The Pope blesses Andreotti at a mass held for Padre Pio.
 3 Cossiga declares that the PPI 'do not have enough line to spin themselves, but enough to tangle everyone else's'.
 4 Minister Piazza and under-secretary Bassanini fall out over reorganisation of the ministries and the public administration.
 5 Prodi duly receives the European Parliament's vote of approval but with less support than expected.
 7 The Polo calls for a single-term bipolarist president not hostile to presidentialism.
10 A row breaks out between Marini, who proposes Rosa Russo Jervolino for the Quirinale, and Veltroni, who supports Ciampi and declares that Amato does not represent the left.
12 After mediation by Amato, the Polo announces that it will vote for Ciampi as President of the Republic right from the first ballot.
13 Treasury Minister Carlo Azeglio Ciampi is elected President of the Republic on the first ballot. Satisfaction is expressed by the press and by the parties, with the exception of the PPI. Giuliano Amato takes Ciampi's place at the Treasury.
14 The Greens, the PPI and a part of the DS once again call for a halt to the NATO bombing of Serbia.
15 Scalfaro resigns in advance to allow the rapid investiture of Ciampi. D'Alema and Prodi quarrel.
18 The Court of Cassation suspends ratification of the annulment of the electoral referendum. Ciampi declares 'I shall be everyone's guarantor'.
19 Massimo D'Antona, former under-secretary and adviser to Bassolino, is murdered in Milan by self-styled Red Brigade terrorists. The controversial bill on party financing is approved by the Senate.
20 The Red Brigades claim responsibility for D'Antona's murder.
21 Bertinotti states that some parts of the Red Brigade document 'can be subscribed to'.
22 Olivetti succeeds in its takeover bid for Telecom, acquiring a 51 percent shareholding. D'Alema declares that the Red Brigades are nothing but murderers.
23 The UDEUR party is founded, with Mastella as its secretary and Irene Pivetti as president.

24 Andreatta launches a fierce attack on Marini. Ecofin asks Italy to stick to the target of a 2 percent deficit/GDP ratio.

25 Amato persuades Ecofin that the deficit should stay at 2.4 percent of GDP. Ciampi meets leading representatives of the institutions and the parties to discuss reforms. The Telecom board of directors resigns.

27 Fossa praises the work of the government.

30 Marini calls for a reassessment of the government after the European elections and Boselli supports him.

31 The Governor of the Bank of Italy asks for reduced spending on health and pensions, a relaunching of investments, more reforms and fewer taxes. D'Alema predicts a long period of stability and good results for his government. Berlusconi and Fini clash once again on the Polo's strategy and leadership.

June

1 Italy's public accounts improve, with the deficit reduced by 10,700 billion lire. D'Alema marks out the route for reform: federalism, a new form of government, and an electoral law through article 138 of the Constitution.

4 Berlusconi claims that the centre-left has fallen apart; according to Veltroni, the Polo is racked by internal divisions.

5 Berlusconi and Fini declare that D'Alema has the political and moral duty to resign if the European elections show that the centre-left is losing ground.

6 Government review, reshuffle and/or crisis are all still on the agenda for after the European elections.

8 Berlusconi argues that D'Alema has the political and moral duty to resign if the centre-left does not gain 40 percent of votes in the European elections.

9 D'Alema says that he does not believe that the country wants to 'send him packing'.

10 Prodi and D'Alema argue over the single party of reformists: should it side with either the European socialists or under a new and different roof?

11 Veltroni declares that he wants to refound the Ulivo and relaunch reformism. Tension between Berlusconi, who accuses Segni of talking nonsense, and Fini, who rejects any sort of a neo-consociational deal with the left.

13 Forza Italia receives the most votes in the European elections; things go badly for Fini and Segni, and indifferently for the

Democrats of the Left. The Bonino List manages to do better than Prodi's Democrats.

14 Buoyed up by his three million preference votes, Berlusconi calls on the government to resign. D'Alema replies that the centre-left garnered more than 40 percent of the votes. Marini, Manconi and Bossi announce their resignations. Emma Bonino offers her votes to anyone willing to commit themselves to the 'liberal revolution'.

15 The centre-left outstrips the Polo in the municipal and provincial elections. Bologna goes to a second ballot.

16 At a tense meeting of the AN's leadership, Fini offers his resignation.

17 Fini launches a referendum campaign – 650,000 signatures against the proportional quota and the public funding of parties – and puts his resignation on hold.

18 Emma Bonino gives Prodi seven days to decide on her reappointment to the European Commission.

19 Pannella calls for Prodi's resignation as designated President of the Commission, because the majority has changed in the European Parliament.

20 Elected by a landslide vote to leadership of the LN, Bossi abandons secession and declares himself willing to cut a deal with the Polo.

21 Bassolino returns to his post as mayor of Naples. Cesare Salvi is appointed Minister of Labour and Antonio Maccanico Minister of Institutional Reforms. D'Alema denounces neo-centrism and the proportionalist drift and announces that he will ask for a parliamentary debate on his government. A statement by Prodi on Italian inflation drives the Euro down.

22 According to Veltroni, the true emergency facing the country is reform of the electoral law. The president of the Anti-Mafia Commission, Del Turco, criticises the use of *pentiti* and the anti-mafia judges.

23 D'Alema (and Amato) who want to reform the pensions system clash with the unions, which are opposed.

24 Veltroni defends the unions. Emma Bonino turns down a UNO appointment in Kosovo and gives Prodi seven days to reappoint her to the European Commission.

25 D'Alema claims that his government is genuinely 'of the left'.

28 The Polo wins the majority of the municipal elections, as well as the elections for mayor in Padua and Arezzo, and for the presidency of the provincial council of Milan. For the first time since the war, the left loses Bologna, where the municipal election is won by Giorgio Guazzaloca, with the support of the Polo. Berlusconi declares that the D'Alema government is 'illegitimate,

losing and in the minority'. Veltroni argues that reform of the pensions system should be agreed with the unions.

29 The DS assert their independence from the D'Alema government. The government scales down the contents of the Dpef (the financial and economic programme). Amato vetoes Emma Bonino's candidature for the European Commission.

30 The Dpef does not set out reforms. Berlusconi declares his candidature for prime minister and attacks the 'dwarves of politics'.

July

1 Cofferati rejects the Dpef, but D'Alema declares that he will not backtrack.

2 Prodi and D'Alema confirm Mario Monti's appointment to the European Commission. Emma Bonino and Marco Pannella stage noisy 'anti-partitocracy' protests, inviting Confindustria to support their 'liberal' referendums.

3 Mauro Zani is elected temporary secretary of the Bologna Democrats of the Left and is given the task of reorganising the party before the congress in November. Amid heated exchanges, Manconi confirms his resignation as spokesperson for the Greens.

4 Martinazzoli proposes that the PPI in the north should wind themselves up and start again from scratch. Monti suggests a pensions pact to D'Alema.

6 D'Alema reaffirms the social and institutional reforms, the coalition, and the government in the Chamber. The Polo is sceptical of the effectiveness of a divided majority.

8 Fazio calls for action on pensions with a view to reducing the tax burden. Visco argues that combating tax evasion only redistributes the tax burden. Ciampi advocates federalism on an official visit to Venetia.

9 The director general of Confindustria, Innocenzo Cipolletta, says that the government can reform the pensions system without the consent of the unions. Under-secretary Laura Pennacchi resigns after falling out with Treasury Minister Amato. With a polemical speech devoid of self-criticism, secretary of the PPI Franco Marini resigns.

10 Minister of Transport Treu serves a back-to-work injunction on striking railway and airline workers, provoking criticism from CISL and UIL.

11 The national council of the PPI freezes Marini's resignation and convenes the party congress for mid-September. FIAT celebrates its two hundredth birthday.

12 European commissioner Mario Monti and the International Monetary Fund insist that Italy's pensions system must be reformed.

14 The Chamber allows the Palermo court to use recordings of telephone conversations between deputy Dell'Utri and a mafia *pentito*. Ciampi insists on the institutional reforms and D'Alema calls for reform of the pensions system. CISL and CGIL clash over regulation of strikes in the transport sector. ISTAT calculates that two and a half million Italian families live below the poverty line.

15 Relations between D'Alema and Prodi thaw, while Veltroni and Parisi hold a four-hour meeting to reach agreement on ensuring that the government lasts until the end of the legislature.

18 Treasury Minister Amato criticises the unions for their social conservatism.

20 After days of tension, an agreement on the 'single judge' is reached, thereby saving the trials in progress. Cofferati again rejects any proposal to reform the pensions system, postponing discussion until the review forseen by law in 2001.

21 President of the Republic Ciampi meets the secretaries of CGIL, CISL and UIL to relaunch concertation. The Prime Minister makes an appearance on the Maurizio Costanzo televison show to reiterate that the pensions system must be reformed.

22 The proposal by Interior Minister Jervolino that conscript soldiers should be used to guard criminals under house arrest is rejected.

24 Buttiglione's CDU, with the exception of minister Folloni, leaves the majority coalition and declares that it intends to 'remake the DC'. The Greens fail to elect a new spokesperson.

25 Brawling breaks out at the LN's congress. Bossi half-heartedly relaunches secession by Padania and expels Comino for his 'treason' in talking to the Polo.

27 D'Alema meets the senators belonging to the ex Ulivo group.

28 The Radicals' three 'referendum days' begin. D'Alema declares that the referendum is a 'worn-out instrument'. Amato threatens to resign if the welfare system is not reformed.

29 A meeting between D'Alema and representatives of the Democrats establishes a state of semi-appeasement between them.

30 Bossi changes the LN's name to *Forza Nord*. Grazia Francescato agrees to lead the Greens until their assembly in the autumn. The centre-left attempts to push through a bill prohibiting party political commercials on television during the last thirty days of electoral campaigns.

31 Treasury Minister Amato and Labour Minister Salvi strongly disagree on reforming the welfare system. There are stormy exchanges at the Radical Congress between party president Bruno

Zevi, who is opposed to the Radicals joining a European parliamentary group that includes Le Pen's Euro-deputies, and Emma Bonino and Marco Pannella, who are in favour of the move.

August

1 Pannella closes the Radical Congress with the declaration: 'Never with the right'. Comino and Gnutti set about organising the *Lega* dissidents.
2 Berlusconi, citing polls on support for FI, clashes with Pannella, who criticises his political line. The tax yield increases and the public accounts improve, with a record surplus in July of 35,400 billion lire.
3 Dini, Mastella, Cossiga and the PPI announce that they will set up a united centre grouping in September. The Democrats are sceptical.
4 The government passes the bill prohibiting party political commercials during the last thirty days of election campaigns.
5 Three former presidents of the Constitutional Court suggest that the D'Alema government's law on equal media access may be unconstitutional.
14 Gherardo Colombo announces that the *Mani Pulite* investigations have concluded.
15 D'Ambrosio and Borelli praise the results achieved by the *Mani Pulite* investigations and say that, despite the politicians, the battle against corruption will continue. There is a chorus of 'silly season' assent for the proposal to use electronic bracelets to tag criminals under house arrest.
16 The Audit Court sounds the alarm on the cost of the pensions system. The government seeks to be reassuring, and the unions say that everything is under control. L'*Unità* proposes that Craxi should be allowed to return to Italy.
17 The merger between Banca Intesa and Comit gives birth to the largest bank in Italy.
18 A new recruit to the parachute regiment, Emanuele Scieri, is found dead at the Pisa barracks. Bullying is suspected.
20 The commander of the Pisa barracks is replaced.
21 The commander-in-chief of the parachute regiment, General Celentano, is dismissed. Veltroni announces an all-out assault on the Polo and declares that the DS are in favour of reforming the pensions system.
23 CGIL and Larizza (UIL) also declare themselves in favour of a mini-reform of the pensions system, although D'Antoni (CISL)

states his opposition. Andreotti is given a standing ovation, to a chorus of 'sei bellissimo', at the meeting of *Comunione e liberazione*.

24 Sofri, Bompressi and Pietrostefani are released. Their retrial is ordered. The replacement of General Celentano is postponed to October; indeed, amid much protest, he will be promoted. Inflation is now a steady 1.6 percent and the deficit is limited to 2.4 percent of GDP.

25 Silvia Baraldini, serving a long sentence in the USA for terrorism, returns to Italy. Minister Diliberto accompanies Baraldini's mother to the airport to meet her, provoking protests and calls for his resignation.

26 D'Alema defends Diliberto. He declares that the government is doing well and promises a million new jobs before the end of the legislature.

27 Cesare Romiti attacks the D'Alema government at the *Comunione e liberazione* meeting, saying that it has failed to deliver on equal media access, on the 'million new jobs', on concertation, on flexibility, and on reforms.

28 Around 1,000 containers of humanitarian aid bound for Kosovo are found abandoned on Bari docks, their contents left to rot.

29 Di Pietro signs the two referendums promoted by the AN and criticises D'Alema for his rash promise of a million new jobs.

September

1 Cofferati gives way on reform of the pensions system, proposing the extension of the contributory system to all workers and access by employees to the 'end-of-service allowance'.

2 Confindustria is severely critical of the 'expropriation' of the end-of-service allowance. Also D'Antoni and, to a lesser extent, Larizza are opposed to Cofferati's proposal. Parisi says that D'Alema can continue as Prime Minister.

3 The government begins the process of transforming an army of conscripts into an army of professionals. The PDCI declare their opposition.

4 Scalfaro returns to politics, attacking Berlusconi and sponsoring Franceschini. Fossa says that he is willing to negotiate on severance bonuses. D'Antoni calls for a referendum among union members on the application to all workers of the contributions-based pension system.

5 Agnelli says that without stable government Italy is losing its competitiveness. D'Alema offers to cooperate with Berlusconi

to achieve institutional reforms. Fini says that the reforms will be made by the referendum.

8 Cossiga proposes a 'maxi-centre' ranging from Prodi to Amato. The Democrats reply that they prefer to work for a centre-left rather than for a new "leg" for the centre as a whole.

9 Success of the majority summit meeting: promises for reform and elections in 2001.

10 Fini splits from Segni: separate lists at the regional elections. The President of the Republic in Naples: work and electoral reform.

13 Ciampi meets Berlusconi in order to find a way out of the impasse blocking the reforms.

14 *Assicurazioni Generali* of Trieste announces a hostile takeover bid for the *Istituto Nazionale delle Assicurazioni* (INA).

15 The newly-elected president of the Sardinia regional council, Mauro Pili, faces a vote of no confidence for having copied his policy statement wholesale from one written by Formigoni, president of the Lombardy regional council.

16 Prodi delivers his farewell address at Montecitorio: 'I am leaving Parliament, not Italy'.

17 Politicians realise the extent of public alarm over crime. Violante declares: 'law and order come before justice'. The Milan judge for committal proceedings rejects Previti's application for yet another postponement of his trial.

18 Senator for life Leo Valiani dies in Milan at the age of 90.

21 A seminar of ministers draws up the programme for the remaining 500 days of the legislature. Employment and the fight against crime are put at the top of the agenda.

22 CISL secretary D'Antoni is severely critical of the government's budget law.

24 The jury in Perugia acquits Andreotti and Vitalone 'for not having committed the offence', i.e., for not having ordered the murder of the journalist Pecorelli.

25 In his speech closing the *Unità* festival, Veltroni relaunches the Ulivo.

27 At an unprecedented meeting, Prime Minister D'Alema, Minister of the Interior Jervolino and around 500 prefects, police chiefs and heads of law enforcement agencies discuss the theme 'fighting crime'.

28 Debate begins on the *Tangentopoli* committee of inquiry proposed by Di Pietro.

29 The government introduces a 15,000 billion lire 'light' budget.

30 At the PPI congress, Marini relaunches the centre-left against the hegemony of the DS.

October

1 Amato rejects the plan to overhaul Telecom, and the Antitrust authority inflicts a 'super-fine' on TIM and Omnitel.

2 Castagnetti is elected secretary of the PPI, gaining almost 70 percent of votes.

4 D'Alema claims that there is no need for a government reshuffle. Violante and Mancino clash over the latter's criticisms of D'Alema.

5 D'Alema promises that the government will last until 2001. Amato presents the budget law to the Senate and calls for reforms to halt the country's decline.

6 Veltroni stakes everything on the Ulivo in his document for the DS Congress. The government conceals a KGB document on spies recruited in Italy.

8 D'Alema says that the list of KGB spies will be made public when the magistrates have completed their inquiries. *San Paolo* and *Assicurazioni Generali* agree that the latter should take over INA.

11 The government delivers the Mitrokhin dossier to the *Commissione Stragi* and to the services control committee.

12 The Mitrokhin dossier contains only twenty names of outright spies. Andreotti addresses the judges in Palermo. Occhetto refuses to sign Veltroni's motion.

13 D'Alema and Veltroni accept Cossiga's proposal for a commission of inquiry on the Mitrokhin dossier.

14 D'Alema writes an affectionate letter to Cossiga; the Democrats reject Cossiga as the proposed chairman of the Mitrokhin commission.

15 A Mitrokhin commission with Cossiga as chairman is no longer feasible because of the Polo's opposition and wrangling within the DS.

16 At the Polo's 'Security Day' meeting, Berlusconi suggests that the majority and opposition should work together against 'the army of evil'.

17 The Democrats call for a new government; Veltroni replies: 'first a new Ulivo, then a new government'.

19 Parisi agrees to stand as a candidate in the Bologna 12 constituency. The Senate's Constitutional Affairs Committee vetoes any commission on the Mitrokhin dossier.

20 Cossiga asks D'Alema to open a formal crisis. The trial of Sofri, Bompressi and Pietrostefani reopens.

21 D'Alema threatens early elections and then retracts: 'no crisis'. The bill on equal media access is approved by the Senate.

22 The committee to promote the new Ulivo meets: Veltroni, Parisi, Castagnetti, Francescato and Dini are present.
23 Andreotti is acquitted in Palermo on charges of mafia conspiracy: lack of evidence is cited.
25 Andreotti attacks Violante and the Anti-Mafia Commission and denounces magistrate Almerighi, who replies with a writ for defamation.
26 At the 'All Iberian' trial for illicit party funding, the sentences on Craxi and Berlusconi are barred by the statute of limitations.
27 D'Alema excludes a crisis, promising a new government or early elections after approval of the Budget Law.
28 Inflation rises to an annual 2 percent in October. Pivetti delivers the UDEUR's ultimatum to D'Alema.
30 Martone, president of the National Association of Magistrates, resigns when accused of failing to defend the Palermo magistrates. Fazio, who predicts inflation at 3 percent, argues with Amato, who declares that it will not rise higher than 1.5 percent.
31 Amato certifies the extraordinary success of the ENEL privatisation and puts more stock on the market. The Pope and the bishops oppose Berlinguer's plans for parity between public and private schools.

November

2 D'Alema defends the Berlinguer Law on school parity. Cacciari announces that he will run for the presidency of the Venetian regional government. D'Alema proposes a government reshuffle, which Parisi says is a 'linguistic lapse'.
4 Cossiga comes out in favour of a second D'Alema term or a government headed by Amato.
6 D'Alema announces that there will be 'no wavering': either a government reshuffle or early elections.
7 Dialogue between Berlusconi and Cossiga resumes.
8 Senate President Mancino proposes the election of a constituent assembly.
10 The direct popular election of the presidents of the regional governments is approved.
11 Borrelli and D'Ambrosio criticise the law on the so-called 'fair trial'. Giuliano Vassalli is elected president of the Constitutional Court.
12 Amato declares that it was the mass parties which built democracy in Italy.

13 D'Alema rehabilitates the DC and the PSI, claiming that their past was not 'entirely criminal'.

15 The High Court in Milan pronounces in favour of house arrest for Craxi in hospital, should he return to Italy. The DS comes out in favour of a single-ballot electoral system.

16 Berlusconi and Fini veto the proposal for a single-ballot electoral system, given that the centre-left refuses to compromise on equal media access. Bank of Italy Governor Fazio presents his political manifesto.

17 Berlusconi proposes the German proportional system. Annual inflation is 2 percent.

18 After fifty-three years as a member parliament, Nilde Iotte resigns from the Chamber for reasons of ill health. Cardinal Giordano of Naples is committed for trial on charges of usury.

19 Veltroni puts forward a new electoral proposal: single ballot, plurality premium, guarantees for minority parties, nomination of the premier, rules to make government crises more difficult. Ciampi opposes a pardon for Craxi, and Veltroni rejects an amnesty for corruption offences.

20 Milan chief prosecutor D'Ambrosio rejects proposals for an amnesty.

21 D'Alema reiterates that reform of the pensions system is necessary.

22 Minister of Labour Salvi and the unions postpone assessment of the pensions system until 2001. Martinazzoli announces his candidacy for the Lombardy regional council but eschews the Ulivo symbol.

25 The Senate institutes the commission of inquiry on the Mitrokhin dossier.

26 Previti, Squillante and Verde are committed for trial in the *Toghe Sporche* case (corruption of Rome magistrates), together with Berlusconi who declares that the investigating magistrates are a 'national cancer'.

28 Ciampi defends the autonomy of the magistracy against Berlusconi's accusations, while also announcing that reform of the pensions system is necessary.

29 The Ulivo regains all five of its constituencies in the by-elections. Parisi also wins in Bologna.

30 Berlusconi accuses Veltroni, D'Alema, Mussi and Angius of using the 'red magistrates' for their political ends. The DS announces that it will sue Berlusconi for slander and defamation.

December

2 Forza Italia is admitted into the European Popular Party: votes against are cast by the Italian PPI, the UDEUR and RI.

4 Former President of the Chamber of Deputies Nilde Iotte dies at the age of 79.

5 Bossi's *Lega* marches on Rome.

6 Tensions erupt in the Democrats between the supporters of Di Pietro and Prodi.

10 Socialist leader Boselli calls for a government crisis and D'Alema's replacement. Berlusconi is ready to strike a deal with the LN and the Radicals.

12 Diliberto announces that he will lift state secret privilege from documents on terrorist bombings. Fini says that an alliance with Bossi cannot be ruled out.

13 La Malfa and Cossiga call for D'Alema's resignation. The Court of Cassation declares all twenty-three referendums to be admissible, unifying two of them.

14 D'Alema announces that the government crisis will immediately follow approval of the Budget Law. The PPI and the Democrats declare themselves amenable to a second D'Alema term, but the *Trifoglio* declares its opposition.

15 Former minister Andreatta is seriously ill after suffering a heart attack in the Chamber.

16 Insistent rumours allege that deputies' votes have been bought to save the D'Alema government. Cossiga leaves the majority coalition.

17 Cossiga announces that he will vote against a second D'Alema term; the SDI says that it will abstain.

18 The Budget Law is approved. D'Alema condemns cash-for-votes, announces his resignation, rejects early elections and calls for a 'radical and immediate clarification'.

19 Cossiga visits Craxi in Hammamet.

20 D'Alema is reappointed and tries to form a government with seven parties: the DS, the Democrats, PPI, Greens, Italian Renewal, PDCI, UDEUR.

21 The second D'Alema government is born with the entry of the Democrats, the exit of the *Trifoglio* and the opposition of Cossiga.

22 The Senate passes a vote of confidence in the second D'Alema government: 177 votes for, 100 against, 4 abstentions.

23 The Chamber passes a vote of confidence in the second D'Alema government: 310 votes for, 287 against, 18 abstentions (the members of the *Trifoglio*).

24 Under-secretary of Defence, Senator Misserville of the UDEUR (a former member of MSI), resigns after comparing D'Alema to Almirante.

27 Boselli declares that D'Alema must negotiate all government measures with the *Trifoglio*.

29 The decree on the end-of-service allowance is issued. The number of under-secretaries falls to 64; Stefano Passigli is appointed to the new post of under-secretary for technological innovation.

30 The Milan stock exchange reaches record levels; the Euro sinks to an all-time low.

Translated by Adrian Belton

1

Introduction:
The Faltering Transition

Mark Gilbert and Gianfranco Pasquino

Unravelling the knots of Italian politics was as elusive a task as ever in 1999. But the key thread, if anywhere, is to be found in the interwoven themes of the creation of the D'Alema government in October 1998 (and its subsequent political fall-out), the difficulty of reforming the electoral law, and hence the hyperfragmented party system, and the short, sharp crisis of the D'Alema cabinet just before Christmas 1999. Short though the crisis was, it jumbled up politics once more and left new loose ends that will gradually unwind themselves in the coming year.

Political Jostling

Having become prime minister as the result of a traditional bout of parliamentary plotting,[1] D'Alema spent most of the first half of 1999 beating off the sustained and insistent attacks on his leadership launched by the deposed former premier, Romano Prodi, and his supporters. Even after Prodi had been nominated to the Presidency of the European Commission on 24 March 1999, the *Democratici per Prodi* (Democrats), which adopted a somewhat Disneyesque donkey as their electoral symbol, continued to jab at D'Alema from a distance. With a view to the looming European elections in June, the Democrats were anxious to raise their political profile with the very many people who had criticised both the manner and the fact of Prodi's defenestration from Palazzo Chigi.

The NATO intervention in Kosovo (fully analysed in this volume by Osvaldo Croci), however, brought about a lull in the squabble between Prodi and D'Alema and allowed D'Alema, after a few initial wobbles, to show off his leadership qualities by keeping Italy firm in its loyalty to its treaty commitments. Paradoxically, though not too paradoxically, the intervention in Kosovo also influenced domestic politics in a second way, by shaping the deployment of the referendum campaign for electoral reform (discussed, below, in Mark Donovan's chapter). Campaigners for a 'Yes' vote were obliged to fight for the attention of the media and public opinion and faced an unexpectedly difficult job in getting their voice heard. The referendum's opponents, who from the beginning knew their only hope was that the referendum might fail to reach the legal threshold for approval, were greatly assisted by the electorate's distraction by the war. The minor parties, and certain factions within Forza Italia, also had an even bigger prize to aim at. They hoped that the referendum's failure to reach its quorum would lead to the election of a supporter of proportional representation (PR) as President of the Republic.

This was because the political debate surrounding the referendum campaign had somewhat improperly, and in a way that is hard to comprehend, linked the election of the President, which was scheduled for May 1999, with the outcome of the referendum. By this line of reasoning, a 'Yes' vote for the abolition of the proportional quota in the electoral law would have favoured the election to the presidential palace of a campaigner for a bipolar, majoritarian democracy, while a failure to reach the minimum threshold would have strengthened the chances of the minority in the country opposed to such reforms. In this second hypothesis, the likelihood was that the presidency would go to a member of the *Partito popolare italiano* (Italian Popular Party: PPI). The PPI's secretary, Franco Marini, with excessive self-confidence and willingness-to-please, said he was happy to put forward 'any man or woman' the other parties liked, but was by strange coincidence himself the best-placed candidate his party could offer. It is also probable that the PPI was counting upon a secret and unwritten rule. Having delivered the prime minister's office to D'Alema, they, as the second-largest party of the governing coalition, could allegedly expect to obtain the presidency for themselves.

These intricate political games (which are described more fully in the chapter by Gianfranco Pasquino) were, however, shaken up by the rise of a widespread and cross-party campaign for the election of a woman candidate to the presidency. In particular, support had gathered around the candidacy of Emma Bonino, a member of the *Partito Radicale* (Radicals: PR) and an incumbent European Commissioner. Moreover, resistance was growing among the *Democratici di sinistra* (Democrats of the Left: DS) to the idea of entrusting the presidency to yet another Christian Democrat. After seven years of president Cossiga and seven of Oscar Luigi Scalfaro, nominating a member of the PPI meant that the *Democrazia cristiana* (Christian Democrats: DC) and its heirs would have had uninterrupted control of the post for twenty-one years. The secretary of the DS, Walter Veltroni, was also hoping to relaunch the drifting ship of institutional reform by involving the opposition in the search for a suitable candidate.

Had Veltroni and the rest of the government majority put forward the name of a member of the PPI, it is unlikely that the opposition would have given much support. The prospect, however, of the presidency being decided, as in the previous election in 1992, by a prolonged and contentious series of parliamentary ballots, at a time when the country was at war, genuinely alarmed both Veltroni (and D'Alema) and the more responsible leaders of the Opposition. Accordingly, when Veltroni nominated the Treasury Minister, Carlo Azeglio Ciampi, the *Polo delle libertà* (Liberty Pole) made a commendable and rapid show of support that both thwarted the PPI's schemes and caused the election on the first ballot of a widely revered candidate.

With Ciampi's election to the presidency, the two men most responsible for Italy's arduous entrance to the Euro – Ciampi himself and Romano Prodi – had received their just deserts in a way that rarely happens in politics, still less in Italian politics. Moreover, the cross-party support expressed for President Ciampi seemed like a harbinger of further cooperation between the government and the Liberty Pole over institutional reform. At least in principle, Ciampi, whose personal political history led observers to assume that he would look favourably at reforms intended to render a bipolar, majoritarian democracy, seemed like a much-needed ray of hope for gloomy institutional and electoral reformers depressed by the failure of the referendum. It is hard to tell which of the subsequent multitude of political initiatives in the field of constitutional reform were caused by Ciampi's election. But it is a fact that the leader of the *Alleanza nazionale* (National Alliance: AN), Gianfranco Fini, mobilised his party in pursuit both of a second attempt to abolish the proportional quota in the electoral law (this, along with nineteen other causes was also backed by the Radicals) and a new attempt to abrogate the recently passed law on the public financing of political parties (discussed in the chapter by Véronique Pujas). In addition, during the autumn parliament finally passed a law instituting the direct election of regional presidents. This law, which might and should have been passed four years earlier, was a prerequisite for any reform turning Italy into a federal state. It is still by no means certain that any step towards federalism will be taken.

The European Elections and their Consequences

Deprived of the presidency, which they had regarded as the ace in their sleeve, and under fire from the Democrats, who regarded them as scarcely less responsible than the DS for the plot against Prodi, the PPI plunged to defeat in the June elections to the European Parliament. Marini was forced to resign. Fought, as usual, over primarily domestic issues, and for the most part over petty party political matters rather than questions of 'European' import, the elections for the European Parliament (amply analysed in the chapter by Philip Daniels) were characterised by a successful, though not staggering, debut for the Democrats and a genuinely striking victory for the Bonino list. The (by now) former European Commissioner owed her success to both her presidential campaign and the deservedly high profile she had won for herself during her spell in Brussels. But it also owed much to the skill with which she exploited the badly drafted law on the public financing of the parties to pay for a strident series of television advertisements.

Seeing that the media entrepreneur Silvio Berlusconi also scored a notable triumph for his party, Forza Italia, the government belatedly deduced that the time had come to pass a law (the so-called *par condicio*) that banned political propaganda during electoral campaigns (see the chapter by Véronique Pujas once more). By so doing, it inevitably laid itself open to the charge that it was acting opportunistically. At the end of the year, the parliamentary bill introducing restrictions on political advertising – which Berlusconi exaggeratedly defined as a gag on free expression – was still to be approved by Parliament and had become pointlessly entangled with the fate of a bill on the conflict of interest for holders of public office.

The European elections saw a redistribution of votes within each of the opposing coalitions rather than a victory for one coalition or the other. The AN, the DS and the PPI were particular losers. In terms of votes and mayoralties won, nor did the June local elections show one coalition strikingly ahead of the other, though the Liberty Pole did do slightly better. But as Gianfranco Baldini and Guido Legnante show in their chapter, the symbolic importance of certain victories can overshadow mere numbers. This is why so much importance has been ascribed to the muncipal elections in Bologna. In Bologna, a local businessman, Giorgio Guazzaloca, was able to take advantage of the internecine warfare within the centre-left coalition between the Democrats and the DS (which was made all the worse by the fact that Bologna is Prodi's home city), and within the DS itself, to break over fifty years of leftist government in Bologna. Guazzaloca's list, 'Your Bologna', was supported, albeit somewhat reluctantly, by the parties of the Liberty Pole, but it also owed its success to the breeze of anti-party sentiment that had also blown life into the movements organised by Emma Bonino and Romano Prodi. Thus far, Guazzaloca's victory reminds us only that one swallow does not make a summer; it remains a model, however, for the Liberty Pole to follow whenever it has to confront a declining left in its electoral strongholds.[2]

The Past and its Burdens

Every time Italy voted in 1999 (the referendum on electoral reform, the presidential election, the European elections and the local elections), the two main coalitions trembled. Quite simply, both coalitions are too diverse to be stable. The centre-left, whose composition is particularly incoherent, is especially prone to being twisted apart by the political winds, which are chiefly blowing from two directions. On one side, a wind of possible progress towards a majoritarian and bipolar form of democracy is fluttering the centre-left coalition, on the other, an insidious draught urges a return to a proportionalist system, or, at least, to some of its more nefarious customs (such as cash payments to the parties).

The trial of the former premier Giulio Andreotti, the emblem of the proportionalist democracy of the First Republic, was, despite a show of false modesty on his part, used as an occasion to sing the praises of the former system. Even Prime Minister D'Alema somewhat clumsily acknowledged that the history of the DC and the PSI could not be regarded as entirely criminal. Andreotti's double acquittal by the courts of both Perugia and Palermo seemed at first as if it would give an impulse to hitherto somewhat inefficacious attempts to rebuild the DC, or something akin to it, and to rewrite the history of the First Republic. Yet, as Jean-Louis Briquet accurately comments in his chapter on Andreotti's acquittals, neither the DC nor the history of the First Republic were on trial at Perugia and Palermo and therefore Andreotti's legal vindication cannot be regarded as a political vindication for either the First Republic, or Andreotti himself. The issue of the links between the Mafia and politics remains one that needs to be addressed. Moreover, for all Silvio Berlusconi's violent attacks on the judiciary in general and 'red-robed magistrates' sympathetic to communism in particular, the judiciary continued to show both considerable independence from politics in 1999 and a skilful ability to correct its own excesses.

The enthusiasm displayed by Berlusconi, the PPI and by the *Centro cristiano democratico* (Christian Democratic Centre: CCD) of Pierferdinando Casini, for the acquittal of Andreotti, lasted only briefly and had no political fall-out. Nevertheless, the former Christian Democrats both in the Liberty Pole and the centre-left *Ulivo* (Olive Tree Alliance) did appear to be looking out for a figure able to group them back together. The election in September of Pierluigi Castagnetti as leader of the PPI diminished, but did not eliminate, this tendency. Throughout the year, the two most mentioned candidates for this role were the trade unionist Sergio D'Antoni, who engaged in frequent spats with the government, and the governor of the Bank of Italy, Antonio Fazio, who spoke out sharply over the government's failure to do more to reduce unemployment and taxation.

It is difficult to say how attractive these individuals would be to the electorate. But the mere fact that they are being spoken of as potential leaders signals both widespread dissatisfaction towards the actual party leaderships and the weakness of the political class, which for a decade now has been obliged to recruit its most authoritive figures from outside of the traditional political parties (Ciampi, Berlusconi, Dini, Prodi). The current electoral law, the 'Mattarellum', has the defect of encouraging the minor parties to blackmail their larger partners ruthlessly, but it also tells against the recomposition of a centre party, and, as Mannheimer and Sani have convincingly shown, there is little public support for the idea in any case.[3] Any new leader would have to seek a home inside one or the other of the major coalitions. Given their seeming 'centrism', both D'Antoni and Fazio could quite easily be recruited by either of the opposing coalitions, which adds just one more Italian anomaly to the list.

One last spasm of excitement was provided for the political class by the publication of a list of Soviet informants contained in the so-called Mitrokhin dossier and by the worsening illness of Bettino Craxi, whose ill health (and subsequent death) was used by the Liberty Pole, the former president, Francesco Cossiga, and the *Socialisti democratici italiani* (Italian Democratic Socialists: SDI) to reopen the argument over whether there should be a commission of inquiry into judicial behaviour during the *tangentopoli* corruption investigations. Silvio Berlusconi's worsening legal position in both Italy and Spain, whose judge Baltazar Garzòn informed the European parliament that he was carrying out an investigation against both Berlusconi and his right-hand man, Marcello Dell'Utri, only raised the tension further. Lashing out in anger, Berlusconi went so far as to accuse leading members of the DS, including the party secretary, Veltroni, of being the masterminds of the judicial plot against him. They sued. Berlusconi may appear to have lost the plot somewhat, but the violence of his reaction was one of several factors which conspired to call the survival of D'Alema's government into question.

The D'Alema Cabinet in Crisis

In fact, the origins of the weakness of D'Alema's government can be traced back to the repeated public requests during the summer of 1999 by the Democrats' chief spokesman, the politics professor Arturo Parisi, for a relaunch of the Olive Tree coalition and a cabinet reshuffle. The Democrats were not against D'Alema's continuation as prime minister, so long as he confirmed his support for the Olive Tree coalition as a concept, but were insistent that he should submit himself, along with all other would-be officials at all political levels, to American-style primaries before he became the coalition's accepted choice. This demand undoubtedly weakened D'Alema and, despite his making a clear expression of his faith in the Olive Tree idea (claiming, for instance, that 'It was I who created the Ulivo'), he was not able to stop the Democrats from continuing to press for the opening of a formal government crisis and for his acceptance of the use of primaries.

Just to confirm that coherence is rare in politics, and especially rare in Italian politics, Arturo Parisi in the meantime had become Romano Prodi's annointed successor for a by-election in the Bologna 12 parliamentary constituency, after a long tug-of-war between the parties that was characterised by the stark absence of any primary whatever. Parisi's candidacy in Constituency 12, in which the Polo stood as its candidate a well-known local doctor, became a symbol of the Olive Tree coalition's desire for a relaunch. The local leaders of the DS were more concerned to avoid repeating the setback of the communal elections. All the Olive Tree's big names – D'Alema, Veltroni, Di Pietro, Castagnetti – 'descended' upon Bologna to support Parisi, who did much less well than Prodi before him and eventually sneaked a narrow victory by a handful of percentage points. The by-election victory thus provided little or no new momentum either for the Olive Tree or for D'Alema's government.

Indeed, all hopes for a 'piloted' or managed government crisis, with a reshuffle taking place after the DS's party conference scheduled for January 2000 and leading to a strengthened administration, vanished when the leader of the SDI, Enrico Boselli, turned his speech at the SDI's party conference on 10 December into a broadside against the government by demanding not just the opening of a formal government crisis, but the replacement of D'Alema as prime minister. Boselli was apparently acting as spokesman for all those within the Olive Tree coalition, such as former president Francesco Cossiga and the Republican leader, Giorgio La Malfa, who were opposed to relaunching the Olive Tree. Together with the SDI, these two figures had added to the horticultural trend in Italian politics by starting earlier in the year a new mini-coalition called the *Trifoglio* (clover leaf).

A tired and exasperated D'Alema declared that he was not holding office just for the sake of it, but to carry out useful reforms, and demanded 'an immediate and drastic act of political clarification'. He called the bluff of the Trifoglio by resigning on 18 December and on 23 December was already in a position to present a new cabinet with the Democrats ensconced in the place of the *Cossighiani*. His first government had lasted 425 days, far less than Romano Prodi's previous administration (861 days). The four-day crisis itself was the shortest in the history of the Italian Republic. Nevertheless, despite its brevity, the crisis had illustrated that certain habits die hard. In the scrabble for votes prior to the new government's initial vote of confidence, it was alleged that certain former members of the *Lega Nord* (Northern League: LN) had sold their votes for the round sum of 200 million lire. The distribution of ministerial posts and under-secretaryships, meanwhile, became an exercise in horse-trading, with political copers like Clemente Mastella of the *Unione dei democratici europei* (Union of European Democrats: UDEUR) taking a leading role. Mastella demanded a ministerial post for the former President of the Chamber of Deputies, Irene Pivetti, whose pregnancy perhaps recommended her for the health ministry, but whose expectations were dashed, to her fierce irritation. The PPI struggled to maintain its position as the second party of the coalition, but had to cede Rosa Russo Jervolino's post as Minister for the Interior to the Democrats' Enzo Bianco. Willer Bordon of the Democrats became Minister for Public Works. Most ministers were reconfirmed in their jobs, but Tiziano Treu carried the can for the international humiliations caused by the ongoing Malpensa airport saga by being sacked from the transport ministry. He was replaced in this jinxed position by Pierluigi Bersani (DS), who had been an outstanding Minister of Industry and who took over his new post with scarcely disguised disgust at having to leave his former job half-finished. With the under-secretaries, D'Alema dished out jobs to all and sundry in a bid to satisfy the appetites of the minor parties in the coalition. In the case of Romano Misserville, an ex-fascist who had passed into the UDEUR and who was rewarded for his opportunism by an undersecretaryship, this generosity rebounded upon the government and caused a scandal that ended only with Misserville's resignation. In all, D'Alema handed out sixty-four undersecretary-ships, not far short of the absolute peak of sixty-nine attained between April 1991 and April 1992 by Andreotti's seventh and last administration.

On 23 December, the Chamber of Deputies rewarded D'Alema with a majority of 310 votes to 287. This already narrow majority would have been even more slender had D'Alema not bought the abstention of the Trifoglio's approximately twenty deputies by promising the parliamentary inquiry into *Tangentopoli* greatly desired by Cossiga and former prime minister Bettino Craxi. The Trifoglio's good will stopped at abstention, however: it threatened to adopt a case-by-case approach to the new government's future legislation. D'Alema had, however, achieved his main goal: surviving until the regional elections in spring 2000, the results of which, he hoped, would inject enough life into his government to enable it to endure until the end of the legislature in 2001. The forthcoming referendum on electoral reform, if it passes, should also reduce the blackmail power of the minor parties by introducing simple plurality voting in all constituencies. Here, however, there is the complication that Silvio Berlusconi has now brusquely adopted proportional representation as party policy, so the referendum will have to be won without the main opposition party's cooperation. Not that cooperation with Berlusconi, in the context of the parliamentary inquiry into tangentopoli, is likely in any case. The inquiry will be used by the Liberty Pole for propaganda purposes and to attack the judiciary, which is bound to erode a majority that contains numerous elements whose hostility to the judiciary is well known. In sum, D'Alema's government looks likely to be an 'Andreotti-style' cabinet, (to borrow the unkind but accurate description of the leftist leader Fausto Bertinotti,) whose chief occupation is surviving rather than governing. It is hard to see how it can direct its energies towards passing major social and economic reforms when its ability merely to cling on to office will be permanently in doubt.

Economic Management and Political Responsibility

The parlous state of D'Alema's government, irrespective of whether its formation was yet another instance of the perennial Italian vice of transformism,[4] has propelled the political parties back to the centre of the political system. In this regard, it represents a victory for its real architect, the evergreen Francesco Cossiga, who perhaps overestimated the Trifoglio's strength, but who managed to land yet another heavy blow in favour of his personal project to recreate a 'centre pole' that would bring Italy's experiment with bipolarity to an end. This plan already has a great deal of support among the very many former supporters of the DC and the less numerous but more avid ex-Socialists. The key for this plan's success is persuading Silvio Berlusconi to detach Forza Italia from the AN (at least before the elections) by convincing him that such a strategy offers the prospect of a permanent hold on power. From October onwards, Cossiga continually signalled his willingness to move closer to the leader of Forza Italia.

This likelihood of the clock being turned back in this way, to a blocked democracy where there is no prospect of alternation between left and right, depends entirely upon the fate of the upcoming and re-presented referendum on electoral reform in the late spring of 2000. A second defeat would certainly shatter any hopes of putting together an electoral reform guaranteeing bipolarism and might well lead to a proportionalist revision of the 1993 electoral law. Berlusconi's recent shift – after years in which he presented himself as the standard bearer for his own personal vision of a majoritarian, winner-takes-all form of democracy – towards a preference for a 'German-style' electoral law is a significant pointer here. Such a reform could be sold to public opinion as being both progressive and 'European', but it would also be grist to the mill of those, like Cossiga, who are hankering after the old regime.

The political uncertainty described in this chapter has its costs. It is not an accident that Italy's economic growth rate is the lowest in the European Union, or that inflation is starting to creep above 2 percent, bringing in its wake a loss of competitivity. But a return to a proportionalist past would do nothing to end the lingering political transition hampering the management of the economy. Having said this, such a judgement may be too hasty. D'Alema's government did complete major privatisations in the energy and transport sectors and, as Dwayne Woods describes in his very readable chapter, also bit on the bullet and allowed a hostile take-over of a bastion of the former state sector, Telecom Italia, by a private company, Olivetti, which financed the move with vast loans from a consortium of international banks.

It should also be said that Italian capitalism seemed convinced of D'Alema's ability to run the economy well. The Milan stock exchange enjoyed a boom year in 1999, with the Mibtel index soaring to unprecedented heights. In part, this boom reflected the avidity with which investors were willing to speculate upon the shares of internet start-ups, but it also owed much to the sound macro-economic management of the government, which kept the public debt under strict control and stayed within the stability pact guidelines for members of the Euro. Deprived by these policies of government debt, savers finally began to turn to the stock exchange in search of higher yields. One wonders whether D'Alema, when he was a militant in the Young Communists, ever expected to preside over the transformation of the Italian economy into fully fledged capitalism; the crucial first step along the much-heralded 'third way' favoured by contemporary socialists.

The government also undertook interesting new initiatives in the labour market and regional development. As Michael Contarino describes in his chapter on the *Patto di natale* ('Christmas Pact'), the government began the year by establishing with the trade unions and the employers' confederation a new agreement for economic development and productivity that carried on the series of reforms in the labour market that began in 1993. Italy is now edging towards the widely acclaimed Dutch model in this field and is doing so, moreover, with a degree of social cohesion that experts believed to be impossible until a few years ago. D'Alema's government also showed great awareness of the problems of the South, but, as Vincent Della Sala shows in his chapter, the state is no longer seeking to resolve them with heavy doses of public money, but with private capital and investment. The new government body coordinating investment in the South, *Sviluppo Italia*, is more like one of the development agencies that have brought thousands of new jobs to the depressed areas of Britain, especially Wales and Northern Ireland, than the old *Cassa per il Mezzogiorno* ('Southern Italy Development Fund'). It remains to be seen whether the new body will be able to reproduce the success of its British counterparts in the absence (despite the implementation of the so-called Bassanini laws[5]) of adequate bureaucratic flexibility and a system of civil law that is both effective and rapid. Local government, moreover, is too often indifferent to private enterprise whereas the criminality widespread in southern Italy represents a serious competitive disadvantage with respect to competitors such as Portugal or Wales.

It is worth underlining, too, that the government's main initiatives in the labour market date back to the beginning of the year before the administration was ground down by political infighting. Urgently needed reforms to the universities, the schools, public transport, the public administration are in the pipeline, but unless the political climate improves, they will have to stay there. Each year that passes, the truth identified by Michele Salvati in a prophetic 1997 article 'Moneta unica, rivoluzione copernicana', ('Single Currency, A Copernican Revolution') becomes ever more evident.[6] In order to stay in Europe, Italy has got to overhaul its entire economic system: no aspect of society or the economy can escape the process of re-engineering. Italy cannot be an anomaly any longer but must become, to use a phrase of D'Alema's by now as worn out as his government, 'a normal country'.

D'Alema himself has written in the past that the path to normality cannot be through the existing political infrastructure. The austerity of the Amato, Ciampi and Dini governments in the course of this decade, and the fundamental reforms to the pensions system and the labour market instituted since the mid-1990s, were rendered possible by the drastic economic situation that the country was facing. But to strengthen these reforms, and to ensure long-term control over public spending, it is necessary to have, in the long run, governments that govern and that can be punished by a dissatisfied electorate. It is necessary, in other words, that politics should be held accountable and that the political class should itself behave responsibly. The endless political infighting during 1999 has shown clearly that both the parties of government and those of the opposition either do not know how or simply do not wish to take on the burden of that responsibility.

Notes

1. S. Fabbrini, 'From the Prodi Government to the D'Alema Government: Continuity or Discontinuity?' in *Italian Politics: The Return of Politics*, eds. D. Hine and S. Vassallo, Oxford, 2000, 121–38.
2. For the significance of this election see D. Campus and G. Pasquino, 'How to Lose a Mayor: The Case of Bologna', *Journal of Modern Italian Studies*, vol. 5, no. 1, forthcoming.
3. R. Mannheimer and G. Sani, 'Reassembling the Centre and the Electoral Spectrum', in *Italian Politics: The Return of Politics*, eds. D. Hine and S. Vassallo, Oxford, 2000, 87–100.
4. This accusation was convincingly disputed by G. Sartori in *Il Corriere della Sera*, 30 December 1999. To give some idea of the state of flux in which the Italian parliament finds itself, a useful letter from the Chief Whip of the Verdi (Greens) to the 5 January 2000 edition of *La Repubblica* estimated that the 'Mixed Group' in the Chamber of Deputies contained fifteen Greens, fifteen 'Republican-Federalists', thirteen members of the CCD, thirteen members of *Rifondazione comunista* (Communist Refoundation: PRC), eight Democratic Socialists and six floaters who had been in Rinnovamento Italiano (Italian Renewal). This left a further twenty-seven 'odds and sods' including a number of escapees from the Northern League. Rather generously, he stated that none of these people could be regarded as 'runaways or traitors'.
5. For an early appraisal, see Mark Gilbert, 'The Bassanini Laws: A Half-Way House in Local Government Reform' in *Italian Politics: The Return of Politics*, eds. D. Hine and S. Vassallo, Oxford, 2000, 121–38.
6. Michele Salvati, 'Moneta unica, rivoluzione copernicana', *Il Mulino* no.1/97, 5–23.

2

FORCED ALLY?
ITALY AND 'OPERATION ALLIED FORCE'

Osvaldo Croci

Introduction

Since the mid-1980s Italy's relations with the United States (US) have been characterised by occasional periods of tension, usually following some unilateral American initiative in the Mediterranean. At the beginning of 1999 it seemed that the two countries were again on a collision course. The US was uneasy about Italian diplomatic overtures to Iran and Libya. Italy, for its part, ignored American advice that it extradite Kurdish nationalist leader Ocalan to Turkey where he was wanted for terrorist activities, and it repeatedly and publicly expressed strong reservations about the rationale and effectiveness of the periodic Anglo-American bombing of Iraq. Then, in early March, came the verdict of an American military court acquitting the pilot responsible for the Cermis accident of February 1998. The Italian government, backed by practically the whole of parliament, reacted by calling for a review and possible re-negotiation of the treaty regulating the use of NATO's military bases in Italy.[1]

The debate over this revision, however, was soon overshadowed by the most important international event in 1999: NATO's 'Operation Allied Force' against Serbia over the Kosovo question. Here too there was plenty of room for disagreement between Italy and the US. During the Bosnian war, for instance, the US began to adopt a policy of ostracism towards Serbia that eventually cast that country in the role of 'villain of the Balkans'. Italy, on the other hand, maintained that stability in the Balkans could not be achieved if the West insisted on disregarding the role, problems, and aspirations of Serbia as the largest state in the region. On the circumstances under which the use of force by NATO could be envisaged, moreover, Foreign Minister Lamberto Dini had affirmed in July 1998 that 'an intervention by NATO in Kosovo without a United Nations Security Council (UNSC) mandate [was] absolutely impossible'.[2] Yet, from 23 March to 9 June, 1999, Italy played a central role in the logistics of NATO's 'Operation Allied Force'. Ironically, the military base from which most of the air sorties against Serbia were launched was Aviano, the base from which the plane responsible for the Cermis accident had taken off.

How can one explain this Italian conversion to a policy of force, especially in view of the fact that the largest member of the governmental coalition, the *Democratici di sinistra* (Democrats of the Left: DS), was, except in name, the same party that had taken a strongly critical stance against the 1991 Gulf War. Given its record in the fight against domestic terrorism, moreover, the DS could hardly be expected to have any sympathy for the terrorist tactics employed by the military wing of the Kosovo Albanian nationalists. The conversion is even more intriguing if one considers that NATO military intervention against Serbia, unlike the Allied one against Iraq, did not have the explicit authorisation of the UNSC and rested therefore on a much shakier legal ground.

This paper examines the position of Italy in the Kosovo war. The first section of the chapter gives a brief account of the origins and development of the problem up to NATO decision to launch air strikes against Serbia. The second section examines the politics of NATO intervention, focusing primarily on the Italian position. The third section focuses on the political debate in Italy during the war. The paper ends with an assessment of the impact of the Kosovo war on the potential development of common foreign and security policy in Europe and the establishment of European identity within NATO.

The Kosovo problem

According to a simplistic explanation presented in the popular media to rally public support behind 'Operation Allied Force', the Kosovo crisis is simply the latest episode in a series of acts of aggression perpetrated by Serbian political leaders in their attempt to create an ethnically pure Greater Serbian state. This explanation ignores the fact that the Kosovo Albanians' demands for independence are not simply a reaction to Serbian repression but represent the playing out of a century-old nationalist movement that from its very beginning has turned to outside powers for support in the realisation of its objectives.[3]

The most proximate origin of the Kosovo crisis can be dated from the Yugoslav constitutional reform of 1974, when Kosovo, until then an autonomous region of Serbia, was granted a new status almost equivalent of that of the six states of the Yugoslav federation. By 1987, however, the Serbian minority within Kosovo had begun to denounce acts of discrimination at the hands of an Albanian majority that had come to exercise almost complete control over the regional administration. In 1988 and 1989, new constitutional changes revoked the extensive autonomy granted in 1974. In 1991, Kosovo declared independence under the leadership of Ibrahim Rugova and his Democratic League of Kosovo. Since only Albania recognised the new state, Rugova, conscious that Kosovo could not resist an armed intervention by Serbia, did not force the issue of independence, opting instead for a strategy of civil disobedience. Kosovo Albanians operated a kind of internal secession by boycotting Serbian and Yugoslav political institutions.

Rugova's peaceful strategy, however, came under increasing criticism by more radical Kosovo Albanian factions, particularly the Kosovar Liberation Army (KLA), a military organisation apparently formed in 1993, that claimed the right to represent all Kosovo Albanians. In 1996 the KLA launched guerrilla operations, attacking police stations and assassinating Serbs as well as ethnic Albanians seen as collaborators. The Serbian police reacted as might be predicted, and the cycle of violence quickly escalated. By mid-1998 the KLA controlled about half of Kosovo's territory. Serbia responded by sending in its army. Given the guerrilla nature of the KLA and its tactics, the army engaged in clean-up operations that often caused civilian casualties. As a result of the intensification of military activities the number of refugees began to increase.

Western powers attempted to mediate the conflict through the so-called 'Contact Group', composed of representatives of the US, Russia, France, Great Britain, Germany and Italy. On 31 March, and on 23 September, 1998, the UNSC issued two resolutions (1160 and 1199) inviting the Belgrade government and the leadership of the Kosovo Albanian community to put an end to violence and to begin negotiating a political solution. Since the violence continued, on 13 October the Atlantic Council issued the so-called 'activation order', authorising NATO's military command to prepare plans to launch aerial attacks against Serbian objectives. Three days later,

Serbian President Slobodan Milosevic and US envoy Richard Holbrooke reached a cease-fire agreement that provided among other
things for the withdrawal of the Serbian army from Kosovo. The
agreement would be guaranteed by the presence of international
observers (the so-called Kosovo Verification Mission) under the
authority of the Organisation for Security and Cooperation in
Europe (OSCE). On 24 October this agreement received the UNSC's
seal of approval (resolution 1203).

The cease-fire was, however, repeatedly broken by the KLA. In
this context, the Serbian army interrupted its withdrawal from
Kosovo and intensified its operations against the KLA. On 15 January 1999, a Serbian military operation in the village of Racak
resulted in the death of forty-five Kosovo Albanian civilians. The
dynamic of events was unclear, and the suspicion existed that the
KLA might have tampered with the scene of the massacre to further its own cause with Western governments and media.[4] At the
end of January the 'Contact Group' stepped up its diplomatic initiatives culminating in a series of meetings at Rambouillet. The two
parties were presented with a non-negotiable peace plan that provided for the withdrawal of the Serbian army and police from
Kosovo. They would be replaced by a NATO force that would
ensure compliance. The administration of Kosovo would be
handed over to a NATO-appointed 'Civilian Implementation Force'.
A final decision on the status of Kosovo would be taken three years
after the implementation of this plan 'on the basis of the will of the
people'. At first both parties rejected the plan. However, on 18
March, following American insistence, the Kosovo Albanian delegation changed its mind and accepted it. The Serbian delegation,
instead, stuck to its original position. In their eyes, the plan was
unacceptable because it represented a blatant violation of national
sovereignty and amounted to a surreptitious granting of independence to Kosovo. Two days later the OSCE verification mission
began to be withdrawn from Kosovo. On the night of 23 March,
after a final attempt by US envoy Holbrooke to extract Serbian
assent to the plan, NATO began its aerial strikes on Serbia.

The politics of NATO's intervention

NATO intervention in Kosovo is neither the result of a genuine concern for human rights ushering the advent of a new era of
moralpolitik nor yet another example of Western imperialism.
More simply, 'Operation Allied Force' is the first intervention
falling within the new mandate that NATO has given itself to deal

with the security challenges and risks perceived to exist in the post-Cold War environment. According to NATO's new 'Strategic Concept', besides meeting its traditional task of repelling an armed attack against the territory of any of its members, the alliance must also be ready to respond to 'new' threats. Among these is the uncontrolled movement of large numbers of people, particularly as a consequence of armed conflicts, which can pose problems for security and stability affecting the alliance.

The Kosovo case is a perfect example of this kind of threat. The flow of refugees into Macedonia threatened the eruption of a conflict there that could have potentially serious consequences for the alliance, first and foremost the possibility that both Greece and Turkey might be drawn into it. The flow of refugees also represented a problem for a number of European countries and, given its geographic proximity, for Italy in particular. So the intervention was primarily designed to contain the conflict and thus stem the flow of refugees. D'Alema, for instance, has argued that NATO's 'activation order' was issued in October 1998 because by that time 'the fear existed that the situation was rapidly degenerating ... Italy felt the emergence more than any other country since it was in the front line of the exodus of refugees.' In early February 1999 he suggested the organisation of a kind of second *Operazione Alba*, namely the deployment of NATO troops in Albania to assist and to provide for refugees there.[5]

Besides the problems posed by refugees, another consideration seems to have played a role in NATO's decision to intervene in the Kosovo crisis, namely the desire to promote a European identity within NATO. As NATO Secretary-General Solana stated in early March: 'The Kosovo Implementation Force should also be the start of yet another new feature of how we manage security today: it should be the start of a stronger European role in NATO'.[6] The US encourages the development of such an identity as long as it implies a greater and more active role for Europeans both in terms of defence spending and willingness and capability to participate in joint actions. The Europeans, for their part, regard the development of such an identity as an obligatory step if Europe wishes to become an equal partner of the US in the field of defence. As put by D'Alema: 'The Italian government believes that the development of a European defence initiative would reinforce Atlantic relations because it would help overcome an obsolete division of labour and would allow a more effective management of current international crises'.[7]

NATO's new strategic doctrine and the effort to develop a European defence identity do not explain, however, why the perceived need to intervene in the Kosovo crisis resulted in the bombing of

Serbia. It would seem that NATO was inexorably propelled towards this option because of the historical lesson it drew from the war in Bosnia. The lesson that Western leaders, and the American ones in particular, drew from the Bosnian war was that Milosevic would yield on Kosovo only if confronted with a clear military threat. They also thought that this time the threat itself might suffice. If it did not, they were convinced that only a few days of bombing would be needed to bring Milosevic back to the negotiating table. The 'activation order' of 13 October was issued as part of a strategy of coercive diplomacy, its aim being to support Holbrooke's negotiating mission to Belgrade. Although the mission yielded the desired result, the 'activation order' was not cancelled because NATO did not trust Milosevic and intended to keep him under pressure. In the words of D'Alema: ' NATO logic ... was to show Milosevic a loaded gun in order to convince him to negotiate. ... We looked to the Bosnian precedent when limited air raids had brought him to the negotiating table. So much so that in the case of Kosovo initial plans provided only for a couple of raids and nothing else'.[8] The perception that Milosevic would yield only if threatened with a military attack also explains why NATO leaders chose not to entrust the question in a more direct way to the UNSC. Both Russia and China face domestic situations similar to that faced by Serbia in Kosovo. Hence, they could not be expected to approve a military intervention against Milosevic.

To what extent did the Italians share this assessment of the situation? The Italian position on the Kosovo question can be summarised as follows. Unlike the Americans, who assumed a progressively more marked pro-KLA attitude and regarded the Serbs as the villains, the Italians, (and Europeans in general), tended to blame both parties for the degeneration of the situation in Kosovo. They thought that a diplomatic solution was possible if one chose to isolate the KLA, support the Rugova faction, and offer the Serbs incentives to give back the degree of autonomy that Kosovo had prior to 1989. Kosovo Albanians, moreover, should be told in no uncertain terms that the path towards independence was impracticable.[9]

When it became clear that diplomatic initiatives were insufficient and NATO began to consider military options, the Italians as well as most of the Europeans leaned towards the idea of establishing a *cordon sanitaire* in Albania and Macedonia in order to stop the flow of personnel, weapons and supplies to the KLA. This would have represented an incentive for Serbia to loosen its grip on Kosovo. The Americans, on the other hand, favoured the option of issuing a threat to Milosevic. This second option eventually prevailed because the Americans, on the basis of their intelligence reports, were able to convince the Europeans that a military threat would bring the desired results. They even maintained that for domestic political reasons Milosevic needed such a forceful external pressure before he could yield on Kosovo.

The Italians, as well as the Germans, however, were not totally comfortable with the issuance of the 'activation order'. Besides doubts about its effectiveness, they were also concerned about its official justification, which was couched primarily in terms of the need to defend human rights in Kosovo. The Italian government is sympathetic to the idea that human rights must be protected even if that requires a redefinition of the principle of national sovereignty. Action, however, should be preceded by the development of clear and realistic criteria of intervention. As Dini has put it: 'The question at this point is simply that of identifying the ways in which one can and must act. ... One must uphold values and principles but one must also put their defence into the context of international realities'.[10] More precisely, Italy recognises that in the post-Cold War security environment NATO must take responsibility for out-of-area missions, whether humanitarian or not, especially at its periphery. Unlike the US, however, Italy does not think that such interventions should be launched without some kind of legitimisation coming from the UN. As a recent *Affari Esteri* editorial puts it:

> Italy stresses the necessity of anchoring intervention by NATO, and other regional security organisations, to UN principles and practices. One must work toward a new and more effective complementarity between the UN and regional security organisations based on the development of clear and widely accepted criteria for the authorisation of the use of force.[11]

It is not surprising, therefore, that the Italian government should have been sympathetic to the Serbian request, at Rambouillet and afterwards, that a UNSC resolution precede the entry of a multinational force into Kosovo.

Italian policy makers voiced these doubts, but, once the American point of view prevailed, they felt they had no choice but to support the decision. As Dini would later recall: 'Italy is part of the alliance and cannot therefore renege on its responsibilities. Fifteen members were in favor of intervention: to disassociate ourselves would have been a pretty dramatic gesture'. Even after the Holbrooke-Milosevic cease-fire agreement collapsed, the Europeans continued to believe that a diplomatic solution was not only desirable but also still possible. They, and the French in particular, took the initiative for organising the Rambouillet meeting, which they regarded as a test of European capacity to manage a crisis at the EU borders. The expectations of the Italian government were certainly optimistic. As Foreign Affairs Under-Secretary Umberto Ranieri wrote on 2 March: 'We now have the prospect of a solution whereas only a few days ago we had nothing and we faced the urgency of having to prepare for a difficult military intervention'.[12]

There is reason to believe, however, that by this time the Americans had abandoned every hope of a diplomatic solution and were simply looking for a *casus belli*. They made sure that the Rambouillet talks would provide it. The Americans insisted, in fact, that the text of the peace plan submitted to the parties for approval undergo some semantic modifications from the version prepared by the 'Contact Group'. More precisely, the new text mentioned that the future of Kosovo would be decided 'on the basis of the will of the people'. This change aimed at obtaining the approval of the Kosovo Albanian delegation, which it did. At the same time, however, the change also assured the rejection of the plan by the Serbs.

It is not clear why the Europeans agreed to this change. It is unlikely that they believed the rationale the Americans offered for it, namely that the term 'people' was sufficiently vague to be interpreted not only as meaning the Kosovars but also the Serbs or even the Yugoslavs. More likely, this is evidence that although desired and organised by the Europeans, the Rambouillet talks, like most of the diplomatic initiatives, were really led by the Americans. Whichever the case, at this point NATO was left with only one option: to implement its threat. The choice of an aerial attack on Serbia, as opposed to a ground intervention in Kosovo that would have made more sense if the main objective had indeed been to protect Kosovo Albanian civilians, was dictated by the perception that the use of ground troops would not have received public support, especially in the US.

Italy and 'Operation Allied Force'

As NATO planes prepared to launch their first bombs against Serbia, the Italian government found itself in the same predicament it had faced after the approval of the 'activation order'. The response was predictably the same. Both predicament and response were best expressed by DS Member of Parliament Michele Salvati in his intervention in support of the government's position on Kosovo in the Chamber of Deputies on 26 March:

> Even if I regard NATO's choice as wrong, and the prelude to even bigger problems down the road, I do not think that we face one of

those extreme situations in which we are morally compelled to disregard such important issues as that of national interest and loyalty to an alliance upon which our security and role in Europe depend. Hence, it follows that full and unconditional respect for NATO decisions is for us an obligation we cannot evade. We can certainly operate within the alliance and follow its proper procedures in order to have the decisions already taken reconsidered ... But our readiness to assume all the responsibilities that our NATO membership entails must not be a matter of discussion.[13]

Of course, any of the many postwar Italian governments would have made the same decision. D'Alema's government, however, had an additional reason to do so. In assuming power D'Alema, as well as his DS colleagues, felt that as former communists they had to prove their reliability as Atlantic partners. As D'Alema would later put it: 'My biggest problem was relations with the US, how they would judge me and my government'.[14]

Bombing Serbia, however, was certain to increase the flow of refugees, the stopping of which was ironically the main reason why NATO intervention in the Kosovo crisis was deemed essential in the first place. Hence, the first move of the government was to begin planning for this emergency. At the European Council meeting in Berlin on 24 March, D'Alema and Dini requested their European partners 'not to leave Italy alone in the face of a possible humanitarian catastrophe.' Even if 'the refugee emergency' was going to be a problem primarily for Italy, it should be treated as a European problem.[15]

To pass what D'Alema seemed to perceive as a personal as much as a national test with flying colours, it was also necessary that support appear to be given with conviction, if not enthusiasm, and not *obtorto collo*. D'Alema knew that this was going to require a difficult balancing act on the part of his government, given the tendency of Italian political parties, factions, and even individual leaders, to regard foreign policy issues as an extension of domestic politics. The Kosovo issue, moreover, because of its nature and novelty, had the potential for cutting across all established ideological and political lines.

More precisely, D'Alema confronted the following difficulties. First, the heterogeneous composition of his coalition government which, besides the DS, included the *Partito popolare italiano* (Italian Popular Party: PPI), the *Unione dei democratici per la repubblica* (Union of Democrats for the Republic: UDR), the *Partito Repubblicano* (Republican party: PRI), the *Socialisti democratici italiani* (Italian Democratic Socialists: SDI), *Rinnovamento italiano* (Italian Renewal: RI), the *Verdi* (Greens), and *Partito dei comunisti italiani* (Party of Italian Communists: PDCI). Within his own party, moreover, there was a left wing still sceptical of NATO and susceptible to anti-American rhetoric. Second, the existence of a traditional pacifist movement linked to the Church and Catholic associations. Third, public opinion that in the long run was likely to be negatively influenced by the proximity of the war. Some Italians could, after all, literally see and hear the war, since most of the air sorties were taking off from bases in Italy.

The strategy chosen by the government was to present Italy's participation in 'Operation Allied Force' as a result of two imperatives: duty towards NATO and humanitarianism. D'Alema argued that Italy had to show its willingness and ability to fulfill properly the function that the new NATO has assigned to it, namely to 'project stability', in the Mediterranean and the Balkans. This was necessary not only because of an abstract sense of duty but also because the price of evading such a responsibility would be a loss of prestige and, even more importantly, missing an opportunity to become a permanent member of the 'noble circle of Great Powers'. Had Italy chosen to sit out like Greece, it would have remained, as D'Alema put it, using a soccer metaphor, 'a second division country'.[16] The government also made great efforts to downplay Italian participation in the military aspect of NATO intervention and to emphasise the humanitarian one instead. Finally, it constantly reminded Italians that its major effort went into trying to put an end to the war by finding ways that could induce Milosevic to return to the negotiating table.

On 25 March, at the European Council in Berlin, D'Alema expressed the view that bombing had already achieved its objective and the time was rapidly approaching when the question could be handed over to politics and diplomacy again. He was immediately rebuffed by US National Security Advisor Samuel Berger, who pointed out that the Italian Premier obviously had not received a correct military assessment of the situation.[17] Although D'Alema later explained that his statement simply betrayed his 'hope that the whole question could be solved as soon as possible', he probably uttered it in order to strengthen the position his government would take in the parliamentary debate on Kosovo scheduled for the following day.

There, the government put forward a motion that took into account the reservations of some of the parties of the majority but left the government ample room to fulfill its NATO duties. The motion called for an end to the air raids as soon as possible, engaged the government to pursue diplomatic initiatives, and guaranteed that Italian planes would engage only in defensive missions. As D'Alema later hinted, the approval of this motion (by 318 votes to 188) signified the signing of an unspoken agreement between the government and its parliamentary majority. The government would fulfill the engagements deriving from the country's membership in NATO, while political parties and individual leaders would be free to voice their criticism of specific aspects of the NATO campaign and Italy's role in it. This compromise did occasionally give the impression of lack of political cohesion but in the end worked out rather well.

Some NATO allies expressed concern about the significance of D'Alema's statement of 25 March, which they feared was a sign of Italy's limited reliability in the war effort. The Italian government reacted by instituting a kind of division of labour within its ranks. D'Alema, whose Atlantic credibility was being tested, devoted himself to justifying and supporting NATO decisions. The task of uttering reservations and occasional criticism of NATO actions passed to Foreign Minister Dini, whose Atlantic credentials, unlike those of D'Alema, were impeccable. On 23 April, for instance, Dini criticised the bombing of the Serbian television building. D'Alema publicly rebuked Dini and affirmed that while politicians were responsible for establishing the broad parameters of legitimate targets they should not discuss or question 'every single target'. At the end of May, Dini suggested that Italy might not take part in a ground invasion unless approved by a UNSC resolution. D'Alema immediately invited him to be more cautious in his public statements. Italy, he then added, would be 'totally loyal' to NATO.[18]

Such a division of labour was not only an artful device designed by the government to cope with parliamentary difficulties but reflected also dilemmas and ambiguities that existed within the executive. The Italian government in fact had to reconcile its duties towards NATO and its role of promoter of political stability in Albania with its policy of supporter of the Yugoslav (Serbo-Montenegrin) federation which it regards as a necessary bastion against German hegemonic ambitions in the Balkans.[19] Besides geopolitical interests, the Italian government also believed it had to safeguard Italian economic interests in Serbia. These might not have been so significant as to justify a dramatic break with Italy's allies but were nevertheless important enough to call for a diplomatic effort to put an end to bombing as soon as possible.[20] Thus, in uttering reservations about some NATO actions, Foreign Minister Dini was not simply playing an assigned role in a carefully crafted representation but was also acting as the spokesman of Italian diplomacy whose position on how to deal with Serbia was considerably less hawkish than that taken by the Italian government and its Atlantic allies. On a more personal level, moreover, Dini seems to have relished the role of 'dissenter' both for personal convictions and because this placed him in a good position should the D'Alema government fall over the Kosovo question and the need arise for a different leader to try to rebuild a new centre-left governmental majority.

The Italian government did occasionally advance suggestions for diplomatic initiatives, but none of them could be seen as undermining NATO cohesion. Indeed, both D'Alema and Dini limited themselves to announcing publicly courses of actions that the alliance had already embarked upon or was seriously taking into consideration. As Dini pointed out, moreover, Italy's preference for a rapid diplomatic solution should not be interpreted as a lack of military resolve: 'To try to construct an opening to peace does not mean being disloyal to the alliance'.[21] The government carefully avoided any unilateral initiative. Close consultation with its NATO allies was the norm. In early May, for instance, the Serbian government contacted the Italian embassy in Belgrade indicating its intention to let Kosovo Albanian leader Rugova come to the West. Before deciding to receive him in Rome the Italian government duly informed its allies. American Secretary of State Albright expressed concern that Rugova might be sent by Belgrade to make public statements in favour of stopping NATO bombing, thus undermining NATO cohesion. D'Alema and Dini promised that they would recommend 'a certain degree of discretion' to Rugova and that they would limit and control his public appearances.[22]

At the political level, the biggest opposition to Italy's participation in 'Operation Allied Force' came from *Rifondazione comunista* (Communist Refoundation: PRC). Although in the opposition, the PRC put pressure on the PDCI and the Greens, both of which were critical of NATO military initiative in the absence of an explicit UNSC resolution, to withdraw from the majority. Such a withdrawal would not necessarily have led to a passing of a motion of non-confidence since the government could have been rescued by the support given to 'Operation Allied Force' by the major parties of the opposition. Under the Prodi government, after all, *Operazione Alba* (the 1997 Italian intervention in Albania) was approved without the votes of the PRC, which at the time was part of the governmental majority, but with those of the *Polo delle libertà* (Liberty Pole). This time, however, the *Polo* clearly stated that should the government lose a member of its coalition, D'Alema should resign. Throughout the war, the PDCI in particular, repeatedly threatened to withdraw their two ministers from the cabinet or leave the majority altogether. Party leader Armando Cossutta even conducted a personal peace initiative that took him to

Moscow and Belgrade. In the end, however, the two ministers remained in the cabinet and the party in the majority.

As could have been expected, the Vatican took a position against the war. Its opposition to NATO bombing of Serbia, however, was less robust than during the Gulf War. This was due both to internal divisions and to the fact that Serbia scorned Vatican diplomatic initiatives. Perhaps as a consequence of this more subdued behaviour on the part of the Vatican, Catholic and pacifist organisations devoted less time to public protest rallies and concentrated their energies on humanitarian activities.[23] Catholic pacifism, however, was undoubtedly the basis for the ambivalence shown towards NATO intervention by outgoing President of the Republic Oscar Luigi Scalfaro. On 23 March he issued a statement reminding Italians that *pacta sunt servanda* ('treaties must be adhered to') but then went on to express strong anti-war sentiments throughout the remainder of his mandate.

Italians reacted to the war with exactly the same mix of certitude and ambivalence exhibited by their government. A poll conducted at the very outset of the war showed that only 25.1 percent of respondents supported NATO air attacks. Yet, 75 percent also felt that Italy should collaborate with its NATO partners. The two positions were not contradictory. As shown in a different poll on the future of NATO that was conducted in the same period, in fact, 79.8 percent of Italians felt strongly that Italy should remain in NATO. At the beginning of April support for NATO intervention increased to over 31 percent. According to some analysts this shift was the result of media obsession with the images of refugees and D'Alema's insistence on the gravity of the situation in his televised address to the nation on 30 March. In May, however, following NATO 'errors', the consequent increase in the number of civilian casualties, and 'a kind of tiredness due to the protracted state of war', support dropped again by 7 percent.[24]

Overall the government encountered few political difficulties. There were some protests, especially in parliament, when in mid-April it became clear that Italian planes were taking part in the bombing raids on Serbia. D'Alema, however, silenced the critics by arguing through some verbal somersaults that these missions were part of that 'integrated and active defence' duty that parliament had approved on 26 March.[25] A similar effort went into presenting Italian participation in 'Operation Allied Force' as having almost exclusively a humanitarian aspect. Thus, on 29 March, the government launched the much-touted *Missione Arcobaleno* ('Rainbow Mission'), the purpose of which was to collect funds for refugees and assist them in camps in Albania and Macedonia. Although plagued by scandals concerning its effectiveness, *Mis-*

sione Arcobaleno was a great success with the public and collected over 120 billion lire by the end of the war. The media helped considerably in this attempt to shift attention from the military to the humanitarian aspects of the conflict by devoting more attention to the role of Italian soldiers active in refugee camps than those involved in military operations. Both the press and D'Alema, especially during his highly publicised visit to refugee camps in Albania at Easter, also engaged in tear-jerking descriptions of supposed Serbian atrocities in Kosovo.[26]

In the end, the Italian government could rejoice that the plan accepted by Milosevic incorporated, both in terms of the way it was developed and of its content, the key points Italy had emphasised all along and around which the position of the allies had slowly converged. The plan was developed by the G8 group of countries, and hence with the active participation of Russia. The deployment of a multinational force in Kosovo was authorised by UNSC resolution 1244 of 10 June 1999. The mood of the Italian government was self-congratulatory. D'Alema, for instance, affirmed: 'It is the peace we have worked for with such unflagging determination and coherence of purpose'. Defence minister Scognamiglio argued, that 'Italy [had] contributed more than other countries to winning the conflict' because 'it [had] carried more than its share of the weight'. As a result the Italian government felt that Italy had proved its loyalty and responsibility, and hence acquired more credibility or, as D'Alema put it: 'The allies now have more respect for us'.[27]

Conclusions

In the conclusion to an essay examining Italy's role in the 1956 Suez crisis, Giampaolo Calchi Novati recently wrote:

> Whatever her incidental interests might be and wherever her sympathies in any given conflict might lie, Italy could not act against the alliance which anyway ensured much greater benefits (security, a protected position in the market, a link with the world of 'major politics', etc.) so that, whenever their positions diverged, Italy had no choice but to side with her allies.[28]

This assessment also applies to Italy's predicament and behaviour in the Kosovo case. This does not mean, however, that Italy has behaved as a 'forced ally', which implies a certain reluctance to act in a common effort and a readiness to exploit any opportunity to escape one's responsibilities. In the Kosovo case, Italy has fully supported NATO collective action while at the same time trying, with some success, to maintain a profile of its own. In an article meant to be an *ex-post facto* rationalisation of Italy's behaviour, Foreign Affairs Under-Secretary Ranieri has argued that Italy has acted on the basis of its national interest as any other 'normal country' would do. Italy's 'national interest' in the Kosovo case, however, 'did not mean the defence of its traditional bilateral interests but participation in a risky, multilateral enterprise designed to promote security in the region' and which was therefore 'essential for the promotion of Italian security as well.'[29] Italy's particular, short-term, interests, in other words, might not have coincided with those of any of its allies but Italy's general, long-term, interest required that the government act with the alliance once the latter had decided on a common course of action.

Italy's contribution to 'Operation Allied Force' cannot therefore be dismissed as yet another example of the country's automatic, and therefore unquestioned, adhesion to American policies. Rather, it can be seen as a confirmation of the existence of a trend towards a more assertive foreign policy based on a newly found self-confidence and enhanced by a more widespread domestic consensus.[30] Such assertiveness, however, at least when understood as the ability to advance one's preferences in the alliance decision-making processes, is likely to become significant only if it can be transposed at the European level. Only the EU as a whole can in fact hope to transform the current lopsided relationship between the US and EU members into a partnership between equals. To do this, however, EU members must address the problem of their political and military weakness. For this reason the Kosovo experience is likely to push the Italian government to play a very active role in the process of European integration in the fields of foreign and defence policy.[31]

From the military point of view Kosovo has highlighted the fact that the Europeans are vastly inferior to the US in military equipment (satellites, sensors, computers, airlift, precision-guided weapons, etc.) needed to fight a high technology war. This was the conclusion that emerged at the Atlantic Council meeting held in Toronto on 21–22 September 1999. What also emerged at the meeting was a political willingness to address this situation. Hence, it seems fair to conclude that, having completed monetary integration, the EU will now turn its attention to the field of defence. More precisely, there is likely to be an effort to boost the so-called 'European defence capability initiative' to close, or at least narrow, the military gap with the US. As D'Alema has repeated often recently, EU members' defence spending amounts to 60 percent of American spending but yields a military capacity, and an ability to project it beyond their borders, of only about 10 percent of that of the US. One can therefore expect an increase in European defence budgets to acquire adequate transport systems, precision-guided weapons and delivery systems, as well as to enhance force compatibility and interoperable technology. In the case of Italy, this modernisation will undoubtedly accelerate the passage to an entirely professional military, something that ironically the DS used to oppose. Progress in defence integration will inevitably require corresponding steps in the field of foreign policy.

Politically, Kosovo has shown that, as long as Europe continues to find it difficult to speak with one voice, the positions and preferences of the US on any issue the alliance faces inevitably emerge as the winning ones. If nothing else, it is certainly symbolic that the EU has proceeded to appoint its first 'foreign minister', a position provided for by the treaty of Amsterdam, precisely during the Kosovo crisis. Even more symbolic, perhaps, is the fact that the person selected for this post was former NATO Secretary-General Solana. One the one hand he, more than anyone else, symbolises a newly found, albeit still precarious, ability of the major European states to cooperate politically and militarily to address a delicate issue at their borders. On the other, his appointment signals that a more politically integrated EU does not aspire to sever its traditional links with the US but only to redefine them. As D'Alema put it in a speech at the Massachusetts Institute of Technology on 4 March, 1999: 'The US and Europe must also cooperate, I believe, on a global level. Sometimes the details do not work out quite the way we want.'[32]

The passage from the realisation of the necessity of a common, in the sense of communitarian as opposed to intergovernmental or lowest common denominator, European foreign policy to its actual development is, however, a process that will most likely prove lengthy and difficult. In the short run, one can only hope that Europe will prove capable of bringing a more balanced approach to Kosovo and the Balkans as a whole. Should the current American tendency to support Kosovo independence remain unchallenged, in fact, the prospect of renewed violence seems much stronger and likely to spread to Macedonia and neighbouring countries as well.

Notes

I would like to thank Raimondo Catanzaro, Mark Gilbert, Brian MacLean, Giuseppe Sciortino, and Gianfranco Pasquino for their helpful comments and suggestions.

 1. On 3 February 1998, an American Prowler plane on a training mission, while flying at a lower altitude and a higher speed than permitted, struck a ski-lift cable causing the fall of a gondola and the death of all twenty people aboard. On the

reactions of the Italian government to the verdict of the American court, see the article by Foreign Affairs Under-Secretary Umberto Ranieri in *L'Unità*, 6 March 1999 and the declarations of Defence Minister Carlo Scognamiglio in *La Repubblica*, 5 March 1999. *Rifondazione Comunista, Comunisti italiani,* and some members of the *Democratici di Sinistra* even called for 'a revision of the Atlantic pact'.

2. Interview in *La Repubblica*, 9 July 1998.

3. For a brief and balanced survey of Kosovo's history, see R. Morozzo della Rocca, *Kosovo. La guerra in Europa. Origini e realtà di un conflitto etnico*, Milano, 1999.

4. See, for instance, *Le Figaro*, 20 January 1999; *Le Monde*, 21 January 1999. One member of the OSCE verification mission stated that 'the Racak tragedy played the same role in Kosovo that the bombing of the Sarajevo market played in Bosnia' ('Che cosa faceva l'OSCE in Kosovo?, *Limes*, 2/1999, 50. Responsibility for the bombing of the Sarajevo market was immediately attributed to the Bosnian Serbs. Later, however, a UN inquiry found that it was the responsibility of the Bosnian Muslims.

5. M. D'Alema, *Gli Italiani e la Guerra. Intervista di Federico Rampini*, Milano, 1999, 11–16. *Operazione Alba* was the name given to a multinational protection force, organised and led by Italy, that was sent to Albania in March 1997 in the wake of the political and economic collapse of that country. Its objective was to promote national reconciliation and democratic normalisation as a basis for economic recovery and thus stop the flow of Albanian refugees to Italy. See G. Sciortino, 'The Albanian Crisis: Social Panic and Italian Foreign Policy' in L. Bardi and M. Rhodes eds, Italian *Politics: Mapping the Future*, Boulder, 1998.

6. Speech at the Royal United Service Institute, London, 9 March 1999 at: http://www.nato.int/ (henceforth the http://www part of the url will be omitted).

7. Speech by D'Alema at the Conference 'Il Cinquantesimo anniversario dell'Alleanza Atlantica: Una nuova NATO per una nuova Europa', Rome, 25 Febbraio 1999 at: palazzochigi.it/

8. D'Alema, *Gli Italiani e la Guerra*, 12–20.

9. The outlines of the Italian position can be found in the speech of Foreign Minister Dini to the Chamber of Deputies on 17 March, 1998. See also R. Morozzo della Rocca, 'La via verso la guerra', in *Kossovo, L'Italia in Guerra*, Quaderni speciali di *Limes*, 1999, 22.

10. L. Dini, 'Una netta visibilità della nostra politica internazionale', *Vita Italiana* no.4 (May 1998).

11. 'L'Europa, la NATO e il ricorso all'uso della forza', *Affari Esteri*, March 1999. See also Dini's speech at the UN Assembly in *La Repubblica*, 12 October 1999.

12. 'La fedeltà alla Nato non si discute', *Corriere della Sera*, 8 March 1999; 'Ranieri respinge le critiche spiega che cosa è successo a Rambouillet', *Il Foglio*, 2 March 1999

13. At camera.it/_dati/leg13/lavori/stenografici/sed513/s090.htm, p. 28.

14. D'Alema, *Gli Italiani e la Guerra*, 3.

15. 'I profughi: allarme europeo', *Corriere della Sera*, 23 March 1999.

16. D'Alema, *Gli Italiani e la Guerra*, 21–22, 38, 52–53, and 109–110.

17. *Ibid.*, 32; F. Rampini, *La Repubblica*, 26 March 1999.

18. G. Luzi, *La Repubblica*, 24 April 1999. Apart from British Prime Minister Blair, all the allies always affirmed that there would be no ground invasion. It seems, however, that towards the end of May this option received serious consideration. See D. Priest, *Washington Post*, 19 September 1999.

19. On the geopolitical reasons for Italian support of Serbia, see Serpicus, 'Why we help Serbia' in *Italy and the Balkans*, special issue of *Limes*, at: limes.net/limesusa.htm

20. In 1997 Italy exported 887 billion lire worth of goods to Serbia. This placed Serbia in fifty-third place as a recipient of Italian exports. Italy, however, ranked second as a source of Serbian imports. In terms of direct foreign investments many small Italian enterprises have recently opened production facilities in Yugoslavia. The biggest investment was that of Telecom Italia. In 1997 it acquired 29 percent of Telekom Serbia at the price of 900 billion lire. See 'Disastro per 5 mila ditte italiane. Crolla l'export verso Belgrado, investimenti a rischio', La Stampa, 19 April 1999.

21. The courses of action advanced by the Italian government included Dini's proposal for a total embargo on Serbia as an alternative to bombing (Corriere della Sera, 4 April 1999), and D'Alema's proposal for a bombing pause to push Russia and China to approve a UNSC resolution (La Stampa, 20 May 1999, Corriere della Sera, 22 May 1999). Dini's remarks are in B. Jerkov, La Repubblica, 21 April 1999.

22. Corriere della Sera, 6 May 1999. Italy was the only country, among those participating in the military operations against Serbia, to keep its embassy in Belgrade open during the conflict.

23. The release of Rugova, for instance, was apparently organised by Monsignor Vincenzo Paglia, a leading figure in the Sant'Egidio Community, a Roman Catholic association that had been very active in the attempt to bridge the gulf between Albanians and Serbs in Kosovo. See Financial Times, 6 May 1999.

24. See Italy Daily-International Herald Tribune, 27–28 March 1999; 'Lo Stato Europa', Limes, 2/1999: 14; and the articles by R. Mannheimer in Corriere della Sera, 2 April and 10 May 1999.

25. F. Venturini, Corriere della Sera, 15 April 1999; A. Minzolini, La Stampa, 15 April 1999. Some MPs of the majority, including many from the left of DS, reacted by signing a document on 22 April that requested a bombing pause and manifested their intention to vote against a ground invasion should it come to that (Il Manifesto, 24 April 1999).

26. See, for example, 'Offerte e aiuti diretti: Italiani più generosi degli Stati Uniti', Corriere della Sera, 1 May 1999. At times this effort went to ridiculous extremes, as when a newspaper headline claimed: 'Our kitchen dishes out 10 kgs. of pasta every 8 minutes; others offer only potatoes' (Corriere della Sera, 19 April 1999). The worst culprit in the process of demonisation of the Serbs was La Repubblica. For an almost hilarious example, see M. Ricci, 'Rubano sangue ai bambini', La Repubblica, 21 April 1999. These exaggerations, moreover, have never been corrected even if, after the entry of the multinational force in Kosovo, it became clear that Serbian atrocities were on a scale not even remotely close to what was earlier reported. The only paper that raised questions about the reliability of accounts of Serbian atrocities based exclusively on KLA information was Il Manifesto.

27. D'Alema, Gli Italiani e la Guerra, 88–89.

28. G. Calchi Novati, 'Italy and Suez 1956: how to be committed and equidistant', Il Politico, no.1, 1997, 43.

29. U. Ranieri, 'Interesse nazionale e multilateralismo: la strategia italiana nei Balcani', Europa Europe, no. 4, 1999, 30–33.

30. On the emergence of this trend see my 'The Italian Intervention in Somalia: A New Italian Foreign Policy After the Cold War?' in Italian Politics: Ending the First Republic, eds C. Mershon and G. Pasquino, Boulder, 1995, 197–215.

31. See, for instance, D'Alema, Gli Italiani e la Guerra, 83–95.

32. Ibid., 138.

3

THE END OF ITALY'S REFERENDUM ANOMALY?

Mark Donovan

The referendum of 18 April 1999 was intended to force parliament, by pressure of public opinion, to revise the mixed electoral system in a more decisively anti-proportional direction. The existing system, introduced in 1993, was a compromise outcome which had resulted from a similar mobilisation against the still powerful parliamentary elites of the so-called First Republic. Subsequently, supporters of proportionality had sought to reinforce their position and the principle of proportional representation, for example via new legislation on party financing. With the failure of the third attempt at constitutional reform via parliament (1997–8) and continuing government instability exemplified by the change of prime minister and cabinet in October 1998, many despaired of the establishment of the much invoked and much contested Second Republic. The failure of the 1999 referendum to reach the quorum, despite a huge majority in favour of its majoritarian implications, led many to conclude that a cycle of referendum-driven reform had come to an end, and with it the chance of achieving a new institutional framework for the Republic. The pressure for reform remained strong, however, and new referendum campaigns for electoral and wider reform were immediately launched.

The Faltering Transition and Reform by Referendum

By the late 1990s, Italians were losing faith in the ability of the new political elites to establish the so-called Second Republic. Talk was of a stalled transition,[1] or even of a return to the First Republic. Despite the 1994 election having ushered in a substantially new party system and parliamentary elite, two successive parliaments, the twelfth (1994–6) and thirteenth (1996–), had produced two 'false starts' to the putative new order. Thus, the 1994 election gave birth to the government of Silvio Berlusconi which was both short-lived and the cause of great concern, thanks to the identity of his coalition partners and to the nature of Berlusconi's own dramatic conquest of governmental authority. Furthermore, the second (and last) government of the legislature, that of Lamberto Dini, consisted entirely of non-parliamentarians and thus challenged the principle of party government and with it the legitimacy of parliament itself.[2] The 1996 election initially seemed to indicate that, despite everything, progress was being made in the restructuring of Italian politics. Thus, the campaign largely focused on a battle between two coalitions competing to form a government, and the victory of the Olive Tree alliance, led by Romano Prodi, over Berlusconi's Freedom Pole, resulted in Prodi forming a government. The electorate had thus determined who became prime minister. From this perspective, even the false start of 1994–6 could be seen in a better light, as part of a learning process. Indeed, with Prodi's appointment, Italy's party system had also seen a clear case of alternation – something the First Republic had never witnessed.

The formation of Prodi's cabinet was swift, and a competent government team went on to achieve a notable success in bringing about Italy's participation in the European single currency in the 'first wave' of adherents. Meanwhile, the issue of institutional reform was left to the party leaders. The secretary of the *Democratici di sinistra* (Democrats of the Left: DS), the government's principal support party, took a lead role, chairing a specially established Joint Committee on Constitutional Reform (the *Bicamerale*). Here, however, was a major imperfection in the nascent system. Massimo D'Alema, the DS leader, was not the prime minister. This was to prove highly damaging. In the autumn of 1998, a few months after the failure of the Bicamerale,[3] D'Alema replaced Prodi as prime minister in a parliamentary manoeuvre that lacked immediate electoral legitimation and flew in the face of the new principles which, supposedly, the political elites were seeking to implement: the direct election of cabinets and their prime minister by the electorate, and the stability of government between elections.[4] Worse, D'Alema's parliamentary majority relied upon the support of MPs originally elected as members of the Liberty Pole. These, led by the former Christian Democrat and President of the Republic (1985–92), Francesco Cossiga, constituted a new quasi-party, the Union for the Democratic Republic (UDR). This was a textbook example of an enduring parliamentary vice: trans-formism.[5] In mid-term, a group of opposition MPs had transformed themselves into government supporters, ignoring their electoral mandates and overthrowing the premier chosen by the electorate.

Given growing public disillusion with the faltering transition, attested to by declining sub-national electoral turnouts, the expectation in 1998 and early 1999 was that public support for the referendum would be very strong – if the Constitutional Court allowed the referendum to proceed. By October 1998 the referendum process was well under way, propelled by the perception that the political elites needed to be compelled to take decisive action by a manifestation of popular will similar to that which in 1990–3 had forced the first major electoral reforms.[6] Support for another referendum promoting electoral reform had grown in 1997–8 against the background of the extremely disappointing deliberations on constitutional reform taking place in the Bicamerale,[7] and in particular the tendency to reinstate the principle of PR.

In fact, the period from 1993 had seen electoral reform at local and regional as well as national level, as well as reform of party financing, and PR continued to figure prominently. New legislation for local elections introduced in March 1993 (in order to avoid a referendum) had introduced a powerful incentive to bipolarisation and government stability via the direct election of mayors. At the same time, nevertheless, a substantially proportional system was retained for the election of local councils, 'corrected' in favour of government stability by a seat bonus awarded to parties supporting the mayor – again allocated proportionally.[8] The new parliamentary electoral systems (slightly different for each chamber) reflected the basic premises of the April referendum in that three-quarters of seats were now elected on a plurality basis. However, the referendum proposals were the result of institutional happenstance, not rational policy-making,[9] and the detail of the legislation was a product of the elites of the so-called First Republic. In fact, the 1992–4 parliament was still dominated by the Christian Democrats (DC), the Socialists (PSI) and their allies. The legislation thus maintained a significant proportional corrective: 25 percent. Subsequent reform of the regional electoral system was based on 80 percent PR allocation of seats, with the remainder allocated – again on a proportional basis – as a bonus to the winning coalition to facilitate stability. Finally, the reintroduction of party financing in 1997 not only overturned the 1993 referendum which had abrogated the public financing of political parties, but powerfully strengthened the small parties and the logic of proportionality. The press had a field day calculating how many 'parties' were allocated funds in the new parliament – the final figure reached over fifty.

In the run-up to the 1994 election, moreover, even the plurality aspect of the parliamentary electoral system was proportionalised via the candidate selection process. This development was extremely important, for it crystallised the extreme fragmentation resulting from the collapse of the old party system. Underlying this development was the strong tendency to bipolarisation focusing on competition for executive office that emerged in 1993–4: for mayorships locally and cabinet formation nationally. In circumstances of strong Left-Right polarisation, majoritarianism was an extremely powerful incentive to the formation of electoral alliances: under the plurality rule, a seat is won by the candidate who gains most votes. Other candidates get nothing. Thus, in 1993–4 an alliance of the Left, the Progressives, made coordinated stand-down arrangements to enhance the parties' chances of winning each seat. Berlusconi responded by creating similar arrangements for a right-wing bloc. In both blocs, the allocation of candidates to seats had to satisfy even the smallest parties which, furthermore, could blackmail the larger parties in to giving them unduly large numbers of 'safe' seats for fear that otherwise the election would be lost.

In addition to the internal fragmentation of Left and Right, it is also the case that despite the substantial bipolarisation of party competition since 1993, Italy does not have a pure two-bloc party system. In 1994, the DC's major heir, the Italian Popular Party (PPI), led an attempt to establish a third, centre pole and although this failed, tendencies towards 'neo-centrism', that is, the recreation of a third pole able to form a government with either Left or Right have been a feature of the faltering transition. Furthermore, whilst the failure of the centrist third pole in 1994 led to the PPI and its allies splitting Left and Right, in 1996 the Northern League stood alone, creating tripolar politics at constituency level in much of northern Italy. On the Left, too, the formation of the Olive Tree in 1995–6 excluded *Rifondazione comunista* (Communist Refoundation: PRC), so that there are 'two Lefts'. Thus, whilst the nascent party system has seen competition for government in a way the First Republic did not, the system is far from stable.

By the summer of 1997 there was a real threat that PR would be re-established as a key feature of parliamentary elections. Whilst electoral reform was outside the remit of the Bicamerale, it came to be recognised that it would nevertheless be integral to the wider reform process. An initially secret accord reached by party elites on 18 June 1997 suggested that such reform was likely to favour the preservation of the small parties and hence party system fragmentation. Once public, the accord became the object of intense criticism and even ridicule, being dubbed the 'pie pact' (*patto della crostata*) on the basis of its allegedly being agreed over dessert at the house of one of Berlusconi's lieutenants. The pie pact was seen, both for its content and for the secretive and extra-parliamentary manner in which it was reached, as epitomising the re-establishment of partyocracy, that is government by parties for parties, not via parliament for the public good. Interest thus grew in the possibility of launching a referendum to demonstrate the public's hostility to PR even though Marco Pannella, the maverick founder of the Radical party, had been condemned for championing a similar referendum in the immediately preceding period.[10]

In the spring of 1998, as the Bicamerale limped to its ignominious end, the campaign began to collect the half million signatures needed to propose the referendum. Italy's foremost political scientist, Giovanni Sartori, gave his qualified support. Despite being no admirer of the use made of the referendum in Italy, he argued that it was the only way to break out of the impasse in which the country found itself. Electoral reform constituted a 'Gordian knot' which no one could undo, yet only the undoing of it would permit the general structural reform that the political system needed. A referendum could, like Alexander the Great's sword, cut through the knot.[11]

The Referendum Campaign: A Haphazard Tool in a Complex Struggle

In February 1998, a Committee for the Defence of the Referendum and Plurality Voting announced that it had devised what it believed to be a legally adequate means of promoting an anti-proportional referendum. The tiny committee comprised individuals close to Pannella but also had links with Mario Segni, who had chaired the successful 1991 and 1993 electoral reform referendums. A major limitation of Italian referendums is that they are purely abrogative. That is to say, they can delete legislation, or parts of legislation, but they cannot make new law. Over the quarter-century in which the instrument has been used, however, Constitutional Court jurisprudence has further specified the requirements for its use. Thus, the Court has ruled impermissible referendums which render it impossible to hold elections until enabling legislation is enacted. As a consequence, referendums have become, with unique regard to electoral legislation, 'quasi-propositive' since legislation resulting from partial abrogation must be capable of immediate application. This was problematic in 1999. Many of the supporters of the referendum did not support the rather haphazard outcome of a successful vote. Rather, they sought to demonstrate public hostility to PR. The symbolic connotation of the vote was what mattered, not the normative detail.

Following a successful referendum, some reformists, not least Pannella, wanted to see an entirely British-type plurality electoral system introduced. Others, including Sartori, supported the introduction of a French-style double ballot at constituency level. To this end, a draft bill was promoted as a popular initiative by the DS Senator Stefano Passigli and by Antonio Di Pietro. Such initiatives require 50,000 signatures to be collected, following which parliament is required to consider them. Such consideration, however, need only be cursory, and since the double ballot had powerful enemies, it found little political backing despite the fact that over 370,000 signatures were raised in support of it. Others again did support the system that would arise, haphazardly, from the convoluted interaction of the law and jurisprudence concerning the referendum. Had the referendum succeeded, one-quarter of parliamentary seats would have been allocated on a regional basis to those losing candidates with the highest votes (see note 5). For example, of the Abruzzo region's fourteen Deputies, eleven would have been elected on a plurality basis in single-member constituencies, while the remaining three would have been the highest scoring candidates defeated in the plurality ballots.

Given the divisions between the supporters of the referendum as to what post-referendum outcome they intended, there was confusion over the aim of the referendum. This was compounded by the transversal (Left-Right) nature of both support and opposition to the referendum. Finally, some supporters of the 'haphazard' outcome argued that, were the referendum won, elections would have to be held on that basis. Any entirely new legislation would betray the people who had been mobilised in support of the referendum.[12] Arguably, this rather demagogic argument ignored the fact that the legislative outcome of a successful referendum would not at all be a rationally derived electoral system put to the people as a proposition *per se*. Whilst the referendum had become 'quasi-propositive' rather than purely abrogative, its propositional content was haphazard rather than intentional so that, whilst legally binding, a successful electoral referendum outcome should be considered indicative rather than definitive.

The signature campaign lasted from April to mid-June 1998. Its leading promoters included: Mario Segni, president of the 1991 and 1993 referendum campaigns; the liberal wing of Forza Italia, prominent members of which had a past in the Radical party; Achille Occhetto, who had overseen the transformation of the PCI into the PDS and backed the earlier referendums; the ex-President of *Confindustria* (the industrialists' association), Luigi Abete; and Antonio Di Pietro, the ex-investigating magistrate who had become the people's hero during the *Tangentopoli* phenomenon of 1992–3 which had done so much to topple the First Republic. Di Pietro played a highly active and visible role in mobilising public support in the signature collecting campaign, using it to raise the profile of his own political movement, 'The Italy of Values' (*L'Italia dei Valori*).

None of the three main parties, the DS, Forza Italia and the *Alleanza nazionale* (National Alliance: AN), strongly backed the campaign. Each was internally divided, and the DS and Forza Italia especially were hostage to the small parties supporting them in parliament. Despite the DS's official support for the double ballot, Massimo D'Alema was unable to take a strong position since the DS-left favoured PR and the party's coalition allies, the *Partito popolare italiano* (Italian Popular Party: PPI), *Verdi* (Greens) and *Rifondazione comunista* (Communist Refoundation: PRC) all condemned any indication of support for the referendum. D'Alema thus tended to criticise the referendum as an inadequate solution to the problem of electoral reform – which it was. But D'Alema's stance muddied the picture, undermining the referendum's primarily anti-PR connotation. Berlusconi also remained equivocal, whilst the AN took no official position until after the signature campaign was over.

Over the winter of 1998–9 the referendum campaigners turned their attention to the President of the Republic and the Constitutional Court, the latter being due to decide on the admissibility of the proposal at the end of January. Neither the court nor the president were regarded as entirely above the partisan fray and the mobilisation raised temperatures considerably, triggering the emergence of 'Yes' and 'No' campaign movements. The winter mobilisation also promoted a rash of proposals to render the court less susceptible to partisan influence.

In the event, on 19 January and in record time, the court affirmed that the referendum could proceed. Pannella's similar proposal, struck down two years previously, had meant abolishing the one-quarter of seats elected by PR and this had been judged to leave a legislative vacuum. The 1999 proposal left unaltered the number of seats, changing only the basis on which they were allocated. The decision meant that the vote would take place between 15 April and 15 July. In the meantime, the political context in which the final phase of public mobilisation would take place had changed considerably, producing intense speculation about the impact of the referendum on the presidential and European parliamentary elections,[13] both due in the early summer. The future structure of the party system and the likelihood of bringing the faltering transition to a satisfactory end were believed to be at stake.

In October 1998, the government of Romano Prodi had been replaced by that of Massimo D'Alema, and this had several consequences. For a start, Walter Veltroni replaced D'Alema as DS party leader and Veltroni was seen as supporting the *Ulivo* (Olive Tree coalition) as the harbinger of a post-socialist, 'Democrat' party. Simultaneously, however, D'Alema's government now depended on Cossiga's UDR which was hostile to the Olive Tree. Exactly what Cossiga intended is not clear. He appeared to harbour illusions of fostering the reunification of the ex-Christian Democratic parties and breaking Forza Italia's link with AN in order to form a moderate centre-right alternative to a social democratic Left which, for its part, would exclude Communist Refoundation. Certainly, the formation of D'Alema's government split the latter, leaving its rump excluded from the cabinet whilst the *Partito dei comunisti italiani* (Party of Italian Communists: PDCI) entered the new coalition. On the Right, however, Cossiga proved unable to break the Forza Italia – AN alliance although his early support for Berlusconi's link-up with the European People's Party (EPP) was later credited with Forza Italia's success, at AN's expense, in the June European election. The significance of all this for the referendum was that the structure of the party system was particularly unstable, and the referendum was a major weapon in the struggle to redefine it. In particular, Romano Prodi became a major protagonist in the referendum campaign, in a bid to reassert his leadership of a restructured Left.

In February, Prodi allied himself with Di Pietro and the recently formed *Centocittà* ('Hundred Cities') movement of directly-elected mayors to form the Democrats, adopting the donkey symbol of the American party of that name. This new movement sought to build an alliance of the Left that tended towards the subordination of the parties within a single, 'super Olive Tree', reinforcing the bipolar dynamic of the party system. The plebiscitary qualities of this approach, that is, the idea that elections comprise a competition between two forces, with the electorate choosing which forms the government, was reinforced by the participation of Centocittà and Di Pietro in Prodi's movement. While Centocittà comprised directly-elected city leaders whose popularity had gained them nationwide reputations, Di Pietro's popularity had led him to be seen as a powerful presidential candidate if that office became directly elected. Similarly, the support given by the leader of the AN, Gianfranco Fini, for the referendum indicated its plebiscitary aspect, for the AN had long favoured a presidential political system. More specifically, Fini hoped to upstage Berlusconi, demonstrating that he was a leader in touch with the people. A successful referendum outcome would have seen Fini assert his right to lead the *Polo delle libertà* (Freedom Pole) in the next election. Indeed, many predicted that a successful referendum would see that election fought over between Fini and Prodi.

In the meantime, the government sought to pre-empt the referendum by reforming the electoral system. Giuliano Amato, a highly respected technocrat (and prime minister, 1992–3) had been appointed as Minister for Institutional Reform, and he devised a proposal, based on a double ballot, which won the support of the government majority as a first step towards seeking opposition cooperation. In reality, however, the DS's allies, not least the PPI, were as hostile to the double ballot as to the referendum. They backed the proposal only to demonstrate government unity, knowing that it would make no progress in parliament.

By the end of February 1999, the UDR had collapsed while the Democrats were consistently showing public support of about 10 percent in the event of elections. However, polls were also showing that the 50 percent referendum quorum might not be reached. The public's confusion about the significance of the referendum was added to when Segni, the Chair of the 'Yes' campaign, signed an accord with Fini proclaiming the founding of a 'liberal-democratic' alliance to counter the projected super-Olive Tree. At face value, Segni's move promoted bipolarism and challenged Berlusconi's much criticised weak leadership of the centre-right. However, contrary to Cossiga's strategy, it came at the cost of aligning himself with AN. Consequently Segni, little trusted on the Right in any case, now confirmed the view of the far Left (PRC, PDCI, Greens and Left-DS) and the PPI that the referendum was a threat to democracy.

At the end of March, after much speculation about D'Alema's interest in 'decapitating' the Democrats, Prodi was nominated President of the European Commission. Two weeks later he was forced to withdraw his European parliamentary candidacy in response to DS-instigated pressure from the European Socialists (PES). In this way, and via Berlusconi's acquisition of legitimacy via accession to the EPP, Euro-politics became a dimension of the war of manoeuvre to restructure Italian politics. At the same time that Prodi was nominated for the Commission presidency, the Kosovo war broke

out. Given Italy's geographic proximity to Kosovo and strong pacifist traditions, the appalling refugee crisis induced by the war dis-
tracted attention from the referendum and made it seem even more
confusing. In fact, it was just beginning to be explained to the public that the referendum proposal took some fifteen minutes to read
and referred to some fifty pieces of legislation. Still, opinion surveys showed an increase in public understanding of the issue in the
month preceding the vote, and there were developments in favour
of the 'Yes' vote. Thus ACLI, the Catholic workers' association
which had strongly supported the original electoral referendums,
came out in support just as the war started and later, when opponents of the referendum suggested that its cost (approximately
£350 million) was a scandalous waste of resources that should be
directed to refugee aid, Confindustria made explicit its support of
the referendum.

In the ten days before the vote, the 'No' camp swung towards rec-
ommending abstention, with the *Lega Nord* (Northern League: LN)
adopting this position explicitly. Other pro-PR leaders mostly took a
more mealy-mouthed defence of the democratic legitimacy and equal
dignity of abstention. Official party positions can be seen in Table 3.1.
The Pole was consistent in its 'Yes' position, but it should be noted
that Berlusconi did not support the referendum, that one of his leading advisers (Giuliano Urbani) was prominent in the 'No' campaign,
and that Forza Italia urged freedom of conscience rather than support
as its official position. The opposition of the DS's key allies is also to
be noted. Most of the UDR was anti, although Cossiga, its founder,
was personally in favour of a 'Yes' vote.

The Result: Interpreting Referendum Failure

That the 50 percent quorum might not be reached was scarcely
conceivable in 1997–8. In the two months before the vote, however, public opinion polls clearly indicated that this was possible.
Shortly after the voting stations closed, polls nevertheless indicated that this last hurdle had been overcome. In live television
debate, various political leaders consequently gave vent to feelings
that would not otherwise have been heard. Most notably, Fini lost
his usual well-measured prudence, reflecting the enormous investment he had made in the referendum. He called for electoral
reform, the introduction of a presidential system of government
and challenged Berlusconi's leadership of the Liberty Pole.

In fact, despite 91.5 percent of the valid vote being in favour of
the proposal, the referendum was lost – by just 207,010 votes, 0.4

Table 3.1 *Formal party positions and explicit dissent*

Party/party system	Yes	Free vote	No	Abstain
Government				
Communist Refoundation			RC	
Green			Green	
Italian Communists			PDCI	
Democrats of the Left	DS		Left-DS	
Democrats	Democrats			
Italian Popular Party			PPI	
Italian Social Democrats			SDI	
Union for a Democratic Republic	Cossiga	UDR		
Dini List	Dini			
Opposition				
Segni Pact	Segni			
Forza Italia	FI (nominally)	Berlusconi	Urbani et al.	
Centre Christian Democrats	CCD			
National Alliance	AN			
Other				
Social Movement – Tricolour Flame			Flame	
Pannella	Pannella			
Northern League				LN

Notes: De facto, most supporters of the 'No' vote shifted to advocating abstention in the closing days the campaign. The table distinguishes the government and main opposition parties. See discussion in text.

percent of the electorate, on a 49.6 percent turnout. So close was the result that it was challenged in court on the basis that the total registered electorate of 49,309,060 included many who were either dead or uncontactable, especially among the approximately two-and-a-half million registered abroad. These latter constituted 4.3 percent of the total and, moreover, had a notoriously low turnout – just 4.5 percent in the 1996 election. The court rejected the appeal, but the grounds on which it did so were not made clear, to the disgust of the referendum's supporters.[14]

Many blamed the failure on the South where turnout fell well below 50 percent (see Table 3.2, but the 'Yes' vote was slightly stronger there than in the North. More importantly, given that turnout is always lower in the South, what proved critical was the marked demobilisation of the North. This trend, first identified in

Table 3.2 *Regional turnout*

Region	Turnout	Yes	No
North	53.9	90.2	9.8
Centre	54.0	92.8	7.2
South	42.8	92.8	7.2
Islands	40.2	92.5	7.5

Source: La Repubblica, 20 April 1999

recent local elections, represented something significantly new in Italian electoral behaviour. Blame was also placed on the major parties, and especially Berlusconi, for failing to mobilise their voters in support of the referendum. Here, organisational weaknesses as well as strategic weaknesses were relevant. Voter polls (see Table 3.3) indicated that some two-fifths of Forza Italia and AN supporters voted 'No' or returned a blank vote, and just over a quarter of DS supporters did the same. Even a marginally more effective mobilisation of their electorates by any of these three parties would have won the day.

The mainstream media reaction to the result was one of intense gloom. Two successive waves of referendums, first in 1997 and now in 1999, had failed to reach the quorum. The fact that the 1999 referendum had been chaired by Segni, who had triumphed in 1991 and 1993, and been backed by a similar range of interests, including Confindustria and ACLI, had not sufficed to mobilise vot-

Table 3.3 *Percentage distribution of party supporters' vote*

Party	Indication	Yes	No	Blank
PRC	N	22	7	71
DS	Y	72	6	22
Green	N	30	6	64
PPI	N	28	5	67
Dini	Y	43	7	50
CCD-CDU	Y	60	2	38
Forza Italia	Y	59	1	40
AN	Y	62	1	37
LN	Abstain	23	3	74
Pannella	Y	68	2	30

Source: Abacus poll, *La Repubblica*, 19 April 1999, with reference to declared support in 1996 election. For party abbreviations, see list of acronyms.

ers. Many concluded that a cycle of referendum-induced institutional reform was over. Mobilisation had given way to demobilisation. The political elite was off the hook, and further reform was therefore unlikely.

The set-back suffered by AN and Segni was marked, and was compounded by their poor joint performance in the European parliamentary election, especially as Berlusconi did particularly well, enabling him to reassert his leadership of the Right. Romano Prodi's new party, the Democrats, clearly also suffered a blow, but went on to do moderately well in the European Parliament election, becoming the second force on the Left with nearly 8 percent of the vote. The success of Prodi's new party was outdone, moreover, by the Bonino list – and as a protégé of Pannella, Emma Bonino was a convinced supporter of the quarter-century-old tactic of attacking the establishment via the referendum instrument. A radical interpretation of the referendum failure is that both the overwhelming 'Yes' vote for anti-PR electoral reform *and* the extent of abstention signalled very extensive public disaffection towards the party system. The difference between the two votes is that one half of the public believed that reform was still possible, the other half did not.[15] There is poll evidence for this. Abstention seems not to have reflected incomprehension either of the question or of the significance of a 'Yes' vote. Least of all did it imply widespread support for PR. What it did reflect was awareness that the parties would determine any subsequent legislation.[16]

Future Prospects:
the Vulnerability of the New Material Constitution

The failure of the April 1999 referendum led to claims that the prominence of the referendum instrument in Italian politics was over. This hasty reaction was rapidly disproved by events reflecting three aspects of its use in Italy. First, the institutional context for its deployment is an almost uniquely permissive one, given that it is available upon popular demand in Italy. Second, a rash of issues with which the referendum has long been associated remain unresolved. Third, the referendum instrument was rapidly 'rediscovered' in the wake of the European Parliament election, and over the summer and autumn of 1999 the political establishment again came under intense referendum pressure to reform the parliamentary electoral system.

In the wake of the double referendum and European Parliament set-back, Fini drove ahead with his strategy of adopting a radical yet liberal and reformist policy profile by launching a referendum campaign on both the public financing of parties and electoral reform. By competing for the radical centre, Fini sought to avoid his party's marginalisation as a party of authoritarian nostalgics, whilst keeping the party with him as he sought to reorientate it. The referendum instrument thus remained a major factor in the battle to restructure the Right as well as – thanks to the Democrats – the Left. At the same time, Bonino's neo-liberal quasi-party succeeded in promoting a raft of referendums on electoral and politico-economic reform.

That the electoral system remained the master political and indeed constitutional issue, in the material, (if not narrow legal), sense of the term, was notably affirmed by Sartori while the signature campaign was in full swing.[17] He lambasted the political élites' obsessive discussion of ways to legislate against the consequences of the 1993 legislation whilst ignoring the need to replace the legislation which had caused the inadequacies in the functioning of the political system in the first place. Specifically, Sartori condemned proposals to prevent the appointment of new prime ministers (and accompanying cabinets) during the lifetime of a parliament, that is the so-called *ribaltoni* and *ribaltini*, meaning, approximately, 'big switch-around' and 'little switch-around'. These expressions refer respectively: (a) to the switch from centre-right to technocratic centrist government in late 1994 and early 1995 (Berlusconi to Dini); and (b) to the shift towards the centre in late 1998 within the Left (Prodi to D'Alema). Without these devices, argued Sartori, Italians would in all likelihood be condemned to more-or-less annual parliamentary elections since the fundamental problem of the blackmail potential of the small parties and the heterogeneity of the forces comprising the alliances would not be resolved without electoral reform. At the same time, Sartori expressed his very great doubt that attempts to restructure the internally divided electoral alliances as more cohesive blocs would work. Party secretaries simply would not cede significant powers to the alliance leaders.

In making these arguments, Sartori summed up the widespread view that without further electoral reform, Italian governments would remain doubly weak, that is, incoherent and indecisive as policy makers as well as vulnerable to being overthrown. There was, too, a widespread belief that the continuing weakness of government put at risk the country's economic and social welfare, not least its continuing participation in the new European currency area, to say nothing of the country's political and civil stability. In effect, electoral reform and the changed structure of the party system had resulted in substantial modifications to Italy's material constitution, yet these remained contested and unconsolidated. At the end of the 1990s, Italy stood suspended between the continuity of the formal constitution and radical, yet vulnerable, discontinuity in the material constitution. Electoral reform could help consolidate the nascent bipolar system or promote its decomposition and a return to government formation at the centre. In this alternative scenario, some form of national coalition government, probably ranging from Forza Italia to the DS, would result from the difficulties of reforming the country's politico-administrative system and cutting back, or at least recasting, Italy's misshapen, inefficient and unjust welfare state. In this uncertain context, the referendum instrument remained a potent weapon to supporters of plebiscitary democratic reform so long as they could effectively communicate the reasons for its use. Opinion polls consistently indicated strong support for effective, presidential government which majoritarian electoral reform could underpin.

Notes

1. M. Caciagli and D.I. Kertzer, (eds), *Italian Politics. The Stalled Transition*, Boulder, 1997.
2. G. Pasquino, 'No Longer a "Party State"? Institutions, Power and the Problems of Italian Reform', in *Crisis and Transition in Italian Politics*, eds M. Bull and M. Rhodes, London, 1997, 35–53.
3. G. Pasquino, 'Autopsia del Bicamerale', in *Politica in Italia: Edizione 99*, eds David Hine and Salvatore Vassallo, Bologna, 1999, 117–38.
4. Sergio Fabbrini, 'Dal governo Prodi al governo D'Alema', in *Politica in Italia: Edizione 99*, eds David Hine and Salvatore Vassallo, 139–59.
5. See M. Donovan, 'Introduction', in *Italy*, Vol.1, ed., Mark Donovan, Aldershot, 1998, xiii–xxi.
6. G. Pasquino, 'The electoral reform referendums', in *Italian Politics A Review. Volume 6*, eds R. Leonardi and F. Anderlini, London, 1992, 9–24; P. Corbetta and A.M.L. Parisi, 'The Referendum on the Electoral Law for the Senate: Another Momentous April', in *Italian Politics. Ending the First Republic*, eds C. Mershon and G. Pasquino, Boulder, 1995, 75–9; M. Donovan, 'The Referendum and the Transformation of the Party System', in *Modern Italy* 1, no.1, 1995, 53–69.
7. C. Fusaro, 'The Politics of Constitutional Reform in Italy: A Framework for Analysis', in *South European Society and Politics*, no. 2, 1998, 45–74; M. Gilbert, 'Transforming Italy's institutions? The Bicameral Committee on Institutional Reform', in *Modern Italy* 3, no. 1, 1998, 49–66; G. Pasquino, 'Reforming the Italian constitution', *Journal of Modern Italian Studies* 3, no. 1, 1998, 42–54.
8. In both this case and in the description of the impact a successful referendum would have had on the current electoral legislation (see below), the detail is simplified.
9. M. Donovan, 'The Politics of Electoral Reform' in *International Political Science Review* 16, no.1, 1995, 47–64.

10. M. Donovan, 'Failure Due to Abuse'? in *Italian Politics. Mapping the Future*, eds Luciano Bardi and Martin Rhodes, Boulder, 1998, 169–186.
11. *Corriere della Sera*, 14 March 1998.
12. *Corriere della Sera*, 23 December 1998.
13. See the contributions by Philip Daniels and Gianfranco Pasquino in this volume.
14. This and the following paragraph is based on: P. Segatti, 'Quando un referendum fallisce', *Il Mulino XLVIII*, no. 383, 1999, 453–60.
15. P. Pombeni, 'Il 18 aprile e il 13 maggio (con appendice il 13 giugno)', *Il Mulino XLVIII*, no. 383, 1999, 470.
16. R. Mannheimer, *Corriere della Sera*, 19 April 1999.
17. *Corriere della Sera*, 13 July 1999.

4

THE MUNICIPAL ELECTIONS OF 1999 AND THE 'DEFEAT' OF THE LEFT IN BOLOGNA

Gianfranco Baldini and Guido Legnante[1]

On 29 November and 13 December 1998, elections were held for the renewal of fifty-eight municipal councils in towns comprising more than 15,000 inhabitants, as well as of four provincial administrations. The feature that most caught the attention of politicians and commentators, apart from changes in the political balance of the coalitions, was the turnout for these elections. For the first time in the electoral history of republican Italy, non-voters in the provincial elections in some cases amounted to more than 50 percent of the electorate. Largely blamed for this fall in electoral participation was the frequency with which voters had been recently called to the polling booths; and this accelerated the process of modifying the law on the direct election of the mayor, it being proposed, amongst other things, that all the administrative elections should be combined into a single annual round of voting.

Partly because of the extremely low turnout for the provincial elections of 1998, when the time came for the administrative elections of 1999 the mass media and political parties focused their attention on the city elections. Given that there was no voting in the metropolitan areas, where elections had been held in 1997, three large cities – Bologna, Florence and Bari – together with a further twenty-five provincial capitals, were the most important towns and cities called to the polling booths. Very soon, however, the changed political circumstances in which the electoral campaigns were fought in the three cities (in Bari the presence of the outgoing mayor and the strength of the centre-right left little leeway for the opposition,[2] while in Florence the mayor's exit had been painlessly handled by the centre-left) concentrated interest on Bologna, where the breakdown in relations between the incumbent mayor and his party, the *Democratici di sinistra* (Democrats of the Left: DS) had brought the start of the electoral campaign forward to mid-1988.

The changes introduced by law 120/99 ushered in an electoral contest where the defeat of the centre-left in Bologna was seen as epitomising the difficulties besetting the government coalition. Analysis of voting in the twenty-eight provincial capitals (which represented about 10 percent of the voting electorate) will furnish a general picture of the city elections of 1999.

Adjusting the System of Direct Election: Law 120/99

The law on direct mayoral elections (no. 81 of 25 March 1993) had been the first item of legislation to react to a surge in demand for the opportunity to vote for individuals rather than party lists. In the space of two years (1993–95) pressure for majoritarian voting gave rise to changes in the electoral system at all levels of government apart from that of the European Parliament. Widely held responsible for the improved performance of the Italian municipal administrations, the law was viewed as one of the possible 'models' for the institutional reforms discussed by the Bicameral Committee chaired by Massimo D'Alema. As has been frequently pointed out,[3] however, because the law of 1993 was the result of a compromise, it did not entirely resolve the ungovernability and instability that had hitherto typified municipal administration. Minor aspects aside,[4] law 120/99 has introduced important changes in the following four broad areas.

The amalgamation of elections into
a single springtime 'election day'.

In an endeavour to counter any further decline in electoral turnout, the law states that elections for the renewal of municipal and provincial councils must, from 2000 onwards, be held on the same day (between 15 April and 15 June). This provision applies both when mandates have expired in the first six months of the year, and when municipal councils have been dissolved or their mandates have expired in the second six months. Elections for the latter councils are to be held jointly with those of the following year.

The duration and renewal of electoral terms

The law restores the duration of the term of office which applied before the reform of 1993 (five years), thereby making it equal to those of the other levels of government (the regional administrations and parliament). It has also settled the controversial issue of the number of permitted terms: 'a third consecutive mandate is permitted if the duration of one of the two previous mandates has been less than two years, six months and one day, owing to causes other than voluntary resignation' (article 2).

Plurality premium

The law reduces (from 50 percent to 40 percent) the share of votes necessary for a mayor elected in the first ballot to obtain the so-called 'plurality premium' (the additional seats awarded to the party obtaining the majority of votes), on the proviso that the opposing list or coalition has not gained more than 50 percent of the vote. This is one of the most important innovations introduced by the law, in that it helps mayors more popular than the lists backing them to achieve a majority.

Cut-off threshold

In order to counteract the excessive fragmentation of municipal councils, especially outside the coalitions, the law imposes a 3 percent threshold for access by 'isolated' lists (that is, those not in coalition with other groupings) to the share-out of seats on the municipal councils.[5]

Voting in the Provincial Capitals

The 1999 election sheds light on the evolution of various features of municipal electoral dynamics already apparent over recent years: the fragmentation or concentration of the party 'offer' and the response of the electorate to that offer, participation rates, the success of parties and candidates, the number of outgoing mayors.

Once again the lists increased in number with respect to the previous election, but there was a fall-off in the average number of candidates for mayoral posts. Whereas the average number of candidates fell from 7.1 to 6.1 in the sixty-six provincial capitals that went to the polls in 1997–8, it rose from 6.3 to 7.2 in the twenty-eight provincial capitals involved in the 1999 elections.[6] At first sight, therefore, the electoral format seemed to have grown more complex. Not only was there greater fragmentation of lists, but there were more mayoral candidates too. This feature reflected the convulsed state of the political alliances and also the fact that several centrist parties, as well as *Rifondazione comunista* (Communist Refoundation Party: PRC) competed on their own in numerous towns and cities.

However, there was no let-up in the growing tendency for electoral results to display a bipolar pattern (Table 4.1). The average value of the bipolarism index increased everywhere, especially in the North (where it had previously been low), reflecting the decline of *Lega Nord* (Northern League: LN). Thus, what the candidatures complicated, the voters simplified. As far as the 'third poles' were concerned, therefore, the strategy of pre-electoral alliances proved more fruitful than using the elections as a 'trial of strength'.

In recent years, falling electoral turnouts have been widely viewed as symptomatic of the crisis in the relationship between parties and voters, and this was again the interpretation offered in 1999. Numerous commentators stressed, however, that the trend has been apparent for at least twenty years, and that it simply accelerated in the 1990s, because of voter disorientation in the face of the constant changes in the party system, the growing view that the vote is a right rather than a duty, and the reduced effort devoted by the parties to electoral campaigning.[7] Table 4.2 compares the figures for 1999 and the previous two years. Various trends of recent years are confirmed: the proportion of abstainers in 1999 was between 20 percent and 25 percent; the increase was more marked in the Centre-North than in the South; non-voters in the second ballot amounted to around 40 percent; and 'additional abstention' (the difference between the turnout for the first and second round of voting) was about 15 percent.

However, voting in 1999 also displays some specific trends. Firstly, the increase in non-voters in Central Italy doubled, and indeed exceeded the proportion in the communes of the North (that stayed around 8 percent), rising by just under 5 percent to just under 10 percent. In the South, where the drop in electoral participation had been practically negligible in 1997–8, the proportion

Table 4.1 *Bipolarism index in municipal elections1997/1998 and 1999*

	North	Centre	South	Total
1997/1998	71.5%	83.1%	82.5%	78.6%
(N)	(24)	(12)	(30)	(66)
1999	79.0%	86.0%	83.6%	83.6%
(N)	(7)	(14)	(7)	(28)

Source: Calculation by authors on the basis of Ministry of the Interior figures.

of non-voters increased by around 5 percent in 1999. This difference is partly explained by the fact that, whereas neither the elections of 1993–4 nor those of 1997–8 were held parallel with other polls, those of 1995 were held jointly with the regional elections, and those of 1999 with the elections for the European Parliament, for which the turnout is usually lower than for the regional ones.

Secondly, in 1999 personal mobilisation, denoted by the percentage of votes for the mayor, seems to have been a less solid bulwark against the increasing inability of the parties to get out their vote. It should be borne in mind that the many of the mayors elected in 1995 had programmes which departed less from the party line than had been the case two years previously, when political turmoil created greater space for more personalised candidatures.

Thirdly, there were slight increases both in second ballot abstention from voting and in additional abstention. Given that voting in the first round was similar to 1997–98, there was a greater proportion of voters who decided not to turn out for the second ballot. The fact that the first round of voting involved other elections as well – albeit ones usually regarded as of lesser importance, like those for the European Parliament – may partly account for this difference.

Table 4.2 *Turnout (as a percentage of total electorate)*

		% North	% Centre	% South	% Total
1st round					
Abstention rate	1999	23.2	23.6	21.8	23.0
	1997/98	25.4	22.2	22.4	23.5
Increase in abstention	1999	8.0	9.5	5.1	8.0
compared to previous poll	1997/98	7.8	4.8	0.7	3.9
Votes for mayoral	1999	9.6	5.8	4.1	6.3
candidates only	1997/98	11.2	8.4	6.1	8.4
(N)	1999	(7)	(14)	(7)	(28)
	1997/98	(24)	(12)	(30)	(66)
2nd round					
Abstention rate	1999	40.1	39.4	39.8	39.8
	1997/98	38.0	34.7	36.3	36.9
Additional abstention	1999	16.1	15.7	20.1	16.8
	1997/98	12.6	10.5	15.1	13.2
(N)	1999	(5)	(3)	(2)	(10)
	1997/98	(19)	(6)	(14)	(39)

Source: Calculation by authors on the basis of Ministry of the Interior figures.

In view of the results in Bologna, it seems obvious that these elections must be read as a defeat for the centre-left, the government and the DS. The centre-left won in eighteen of the twenty-eight provincial capitals – twice the number gained by the Polo – while in Potenza the candidate of the *Unione dei democratici europei* (Union of European Democrats: UDEUR) eliminated the candidate of the Polo delle libertà (Liberty Pole) in the first round and then went on to defeat the Ulivo (Olive Tree coalition) candidate in the second ballot. Yet before the elections the centre-left governed twenty-four provincial capitals (all seven in northern Italy and the fourteen in the centre of the country), while the Polo governed three, with one being from neither coalition. Whereas in the South both the main coalitions held on to their mayoral posts, in the other areas of the country an Olive Tree mayor was replaced by a Liberty Pole candidate in at least six municipalities.

The success of the Liberty Pole was by no means a foregone conclusion, since it was achieved in areas that were traditionally hostile, or else by defeating outgoing mayors. This ability to overcome adverse electoral conditions was an achievement of great importance for the parties belonging the Liberty Pole. The shrewd selection of candidates, and of the content and style of electoral campaigns, and the ability to exploit the errors of opponents led to successes of great political and symbolic significance which sometimes transcended, as in Bologna, simple city politics.

Rather than just giving a synchronic analysis of the results, a more useful indicator of the performance of individual parties is comparison with their results in past municipal elections. Table 4.3 classifies the performances of the parties (for elections where such comparison is possible) according to whether they gained less than 90 percent, between 90 percent and 110 percent, and more than 110 percent of the votes obtained in municipal elections of the past. The only parties able to increase their votes with a certain frequency are PPI and FI (26 percent and 19 percent in the municipalities considered). The other main parties lost votes in at least three elections out of four, and the PRC has done so in all elections. The figures do not vary even in the six municipalities in which there has been a change of mayor or municipal council. Overall, therefore, very few parties can claim absolute victory when account is taken of previous elections, given that two aggressive new contenders – the *Lista Bonino* (Bonino List) and *I Democratici per Prodi* (Democrats), Di Pietro and various mayors – entered the fray, attracting voter support from across the political spectrum.

In recent years, the winners of the municipal elections have often been the outgoing mayors. In 1999, indeed, fully fifteen of

Table 4.3 *Relative party performance in 1999 and in 1995 (percentage of municipalities)*

	< 90 %	90–110 %	> 110 %	N
DS	75	14	11	(28)
PPI	57	17	26	(23)
PRC	100	0	0	(27)
AN	73	23	5	(22)
FI	67	14	19	(21)
Lega	83	8	8	(12)

Source: Calculation by authors on the basis of Ministry of the Interior figures.

the nineteen mayors stepping down on conclusion of their terms of office were re-elected. Moreover, only outgoing mayors managed to win the second ballot after starting in second position. Those defeated were the mayors of Bergamo, Padua, Imperia and Ascoli Piceno, while 'new' candidates lost control of the city governments in the defeats suffered by the Olive Tree in Bologna and Arezzo. Table 4.4 summarises the votes cast for outgoing mayors and the values of two indices – vote personalisation and voting appeal – used respectively to estimate their electoral performance relative to the lists supporting them, and their performance relative to other candidates.[8] Almost everywhere, outgoing mayors had greater shares of personalisation than their supporting lists, and they also attracted the largest share of the personalised vote (for the mayoral candidate alone) and of the split vote (for a mayoral candidate and for a list standing against him/her). In the Centre of Italy one notes scant personalised voting, although this is nothing new, and it was similarly low in the South, although in that part of the country outgoing mayors performed slightly better in terms of personalisation, and above all attracted larger shares of the split vote, owing to fierce competition among mayoral candidates and among the lists of candidates for the municipal councils.[9]

Two outgoing mayors (in Cremona and Foggia) benefited from the lowering of the threshold for the plurality premium to 48 percent. In all twenty-eight provincial capitals the elected mayor now has a majority of councillors belonging to the lists that supported him or her.[10] In neither Cremona nor Foggia did the coalition which backed the second-placed candidate perform well enough to affect the winning coalition. Although the adjustments made to the law mean that it is theoretically possible for a mayor to be elected without a majority, this eventuality now seems much less likely.[11]

Table 4.4 *Results obtained by incumbent mayors: indexes of personalisation and attraction for incumbents and their opponents*

City		Personalisation Index				Attraction Index			
		Incumb	Opp1.	Opp2.	Opp3.	Incumb	Opp1.	Opp2.	Opp3.
Vercelli	Wins run-off from second place	0.42	0.07	0.10	0.07	0.57	0.20	0.17	0.04
Biella	Wins run-off from second place	0.27	0.14	0.26	0.08	0.55	0.32	0.08	0.02
Verbania	Wins run-off	0.23	0.09	0.07	0.06	0.65	0.25	0.04	0.02
Bergamo	Loses run-off	0.16	0.10	0.19	0.23	0.35	0.31	0.24	0.06
Cremona	Wins first ballot	0.31	0.11	0.04	0.02	0.76	0.17	0.02	0.01
Padova	Loses run-off	0.27	0.20	0.24	0.20	0.49	0.39	0.05	0.03
Imperia	Loses first ballot	0.14	0.04	0.13	0.09	0.60	0.31	0.06	0.03
Total North		*0.26*	*0.11*	*0.15*	*0.11*	*0.57*	*0.28*	*0.09*	*0.03*
Forlì	Wins first ballot	0.06	0.03	0.02	0.02	0.73	0.11	0.04	0.02
Modena	Wins first ballot	0.04	0.10	0.03	0.03	0.35	0.55	0.02	0.01
Reggio E.	Wins first ballot	0.07	0.10	0.04	0.03	0.60	0.34	0.02	0.02
Livorno	Wins first ballot	0.06	0.07	0.05	0.13	0.53	0.29	0.08	0.10
Prato	Wins first ballot	0.08	0.09	0.04	0.12	0.53	0.36	0.02	0.06
Ascoli P.	Loses first ballot	0.12	0.11	0.05	-0.02	0.34	0.59	0.04	-0.01
Pesaro	Wins first ballot	0.08	0.03	0.12	0.26	0.48	0.07	0.15	0.21
Total Centre		*0.07*	*0.08*	*0.05*	*0.08*	*0.51*	*0.33*	*0.05*	*0.06*
Teramo	Wins first ballot	0.07	0.03	0.00	-0.05	0.73	0.22	0.00	-0.02
Campobasso	Wins first ballot	0.10	0.06	0.24	–	0.67	0.30	0.03	–
Avellino	Wins run-off	0.03	0.08	0.04	-0.14	0.25	0.30	0.08	-0.18
Bari	Wins first ballot	0.07	0.08	-0.02	0.00	0.54	0.39	-0.01	0.00
Foggia	Wins first ballot	0.19	0.04	-0.14	-0.07	0.66	0.06	-0.22	-0.02
Total South		*0.09*	*0.06*	*0.03*	*-0.07*	*0.57*	*0.25*	*-0.02*	*-0.05*
Total		*0.15*	*0.08*	*0.08*	*0.06*	*0.55*	*0.29*	*0.05*	*0.02*

Source: Calculation by authors on the basis of Ministry of the Interior figures.

The case of Bologna

Besides systemic figures, proper understanding of the dynamics that led to the historic defeat of the Left in Bologna by Giorgio Guazzaloca requires retrospective analysis of the political situation in that city. The electoral defeat of the centre-left, and of the DS in particular, may be interpreted in the light of four main factors: the crisis of the DS as the predominant party; changes in Bolognese society, so often ignored by the party; the long internal battle over choice of a candidate; and the party's underestimation of the magnitude of the challenge raised by Guazzaloca.

In the early 1990s the *Partito democratico della sinistra* (Democratic Party of the Left: PDS) in Bologna had been able to curb the decline that the party was suffering at the national level and to preserve most of the hold on the city enjoyed by the old *Partito comunista italiano* (Communist party: PCI), albeit amid organisational cut-backs and a slide in its electoral dominance.[12] But the heirs to the PDS, the DS, succeeded in the difficult task of losing its grip on the city that had stood as a 'model' for the PCI at the national level. The clashes that characterised the DS's electoral campaign stemmed from a the turnover in municipal office-holders in 1996. In the space of a few months, following the general elections and the subsequent formation of the Prodi government (March–June 1996), all the city's top-level political posts changed hands, from the presidency of the regional administration to the regional secretaryship of the party; and most importantly, so too did leadership of the federation. The election of Alessandro Ramazza in June 1996 was a major shift for the party as the new leadership joined battle with the mayor Walter Vitali over various crucial aspects of the city's administration.[13]

In several respects Vitali personified the political transition of the party in Bologna. He was the last mayor nominated under the old system, although unlike almost all his predecessors he did not fit the mould of a party boss, and he was also the first mayor to be confirmed under the new system. The fact that he was also the last leftist mayor of the century can be explained by the conflicts that involved his administration; conflicts provoked not so much by the opposition – often weak and willing to accept the 'implicit consociationalism' that had arisen in relationships between the PCI and the DC[14] – as by his own party itself. The ill-concealed ambition of Secretary Ramazza to take Vitali's place at the conclusion of his term, although it was in itself entirely legitimate, probably underestimated the changes that had meanwhile taken place in the party and in the city.

Among the Democrats of the Left, in fact, besides the increasingly evident sterility of the debate leading up to the second national congress of 1997,[15] the secretary of the federation could no longer rely – despite the share of votes that he had garnered when re-elected as local party leader – on the dominance that the PCI leaders had enjoyed under a proportional electoral regime.[16] Times had changed. Ramazza's party was only apparently monolithic: as well as its internal factions, it seethed with personal ambitions and cross-party alliances. Moreover, there was a mayor in office who, although widely criticised, was not prepared to step aside unless he could play a decisive part in choosing a suitable 'heir'. The clashes between Vitali and Ramazza intensified as they set about choosing the nominees. The ousting of Giorgio Guazzaloca from the presidency of the Chamber of Commerce was emblematic for two fundamental reasons. Firstly it signalled an attempt by the party to overcome the crisis by taking over posts that hitherto had been 'granted' to members of the opposition.[17] Secondly it had a crucial bearing on the elections that followed because it sparked in Guazzaloca the idea that he might stand as a candidate for mayor.

The crisis of the party, combined with the progressive breakdown of the mechanisms (notably the mayor/neighbourhood coordination that placed Bologna in the forefront of urban policy-making in the 1960s and 1970s[18]) that had helped to construct the 'Bologna model', bred the image of a city nostalgic for its past and fearful of its future. In recent years, the social structure of the city had changed profoundly, with a constant decline in its population accompanied by a marked increase in immigration from outside the EU and the overall ageing of its population.[19]

The elderly obviously had priorities which differed from those of the rest of the city's population: the guaranteeing of personal safety, as well as the general quality of services, were their most pressing needs. Polls conducted by research institutes in the early months of 1999 depicted a situation of generalised alarm over law and order in Bologna. Almost 90 percent of the interviewees said that the safety of citizens and the prevention of crime was of great or significant importance. And almost 80 percent of them declared that the number of non-EU immigrants in the city was a problem of equal seriousness.[20] Also eloquent were the protests lodged with mayor Vitali in the form of letters or petitions[21] – from all sectors of society and frequently from citizens declaring themselves as leftists – complaining about the decay and squalor of the city, and the authorities' seeming inability to cope with it. Vitali's administration was beset by problems and gave the impression of no longer being able to distinguish between the tasks (and responsibilities) of the city council and those of the police force in dealing with social alarm.

Amid substantial underestimation of the magnitude of the problem of law and order in the city, relations between Vitali and the DS deteriorated further after the electoral defeat of Parma (Table 4.5). The demise of various pretenders (besides the mayor and the secretary, Mauro Zani, a leading member of the party, who was first 'forced' to stand and then sacrificed to internal power struggles, was also in contention) removed all the front runners, and the choice fell on a minor player.

The device of holding primaries – hailed as guaranteeing a candidate selected by popular choice – did not prove as significant as its proponents had hoped. Once Silvia Bartolini had presented her candidature with the blessings of the federation, the primaries were no more than a bogus exercise in direct democracy, given that the result of the election was obvious from the outset. In fact, the coalition parties took pains not to put up any serious challenger, such as councillor Flavio Delbono, who later became leader of the *Democratici* in the municipal council.

Table 4.5 *The principal stages of candidate selection (June 1998–March 1999)*

1998

7 June	Municipal elections in Parma. Outgoing mayor Lavagetto is defeated in the run-off by the centre-right's candidate (Ubaldi) who benefits from the support of a civic list.
9 June	DS Regional secretary Matteucci says: 'no mayor should feel irremovable'.
20 June	Ramazza: 'We are counting on Vitali'.
22 September	DS leaders suggest Delbono (assessore al Bilancio) as alternative candidate to Vitali.
24 September	Vitali decides to stand down to get away from climate of 'conflict and backstabbing'.
25 September	Ramazza denies he is a candidate for mayor of Bologna. The DS accepts Vitali's withdrawl.
22 October	The PPI says the candidate for mayor need not necessarily be from the DS.
19 December	Guazzaloca announces he will run.

1999

January 13	Vitali says he will step down if Ramazza does too.
14	Veltroni. Matteucci and Ramazza ask Zani to run as a compromise candidate.
15	At the DS Congress Ramazza puts himself forward as guarantor for the choice of candidate. There is a split in the leadership between those who want Ramazza to run for mayor and those who prefer Silvia Bartolini.
17	Istituto Cattaneo-Bpa poll rates Bartolini as the best candidate to beat Guazzaloca, though high levels of 'don't knows' are recorded.
20	Matteucci and Ramazza discuss the candidacy with Veltroni in Rome: no outcome.
21	Zani withdraws from consideration with a polemical letter in which he declares he wishes to avoid a 'clash of personalities rather than programmes'.

continued

Table 4.5 *The principal stages of candidate selection (June 1998–March 1999)*

January 22	20 out of 25 members of the DS executive committee, headed by Imbeni, indicate a preference for Bartolini. The Greens agree. The PPI is undecided.
27	The Ulivo parties broach the idea of primaries to choose the candidate.
February 2	Inner divisions are exposed to public scrutiny during Gad Lerner's programme, Pinocchio. Zani and Imbeni back Silvia Bartolini.
9	Andreatta asks Veltroni to convince Vitali to withdraw his resignation.
11	Veltroni cannot accept Andreatta's proposal because Vitali is only disposed to return if asked by the coalition as a whole.
15	Antonio La Forgia, after resigning from the presidency of the regional council, joins the Democrats.
21	At the DS provincial conference, Veltroni does not bestow the candidacy on Bartolini since no decision has yet been made on the issue of primaries.
26	The Ulivo decides it will hold primaries. The leadership committee of the DS approves the decision by 62 votes to 1 with 7 abstentions.
March 5	Delbono refuses to stand for the primaries.
19	The primary candidates are announced: besides Silvia Bartolini, Maurizio Cevenini, deputy leader of the DS group in the municipal council, the animal behaviourist Giorgio Celli for the Greens, and the Catholic journalist Giuseppe Paruolo of the magazine *Il Mosaico*, all decide to run.
27	21,688 bolognesi vote, surpassing even the highest expectations.
28	Silvia Bartolini obtains 17,224 votes (79.9%), Cevenini. 1,876 (8.7%), Celli 1,363 (6.3%), Paruolo 1,071 (4.9%). Bartolini is made official candidate for the Ulivo.

Bartolini possessed positive qualities but was undeniably hampered by her political past. Fielding a woman as candidate, and a young one to boot, might certainly have helped to give the party a new image. And seeing that the woman in question was also well known for her battles on behalf of the socially excluded, her position seemed stronger still. But it was precisely these qualities that penalised Bartolini in the eyes of the conservative voters 'by allegiance' concentrated among the elderly residents of the city (who constituted the traditional stronghold of the PCI-PDS). Indeed, the fact that she was a young woman, and childless, and that she had defended gays, transsexuals and immigrants, hampered her attempt to build an alliance with the centrist sectors of the coalition, and also set the hard core of the communist (or ex-communist) electorate against her. But it was above all Bartolini's career as a political functionary, nurtured in the fold of the PCI since adolescence (a member of the city council at 19 years of age, a councillor in the Imbeni administration when she was only twenty-seven, before being dropped by Vitali in 1993), that was her greatest electoral handicap.

Analysis of the electoral returns reveals the explicit intent of the leftist electorate to punish the DS. Comparison with voting in the provincial and European elections shows that more than 25 percent of DS voters rejected the party's candidate, either by defacing their ballot slips or refusing outright to vote[22] (Table 4.6). And yet the signals had long been apparent: as early as 1995 the party had obtained many fewer votes in the municipal elections than in provincial ones. Moreover, the few hundred votes that had enabled Vitali to avoid a second ballot had postponed discussion of the lack of leadership shown by the mayor, which was due to the electoral method used two years previously.[23]

Voting in Bologna was influenced by a wide variety of factors: besides the crisis of a party increasingly oblivious to the mood of local society, there was the inability of recent administrations to address the new social make-up of the city, the candidate's political past, and the uncertainty of an electoral campaign which sought to steer a middle course between breaking with the previous council and forming a coalition. But without a capable and determined opponent, it would have still been difficult for the Left to lose Bologna.

Giorgio Guazzaloca, mainly owing to his prominence in the Bologna business community, was certainly not a newcomer to the city's political stage. Although this was his first electoral contest, the future mayor had long-standing contacts in city hall and national politics. Yet he had never taken up any clear-cut political position, preferring to work behind the scenes of the city power system in substantially peaceful connivance with the governing PCI-PDS, until the rebuff of his ousting from the Chamber of Commerce.

It was above all the strategy pursued by Guazzaloca during the electoral campaign that enabled him to capitalise on the errors of his opponents, and primarily by presenting himself as a 'non-party' candidate, nostalgically evocative of the Dozza administration and unremittingly hostile (at '360 degrees') to political distinctions in terms of left and right. By creating the civic list *La Tua Bologna*, which became the second largest party in the city, Guazzaloca emphasised the personalised nature of the contest, seeking strenu-

Table 4.6 *Municipal, provincial and European elections in Bologna (1995/1999)*

	Municipal elections 1995		Provincial elections 1995		Municipal elections 1999		Provincial elections 1999		European elections 1999	
	Voti	%	Voti	%	Voti	%	Voti	%	Voti	%
DS (Due torri*)	104,276	38.6	124,462	45.3	57,111	25.3	69,450	30.3	78,373	30.9
Forza Italia	44,723	16.6	78,985	28.8	25,846	11.5	43,494	19.0	44,958	17.7
	Bol. nuova									
CCD			–	–	Con La tua Bologna		3,842	1.7	2,898	1.1
AN (-Segni nel 1999)	46,840	17.4		–	24,699	11.0	34,698	15.1	31,701	12.5
Democr. per Prodi	–	–	–	–	25,927	11.5	27,729	12.1	29,691	11.7
PPI	17,049	6.3	21,793	7.9	3,859	1.7	3,673	1.6	3,709	1.5
Lista Bonino	3,816	1.4	9,256	3.4	–	–	–		25,760	10.1
	(Pannella)		(Pannella)							
RC	20,718	7.7	20,567	7.5	11,194	4.9	12,497	5.4	11,487	4.5
Verdi	14,136	5.2	12,028	4.4	5,757	2.5	7,090	3.1	5,789	2.3
PCDI	–	–	–	–	8,810	3.9	10,862	4.7	3,768	1.5
F. tricolore	1,028	0.4	–	–	6,363	2.8	–		2,701	1.1
Lega	4,608	1.7	7,474	2.7	4,100	1.8	5,710	2.5	3,468	1.4
La tua Bologna	–		–	–	35,072	15.6	–	–	–	–
Governare Bologna	9,194	3.4	–	–	6,724	3.0	–	–	–	–
Salviamo Bologna	–		–	–	4,008	1.8	–	–	–	–
Others	3,374	1.3	–	–	5,861	2.6	9,946	4.4	9,525	3.7
Valid votes	269,762	77.2	274,565	78.6	225,331	66.9	229,261	68.0	253,828	75.3
Total voting	303,655	86.9	304,441	87.1	239,626	71.1	247,767	73.5	266,051	79.0
Total electors	349,260		349,347		337,064		337,064		337,064	

* Between 1947 and 1995 the PCI-PDS list was known as the PCI (PDS) – 'two towers' list. In 1999, the words 'For Bologna' surrounded the 'two towers' symbol.
Source: Ministry of the Interior.

ously (and shrewdly) to keep his distance from the parties supporting him, which he invited to stay 'two steps behind'.

In the months following the election, first the formation of the municipal council, and then the convention to set up an outright 'mayor's party',[24] highlighted the difficulties faced by the new mayor in keeping the coalition parties at bay. These were also months that saw profound discussion within the DS which led to a change of the Federation's leadership. The victory – albeit slim – by Romano Prodi's right-hand man Arturo Parisi in the by-election held on 28 November, (to fill the seat left vacant by Prodi on his appointment as President of the European Commission), helped relaunch the Olive Tree coalition. It also ensured that the strategy of detachment from the parties, initiated by Guazzaloca and partly taken up by Parisi's rival Sante Tura, too, was once again rewarded by the voters, so that it became the strategy to follow in every political contest.

Mayors, Parties and Voters: A Balance-sheet of Seven Years of Direct Elections

Given that with the elections of 1999 almost all the Italian communes had voted at least twice to elect their mayors directly, medium-term analysis is now possible. It may be helpful to recall the main purposes of law 81/93: greater clarity of political responsibility and the increased stability of local governments, to be pursued at least in part through the subtraction of mayors from party manoeuvering in the city councils by giving them direct popular legitimacy.

At least in the provincial capitals, the councils now appear to be more stable than before, although there are still odd cases of early dissolution. Of the twenty-eight provincial capitals which went to the polls in 1999, only Terni had been dissolved early, compared with nine out of sixty-six in the two-year period 1997–8.[25] The calling of elections now tends to replace the search for new municipal coalitions in order to deal with crises.[26] Stability seems increasingly to depend on the figure of a directly elected mayor, rather than on the political parties: in recent years, in fact, the Italian political scene has displayed constantly shifting alliances and trade-offs within parties, whose restructuring cannot be yet said to be complete. So far as the transformation of the electoral result into the majority of seats goes, however, the reform has undoubtedly been a major step forward: the elected mayor is now usually backed by a majority in the council that consists of the parties that explicitly supported him/her in the elections.

The reform has been less influential on the relationship between mayors and parties. But with a neo-parliamentary system it is only possible to undertake a pact with the electorate and then wait for a vote of no confidence in the mayor to lead to new elections. The main issues of conflict between mayors and parties now arise when the mayor nominates the municipal council, and over certain policy choices. Several mayors have had to deal with encroachment by the parties on the inner circle of municipal power, after their campaign promises to 'back off'. In Trieste, for example, the equilibrium between Illy's first electoral campaign, when he was accused by his opponents of being a 'slave to the parties', and his campaign for re-election, when he was charged with supporting a 'party-less democracy', is fragile and shifting.[27]

It is however evident that the directly elected mayors have greater latitude for manoeuvre than previously, and that by and large voters are appreciative of their efforts. Put briefly, the outgoing mayors who sought re-election in the period 1997–8 managed to (a) win in around 70 percent of the provincial capitals in which they stood; (b) make up for lost ground in the second round of voting; (c) win even if the coalition supporting them was incomplete; (d) attract a large part of the personalised and split vote.

The greater visibility of elected mayors and of mayoral candidates has had two consequences. Firstly, outgoing mayors enjoy a celebrity status that has on occasion deterred opposing coalitions from fielding strong candidates against them (cases in point being Rome, Naples and Venice). But when their reputations have been tarred, they may suffer stunning electoral shocks (sometimes, as in Turin, resolved at the last minute of the second vote) or crushing defeats (as in Parma and Grossetto). Secondly, although the public visibility of outgoing mayors is greater, it is a resource available to all candidates. It is this that explains the sensational success of Guazzaloca in Bologna and of Luigi Lucherini in Arezzo after they fashioned their greater party independence into an electoral resource, to the detriment of the candidates put up against them by the city's previous governors. The joint operation of these factors is exemplified by Parma, where an unpopular mayor was defeated by a good candidate with no party affiliations.

In general, although party mobilisation is still decisive in determining the outcome of municipal elections, those of recent years have confirmed that the breakdown in relations between parties and voters still persists. Voters often and willingly choose only the mayoral candidate and not the party; even more often, and perhaps even more willingly, they do not turn out to vote. Those votes that they do cast, moreover, comprise a personal or personalistic component which in the North is apparent in the widespread use of the personalised vote, and in every part of the country (but mainly in the South), in the use of preference votes for municipal councils.

It is more difficult than in the past to discern a distinct pattern in the relations between parties and voters. The Bologna elections, for example, have shown that voting 'by allegiance' probably no longer exists:[28] there are numerous voters who prefer one or the other party when the electoral campaign gets under way. At least in the municipal elections, however, where the monocratic nature of the mayoral office is evident, and with it a high degree of personalisation, the personal characteristics of the candidates become an additional criterion of choice which may upset even the most entrenched political equilibria.

The introduction of direct elections has not only increased the particularity of each individual municipal council, but also the specificity of each of them from one election to the next. The presence of the outgoing mayors, and their impact on the contest, introduces a certain degree of uniformity, but a mayor may stand for re-election only once. Thus, if not every five years, at least every ten, the political forces are now compelled to propose candidates and devise programmes to the liking of the voters. Those who have governed and are now seeking re-election have an initial advantage, but only if their previous track record as mayor has an electoral pay-off. For all candidates, both outgoing and new, their independence from the parties and their knowledge of their cities' problems are factors which grow increasingly indispensable, on pain of resounding defeat.

Translated by Adrian Belton

Notes

1. This essay is the result of joint reflection and analysis by the authors. As regards its final version, the introduction, sections 1 and 3 may be attributed to Gianfranco Baldini, and sections 2 and 4 to Guido Legnante. We wish to thank Paolo Marcotti for his assistance in processing the electoral data.
2. However, relations between the mayor and the coalition had been severely strained in 1997. The mayor resigned and the party secretaries in Rome intervened to appease the conflict by sending such a major player as Giuseppe Tatarella – who died a few months afterwards – as Councillor for Culture and Tourism (see F. Chiarello, 'Travagli urbani a Bari. Trasformazioni sociali e governo locale in una città del Mezzogiorno', *Quaderni di sociologia*, no. 14, 1997: 21–42).
3. G. Baldini and G. Legnante, 'Dal sindaco dei partiti a partito dei sindaci?' In *Politica in Italia. Edizione 98*, eds L. Bardi and M. Rhodes, Bologna, 1998, 45–67. See also: L. Vandelli, *Sindaci e miti. Sisifo, Tantalo e Damocole nell'amministrazione comunale*, Bologna, 1997.

4. The text of law 120/99 of 30 April 1999 can be consulted on the Chamber of Deputies website: www.camera.it. On the law see the comments by S. Vassallo, 'Sistemi elettorali, forma di governo regionale e ordinamento federale dello Stato. La politica dei piccoli passi', *Le istituzioni del federalismo*, no.1, 1999, 433–46.

5. As if to offset the law, the minimum number of signatures required for presentation of lists and candidatures was significantly reduced.

6. Analysis has been made only of provincial capitals. Previous studies have shown that the dynamics highlighted here were substantially the same in smaller communes. See G. Baldini and G. Legnante, *Città al voto. I sindaci e le elezioni comunali*, Bologna, 2000, from which the figures on the two-year period 1997–98 have been taken.

7. On abstention from voting see R. Mannheimer and G. Sani, *Il mercato elettorale. Identikit dell'elettore italiano*, Bologna, 1987, 33–49; G. Sani, 'L'elettore assente', in Political Trends, no.8, 1999, 33–44; A. Mussino, (ed), *Le nuove forme di astensionismo elettorale*, Rome, 1999.

8. The *index of personalised voting* is given by the ratio between the votes gained by the mayoral candidate and the sum of the votes gained by the lists supporting him/her, from which 1 is subtracted. The value of the index is 0 when the candidate and the lists supporting him/her obtain the same number of votes, it is greater than 0 when the candidate gains more votes than his/her supporting lists, and less than 0 in the reverse case. The *index of voting appeal* is given by the ratio between, on the one hand, the difference between the votes gained by the mayoral candidate and the sum of the votes obtained by the lists supporting him/her and, on the other, the total of personalised votes (for the mayoral candidate alone) and split votes (for the mayoral candidate and for a list opposed to him/her) cast in a commune. The index is higher, the greater the difference between the votes for the mayoral candidate and the lists supporting him/her and the lower the amount of personalised and split voting in the commune. For a discussion see G. Legnante, 'Personalizzazione della politica e comportamento elettorale. Con una ricerca sulle elezioni comunali', *Quaderni di Scienza Politica*, no. 3, 1999, 49–141, and Baldini and Legnante, *Città al voto*.

9. In *Città al voto*, we show the importance of preference voting in explanation of the results achieved by the parties and of the difference between votes for mayoral candidates and the lists supporting them.

10. These majorities are still vulnerable to the pitfalls of a 'neo-parliamentary' form of government. See A. Agosta, 'Sistema elettorale e governo locale: gli effetti politici e istituzionali della riforma del 1993', in *Votare in città. Riflessioni sulle elezioni amministrative in Italia*, ed. S. Operto, Milan, 1999, 31–58.

11. In 1997 and 1998 (424 municipal elections) this happened in autumn 1997 in Paternò (Sicily), where the coalition of lists supporting the winning candidate was eliminated in the first round of voting, gaining only 39.1 percent of the votes.

12. On this see G. Baldini, P. Corbetta, and S. Vassallo, *La scanfitta inattesa. Come e perché la sinistra ha perso a Bologna*, Bologna, 2000.

13. See the chapter by Vassallo, in *La scanfitta inattesa*.

14. On the mechanisms of local government and on the PCI in Emilia see F. Anderlini, *Terra rossa. Comunismo ideale e socialdemocrazia reale*, Bologna, 1990.

15. See the chapter by Baldini in *La scanfitta inattesa*.

16. Emblematic in this regard is the ascent to mayoral office by Renzo Imbeni (mayor from 1983 to 1993), who succeeded Renato Zangheri after serving as secretary of the federation (an office which he had held since 1976).

17. And not affiliated with the PCI-PDS, like Giancarlo Sangalli, chairman of the CNA, elected in 1998.

18. See on this G. Pasquino, 'Democrazia e istituzioni a Bologna', 1945–1985, in *Storia illustrata di Bologna*, 5 vols, Milan, 1990, vol. 5, 1–20.

19. See M. Barbagli and M. Pisati, *Rapporto sulla situazione sociale a Bologna*, Bologna, 1995. See also the study by the Istituto Cattaneo and BPA, *Bologna che Cambia*, which calculates that the percentage of over-60s in the city increased from 25.6 percent at the 1970 elections to 36.8 percent in 1999.

20. Ibid.

21. *Egregio signor sindaco. Lettere ai cittadini e risposta dell'istituzione sui problemi della sicurezza*, ed. M. Barbagli, Bologna, 1999.

22. See the Appendix for analysis of the second ballot of 27 June 1999.

23. Vitali's nomination by the municipal council relieved him from having to build the resources of personal leadership that he would otherwise have needed in a direct election.

24. The movement, which took the name *La Tua Bologna*, was created on 19 October 1999. According to article 9 of its statute, Guazzaloca was to be its 'honorary President … appointed for life'.

25. Respectively in Trieste, Udine, Vicenza and Vibo Valentia six months before expiry of their terms of office; in Catanzaro, Cuneo, Frosinone and Lecce one year before; and in Brindisi after only eighteen months.

26. However, pacts in municipal councils have not entirely fallen into disuse, especially at times of political turbulence. The case of the Formentini administration in Milan shows that a mayor may find that the majority that elected him/her falls apart in the municipal council, however cohesive it may have appeared at the time of the elections (only the Lega Nord list qualified for the plurality premium, so this was not even a coalition *giunta*).

27. See P. Segatti, 'La complessa stabilità di Trieste' in *Il Mulino*, no. 3, 1997, 483–92.

28. On voting patterns see A. Parisi and G. Pasquino, 'Relazioni partiti-elettori e tipi di voto', in Continuità e mutamento elettorale, eds A. Parisi and G. Pasquino, Bologna, 1977, 215–49; A. Parisi, 'Appartenenza, opinione e scambio', in *Sulla soglia del cambiamento. Elettori e partiti alla fine della prima Repubblica*, Bologna, 1995, 359–92; G. Legnante, 'Le tipologie del comportamento elettorale in Italia', in *Quaderni di scienza politica*, no. 2, 1998, 111–72.

5

The 1999 Elections
to the European Parliament

Philip Daniels

The fifth elections to the European Parliament were held in Italy on 13 June 1999 against a background of domestic political turbulence. The centre-left government of Massimo D'Alema, which had taken office in October 1998, was inherently tenuous, based as it was on a broad, multi-party majority including several MPs who had been elected with the opposition centre-right coalition in the 1996 national elections. At the same time, the party system was still highly fluid: new parties and political formations were entering the electoral arena and party identities and electoral alliances were characterised by instability. This turbulence in the party system was manifest in the 1999 European elections in which twenty-six parties and movements presented lists, many contesting European elections for the first time. In contrast to the majoritarian mechanisms used in national parliamentary and local elections, the proportional electoral system used for European elections, with its relatively low threshold for representation, encourages the proliferation of party lists and offers few incentives for the parties to form electoral alliances.

As in earlier European election campaigns, domestic political issues were more prominent than partisan divisions over European policy. While the parties alluded to European themes in their official election literature, they tended to focus their campaigns on domestic issues which differentiated the parties much more than

European policy and were of more immediate concern to the voters. For the parties, the European elections serve primarily as a barometer of their support in the national political setting and the results are interpreted largely in terms of their impact on domestic politics. The results of the 1999 European elections indicated a shift in the balance of party strengths within the two competing centre-left and centre-right political alignments and a marked fragmentation of the party system. In addition, the outcome of the elections had an important impact on inter-party competition and alliance strategies in the domestic political arena. The European dimension to the results was also significant, with important changes in the make-up of the Italian representation in the European Parliament.

The Domestic Political Context and the Election Campaign

The 1999 European elections took place against the backdrop of an uncertain domestic political situation. The political transition which had begun in the early 1990s appeared to be faltering and the party system showed few signs of settling into a stable format. The fluidity of political alignments and shifting party identities raised doubts about the system's evolution towards a more stable, bipolar party competition. The formation of the D'Alema government in October 1998 added to this uncertainty, bringing into the parliamentary majority centrist elements which had been part of the centre-right electoral alliance in the 1996 national elections and a group of communist parliamentarians. The broad, multi-party character of the D'Alema government made it intrinsically precarious and hampered effective policy-making, a throwback seemingly to the pattern of unstable governments of the First Republic.

In this fluid and evolving political context, competition among parties in the same electoral alliances has often been as intense as that between the rival centre-right and centre-left blocs. In the run-up to the European elections, parties in both electoral alliances viewed the contests as an opportunity to strengthen their own position relative to that of their closest allies. This competition was particularly pronounced on the centre-left of the political spectrum where the entry of a new movement, the *Democratici per l'Ulivo* (the Democrats: informally known as the *Asinello* after the donkey adopted as the party's electoral symbol), intensified the endemic rivalries.

The Democrats were the principal novelty in the 1999 European elections. The new political movement, led by the former prime minister Romano Prodi, was formed in February 1999 with the support of leading mayors of the *Centocittà* ('Hundred Cities') movement and the 'Italy for Values' movement led by the former investigating magistrate Antonio Di Pietro. The new movement represented an attempt by Prodi to strengthen his position on the centre-left of the political spectrum and to challenge the ascendancy of the Left Democrats in that alliance. The collapse of the Prodi government in October 1998, when *Rifondazione comunista* (Communist Refoundation: PRC) withdrew its parliamentary support, had provoked a crisis in the governing *Ulivo* (Olive Tree) alliance and exposed Prodi's political vulnerability in the absence of his own political base. The new D'Alema government, supported by a more centrist parliamentary majority, was viewed by Prodi as a betrayal of the Olive Tree alliance which had won the 1996 elections.[1] The Democrats made little secret of their desire to unseat D'Alema before the next national parliamentary elections.

The formation of the Democrats and Prodi's decision for the new movement to contest the European elections worsened inter-party relations within the centre-left coalition. The *Partito popolare italiano* (Italian Popular Party: PPI) felt particularly vulnerable to the new formation which sought to attract support from the plethora of centrist political formations. Relations between Prodi and Prime Minister D'Alema also deteriorated significantly despite the Democrats' continued support for the government. D'Alema viewed the Democrats as a direct threat to his premiership and he feared that the new political movement would further fragment the centre-left coalition and undermine his governmental majority. The resignation of Jacques Santer as President of the European Commission in March 1999 added a new twist to the Prodi–D'Alema rivalry. A number of member-state governments suggested Prodi as a possible replacement for Santer and his nomination was supported by D'Alema. Cynics regarded this as an attempt by D'Alema to undermine Prodi's domestic political challenge. While such a scenario would be convenient for D'Alema, it must be remembered that Prodi's candidature had been proposed by other member-state governments, impressed by Prodi's role in securing Italy's qualification for membership of the first wave of the single currency in January 1999. The nomination clearly posed a dilemma for Prodi, who was attracted to the position of President of the Commission but recognised that this would inevitably restrict his political activities in the domestic arena. Despite his reservations, Prodi accepted the nomination and secured the position of President of the Commission in March 1999. Prodi's appointment effectively removed him from the domestic political scene in the longer term but in the run-up to the European elections it gave him and the Democrats extensive national media exposure. Most importantly, in the context of the European elections, Prodi's appointment as President of the Commission established a visible link between the Democrats and the European political arena.

This strong European connection was also true of another novel formation contesting the European elections, the Emma Bonino List. This list was in essence the *Partito Radicale* (Radicals) in a new guise and Bonino, a member of the Santer Commission, gave it a strong European identity. The party was helped by the popular campaign in support of Bonino's efforts to become the new President of the Republic in spring 1999. Although unsuccessful in her bid to become Italy's first female President, the Bonino campaign became an enormous media event and gave her weeks of publicity in the run-up to the European elections.

The European election campaign followed the pattern of earlier contests with national political issues given more prominence than European themes. National political issues tend to be of more immediate concern to voters and differentiate the parties more than their largely consensual pro-European positions.[2] Given the fluid character of domestic politics, the European elections took on an added importance for the parties. This was clearly evident in the way that many of the parties campaigned in the elections. For example, Silvio Berlusconi, the leader of the main opposition party, Forza Italia, attempted to turn the elections into a referendum on the D'Alema government, claiming quite arbitrarily that a combined vote of below 40 percent for the parties in the governing coalition would indicate that it had lost legitimacy and should resign from office. The domestic political importance of the vote was also evident in the intense inter-party competition among parties belonging to the same political alignment; for example, the *Alleanza nazionale* (National Alliance: AN), the former neo-fascists, saw the elections as a chance to challenge the ascendancy of Forza Italia in the centre-right coalition, while on the centre-left the competition for votes between the newly-formed Democrats and the largest party on the centre-left, the *Democratici di sinistra* (Democrats of the Left: DS), assumed a central importance.

Although domestic politics dominated the elections, European themes were not entirely absent from the campaign. Italy's support for NATO intervention in the war in Kosovo, a policy which divided the governing coalition, had a clear European dimension and reopened the debate about the desirability of a common European defence and security policy. This European dimension was also apparent in the government's continued efforts to introduce pension reforms, a policy made more urgent by the fiscal constraints imposed on Italy as a result of its membership of the single currency. Finally, Prodi's appointment as President of the Commission provoked controversy regarding the legitimate role he should play in the European election campaign.

The Results

The turnout of 70.8 percent was the lowest in Italy since the introduction of direct elections to the European Parliament in 1979. This continued the trend of decline in electoral participation in European elections: in 1979 the turnout was 84.9 percent, in 1984 83.4 percent, in 1989 81.5 percent and in 1994 74.8 percent. In comparison with the 1996 parliamentary elections, there was a decline in turnout of almost 6.4 million voters. The decline in electoral participation in the 1999 European elections might have been greater had administrative elections not been held on the same day. In addition, post-election analyses indicated that the Bonino List and the Democrats mobilised voters who had abstained in the 1996 elections.[3] The decline in turnout in Italy is not exceptional, however, and electoral participation in European elections remains higher than in all other EU states where voting is non-mandatory (only Belgium and Luxembourg, both with compulsory voting, recorded higher turnouts in 1999). The 1999 decline in turnout was consistent, however, with a general long-term trend in Italy which has seen a rise in rates of abstention in both national parliamentary and local administrative elections. In the 1999 European elections, the decline in voting was largely attributable to national specific factors: the stalling of Italy's political transition is likely to have contributed to a sense of voter disenchantment; the lacklustre campaigns of most of the parties failed to mobilise voters; and the growing complexity of the party system, with the proliferation of parties and shifting alliances, is likely to have left many voters perplexed and disillusioned.

Nineteen of the twenty-six lists standing in the European elections won seats in the European Parliament. This compares with the thirteen lists which secured representation in the 1994 European elections. The 1999 elections produced a significant turnover in the Italian delegation in the Parliament; of the eighty-seven MEPs elected in 1994 only twenty-two (25.3 percent) returned to the Parliament.

There were three principal winners in the elections: Forza Italia emerged as the largest single party, the Emma Bonino List became

Table 5.1 *European Elections 1994 and 1999 and the Chamber of Deputies 1996*

Elections	European 1999		National 1996	European 1994	
Party Lists	%	Seats Won	%	%	Seats Won
DS	17.3	15	21.1	19.1	16
PDCI	2.0	2	–	–	–
DEMOCRATS	7.7	⎫	–	–	–
SVP	0.5	⎬ 7	–	0.6	1
Union Valdotaine	0.1	⎭	0.1	0.4	–
PPI	4.2	4	6.8	10.0	8
UDEUR	1.6	1	–	–	–
CDU	2.2	2	5.8[a]	–	–
RI	1.1	1	4.3	–	–
PRI-LIB-ELDR	0.5	1	–	0.9[b]	1
SDI	2.2	2	–	1.8[c]	2
Greens	1.8	2	2.5	3.2	3
PRC	4.3	4	8.6	6.1	5
Forza Italia	25.2	22	20.6	30.6	27
AN	⎫		15.7	12.5	11
	⎬ 10.3	9			
Segni Pact	⎭			3.3	3
CCD	2.6	2	5.8[d]	–	–
MS–Fiamma Tricolore	1.6	1	0.9	–	–
Socialist Party	0.1	–	–	–	–
LN	4.5	4	10.1	6.6	6
Emma Bonino List	8.5	7	1.9[e]	2.1	2
Pensioners' Party	0.7	1	–	–	–
Others	1.0	–	1.6	2.8	2
TOTAL	**100.0**	**87**		**100.0**	**87**

[a] Joint list with CCD in 1996
[b] PRI and PLI stood separately in 1994
[c] In 1994 PSI/Democratic Alliance
[d] Joint list with CDU in 1996
[e] Pannella – Sgarbi List in 1996

Source: Author's elaboration of Ministry of the Interior data

the fourth largest party and the Democrats made an electoral breakthrough.

Forza Italia was the only major party to record an increase in its vote compared to the 1996 parliamentary elections, rising from 20.6 percent to 25.2 percent in the 1999 European elections.[4] The party achieved the highest vote in four out of the five multi-member constituencies, recording its best performance of 29.6 percent in the North-west constituency.[5] Silvio Berlusconi stood as a candidate in all five constituencies and came top of the poll in each, recording a record of just under 3 million preference votes.[6] The party's expensive media campaign is likely to have contributed to its strong performance; in contrast to most of the other parties, Forza Italia spent heavily on television election spots, significantly outspending all other parties.[7] Forza Italia's electoral success indicated that Berlusconi's strategy of moving the party towards a more centrist position had been correct. In addition, the party's more moderate and responsible opposition, as shown for example in its support for the government during the war in Kosovo and in its vote for Carlo Azeglio Ciampi as the new President of the Republic, brought electoral dividends. Forza Italia's strong performance, coupled with the electoral decline of the AN, strengthened Berlusconi's claims for leadership of the centre-right coalition, the *Polo delle libertà* (Liberty Pole), and his ambition to be the Pole's prime ministerial candidate at the next parliamentary elections.

For the AN, which stood on a joint list (known as the 'Elephant', after its symbol) with the *Patto Segni* (Segni Pact), the European election results represented a significant defeat. The joint list polled 10.3 percent of the vote compared to the 15.7 percent for the AN in the 1996 legislative elections, a loss of more than 2.6 million voters. Post-election analyses indicated that the party had lost significant numbers of votes to both FI and the Bonino List.[8] The party's decline threatened to undermine the attempts by Gianfranco Fini, the party's leader, to project a new image and identity for the AN as a modern conservative party.[9] The outcome of the elections suggested that Fini's strategy to move the party onto a new political terrain had reached its limits in electoral terms. At the same time, the results effectively extinguished Fini's hopes of supplanting Berlusconi as the leader of the Liberty Pole electoral coalition. In the aftermath of the elections, Fini offered his resignation as leader but this was turned down by the party's executive. He was, however, heavily criticised by elements in the party who accused him of diluting the AN's political identity, of making a tactical error in joining in an electoral pact with Segni and supporting the multiple referendum initiatives, and of concentrating too much on attacking Berlusconi, the party's closest ally.

The *Lega Nord* (Northern League: LN) also suffered a significant electoral setback with a decline from 10.1 percent of the vote in the 1996 national legislative elections to 4.5 percent in the June 1999 European elections. In the North-west constituency the party's vote fell from 21.8 percent of the vote in 1996 to 10.5 percent in 1999, while in the North-east constituency the party declined from 18.7 percent to 6.9 percent over the same period.[10] During this time the League, as a result of its own choices, was largely marginalised on the national political stage. The party's lack of a clear political project and the oscillation in its demands from separatism to greater devolution is likely to have damaged its standing. In addition, the anti-Europeanism of the party may have alienated that part of the northern electorate made up of producers. The party's sympathy with the Serbian position in the Kosovo conflict and its anti-Americanism are also likely to have cost it votes in the European elections. The League's leader, Umberto Bossi, blamed the defeat on the party's more moderate stance and promised a return to a more radical politics.

The European elections were also a disappointment for many of the parties in the governing centre-left coalition. The vote for the DS fell from 21.1 percent in the 1996 legislative elections to 17.3 percent. The party did not benefit from having its former leader, Massimo D'Alema, holding the office of prime minister.[11] Rather, incumbency in office during a difficult period of government is likely to have eroded support for the DS, in common with the pattern of European elections in other member states. The D'Alema government's efforts to introduce pension reforms and a more flexible labour market, in line with the demands of European economic integration, proved unpopular with sections of the party's leadership and the party's social base. Post-election analyses of the flow of the vote among the parties indicated that the DS had lost most votes to Prodi's Democrats.[12] Walter Veltroni, the party secretary, interpreted the results as a clear signal that the party had stagnated in electoral terms and would need to renew itself to rediscover its innovative capacity.[13]

The Democrats made a significant breakthrough in their first electoral test, winning 7.7 percent of the vote and picking up support from parties across the centre-left of the political spectrum.[14] The Democrats overtook the PPI and became the second largest political force on the centre-left.

The Emma Bonino List also achieved a notable success, emerging as Italy's fourth largest party with 8.5 percent of the vote. This result represented a significant advance on the 1.9 percent polled by the Radicals in the 1996 national parliamentary elections; in absolute terms, the political movement won more than 1.9 million extra voters in 1999. Bonino had enjoyed months of media coverage, focusing on her role as coordinator of the EU's humanitarian relief in Kosovo and her attempts to become the new President of the Italian Republic, and in contrast to most of the other political forces contesting the elections she had brought a distinctively European appeal to her campaign. The party conducted a vigorous electoral campaign, making much of Bonino's success as a European Commissioner and spending heavily on television electoral spots (only Forza Italia spent more). Bonino attracted support from across the political spectrum and also appealed to those electors, particularly the young, detached from the traditional parties.[15]

The European elections were a further setback for the principal parties descended from the *Democrazia cristiana* (Christian Democrats: DC). The PPI and the *Cristiani democratici uniti* (United Christian Democrats: CDU) polled 4.2 percent and 2.2 percent respectively, down from the 10 percent they won as a single party in the 1994 European elections. The PPI, as it had feared, saw a major haemorrhage of its voters to the Democrats.[16]

Of the other major parties, Communist Refoundation saw its vote halved from 8.6 percent in the 1996 national elections to 4.3 percent in 1999. The PRC was damaged electorally by its decision to return to opposition in October 1998, a move which brought down the Prodi government and provoked a split in the party. The new breakaway party, *Il Partito dei comunisti italiani* (The Party of Italian Communists: PDCI), polled 2 percent of the vote in the 1999 European elections. The PRC's opposition to NATO's intervention in Kosovo is also likely to have cost the party votes. The Greens (*Verdi*) saw a decline in their vote from 2.5 percent in the 1996 national elections to 1.8 percent in 1999, a result which went against the trend of rising support for Green parties in most other EU states in 1999. Once again, opposition to NATO's intervention in Kosovo appears to have damaged the Italian Greens' electoral performance.

The Political Significance of the European Elections

The post-election interpretation of the results focused almost exclusively on their importance for the domestic political arena and, in particular, on their impact on inter-party competition and alliance strategies. Prime Minister D'Alema interpreted the results as a relative success for his governing coalition, particularly when compared to the election performances of other EU member state governments such as those of Blair and Shroeder. A fall in support for governing parties is a common pattern in European elections, most frequently in those cases where a government is in its mid-term of office or beyond. Although successive treaty reforms since the mid-1980s have introduced incremental enhancements of the European Parliament's powers, European elections remain essentially 'second order' elections: voters are not choosing a national government and they are more willing to abstain, to switch votes and to vote against governing parties.

Given the 'second order' character of European elections, D'Alema could reasonably claim that the results would have no impact on his government and would not necessitate a government reshuffle. The combined vote for the parties making up the D'Alema governing coalition was 41.2 percent (see Table 5.2), in excess of the arbitrary 40 percent which Berlusconi had claimed would be the minimum for the government to be able to claim legitimacy. D'Alema made much of the fact that the Liberty Pole alliance had failed to reach the 40 percent threshold set by Berlusconi, polling a combined vote of 38.1 percent.[17]

While the relative strengths of the centre-left and centre-right alliances were largely unaltered, at a political level much had changed as a result of the European elections. D'Alema's positive interpretation of the results disguised some worrying features of the elections for both his government and his party. First, the European elections highlighted the fragmented nature of the government's parliamentary majority and D'Alema's dependence on parties with very little support in the country; of the twelve separate lists from the centre-left coalition which stood in the elections, nine polled a vote of 2.2 percent or less, while the remaining three lists won 17.3 percent (the DS), 7.7 percent (the Democrats) and 4.2 percent (the PPI). Second, the two largest parties in the coalition, the DS and the PPI, both declined significantly; the DS, the largest party in the 1996 national elections, fell almost 8 percent behind Forza Italia in the European elections. Third, the electoral breakthrough of the Democrats indicated a significant rebalancing of the forces in the centre-left coalition and a relative weakening of both the DS's and the PPI's bargaining power. Fourth, the resignations of Franco Marini as leader of the PPI and Luigi Manconi as leader of the Greens, following their parties' poor results, added to the uncertainties surrounding the stability of the centre-left coalition.

The European election results confirmed both the highly fluid character of partisan identities and the fragmented nature of the Italian party system in the 1990s.[18] Electoral mobility remained high although the movement of voters was primarily intra-bloc rather than inter-bloc, thus leaving the relative strengths of the

Table 5.2 *Results of the European Elections, 13 June 1999*

Party Lists	Valid Votes	%	Seats Won
DS	5,395,287	17.3	15
PPI	1,319,484	4.2	4
Greens	548,899	1.8	2
Republicans/Liberals/ELDR	168,178	0.5	1
Democrats *	2,407,918	7.7	
SVP *	155,749	0.5	7
Union Valdotaine *	41,227	0.1	
Sub-total Olive Tree	**10,036,742**	**32.1**	**29**
RI-Dini List	353,805	1.1	1
SDI	671,820	2.2	2
UDEUR	499,498	1.6	1
CDU	670,063	2.2	2
PDCI	622,252	2.0	2
Sub-total Government Majority	**12,854,180**	**41.2**	**37**
PRC	1,328,491	4.3	4
Total Centre-Left	**14,182,671**	**45.5**	**41**
Forza Italia	7,829,442	25.2	22
AN – Segni Pact	3,202,821	10.3	9
CCD	806,422	2.6	2
Sub-total Liberty Pole	**11,838,685**	**38.1**	**33**
MS-Fiamma Tricolore	495,342	1.6	1
Socialist Party	42,554	0.1	-
Total Centre-Right	**12,376,581**	**39.8**	**34**
LN	1,395,535	4.5	4
Emma Bonino List	2,631,118	8.5	7
Pensioners' Party	232,166	0.7	1
Others	291,446	1.0	-
Total Others	**4,550,265**	**14.7**	**12**
Total	**31,109,517**	**100.0**	**87**

* Joint lists

Source: Italian Ministry of the Interior data

competing centre-left and centre-right alliances largely unchanged. The fragmentation of the party system was exacerbated by the proportional representation system used for European elections; the low threshold for representation enabled nineteen of the twenty-six lists contesting the elections in 1999 to secure seats in the European Parliament. Other features of the results indicated the fragmentation of the party system: only five parties polled more than 5 percent of the vote and three got little more than 4 percent; of the remaining eighteen lists which contested the European elections, the highest recorded vote was 2.6 percent, yet eleven of these lists won seats in the European Parliament. The fragmentation highlighted the need for further electoral reform to bring about a more far-reaching restructuring and simplification of the party system. The 1999 European election results demonstrated that a modification of the proportional system for European Parliament elections, perhaps with a national percentage threshold for representation, would need to be part of any package of electoral reform.

The outcome of the European elections was also important in terms of the parties' alliance strategies in the domestic political arena. Many of the leading parties approached the elections as an opportunity to strengthen their relative positions within either the centre-left or centre-right electoral alliances. As a result, the competition between allies and proximate parties in national politics was often more intense than that between domestic political opponents.

On the centre-right of the political spectrum, the results of the European elections strengthened Berlusconi's position in relation to Fini and the National Alliance and vindicated his strategy of moving Forza Italia towards a more centrist political space. Fini's attempts to recreate the AN as a modern European conservative party did not bring electoral rewards and the party's defeat set back his efforts to challenge Berlusconi's leadership of the centre-right. The AN had failed in its efforts to bypass Berlusconi and to extend beyond its traditional right-wing location through its alliance with Segni. As a result, for the foreseeable future the AN appeared to be consigned to a peripheral right-wing political space in the Liberty Pole alliance.

The LN's electoral decline indicated that the party would have to abandon its self-imposed isolation and seek electoral allies. As a result of its electoral weakening it has much less to offer potential allies in terms of votes, yet in many northern constituencies it is likely to remain crucial to the Liberty Pole's hopes of winning a national majority in the next parliamentary elections.

On the centre-left of the political spectrum, the breakthrough of the Democrats in the European elections brought the bargaining power as a counterweight to the DS which Prodi had sought in launching the movement, and signalled an important shift in the axis of the alliance. In the aftermath of the elections the leaderships of both the DS and the Democrats addressed the issue of the renewal of the centre-left *Ulivo* (Olive Tree alliance). There were, however, important differences between the two parties' conceptions of the so-called 'Olive Tree Two'. According to D'Alema, the centre-left parties in the governing majority should move towards a federation which would present itself under a single name and symbol at the next national parliamentary elections.[19] The Democrats, however, dismissed this federal conception of the 'Olive Tree Two', fearing that the DS, as the largest single party, would be hegemonic in such an alliance and that it would be nothing more than a simple arithmetical summation of the various parties which would retain their distinct identities.[20] The Democrats' alternative conception proposed 'a common home' for all reformist forces, prefiguring the longer-term objective of a move to a single party. Within this 'common home', according to the Democrats' party secretary, the political scientist Arturo Parisi, the Democrats would not simply be the centrist component of the centre-left but would locate themselves at the centre of the centre-left. For the Democrats, a new centre-left alliance should be based on clear rules, a shared programme and its prime ministerial candidate should be chosen in primary elections, a proposal designed to curtail the perceived dominance of the DS. Before any renewal of the centre-left alliance, however, the Democrats' first priority following the European elections was to consolidate their position with the transformation of the movement into an organised political party.

At the heart of the differences over the future of the centre-left coalition was an ongoing struggle for ascendancy among the parties, particularly between the Democrats and the DS. Although faced with an electoral imperative to present a more united and cohesive alliance, the parties remain competitive and with quite different visions of how the alliance should evolve. In the aftermath of the European elections, for example, the Democrats made it clear that their conception of a reformist alliance would not be socialist in character and that they would not be joining the Party of European Socialists (PES) in the European Parliament.

The strong electoral performance by the Bonino List posed a new challenge to both the centre-right and centre-left electoral alliances. Both recognised that if the Bonino List were to attract a similar level of electoral support in a subsequent national election, it could become a critical player in determining a victory for either the centre-left or centre-right electoral coalition. In the aftermath of the European elections both Berlusconi and D'Alema made efforts to forge closer political links with Bonino. Berlusconi pointed to the affinities between Bonino's political project for a 'liberal revolution' and his own political programme, and he recalled that his government had nominated Bonino as European Commissioner in 1994. D'Alema also expressed his admiration for Bonino and revealed that he had invited her to enter his new government in October 1998. His attempts to build closer links with Bonino were undermined, however, by his government's failure to renominate her as European Commissioner in the new Prodi Commission.[21] In spite of the various advances, Bonino and the maverick leader of the Radicals, Marco Pannella, remained noncommittal about any future electoral alliances, claiming that they would only cooperate with those parties which supported a package of referendums on electoral, social and economic reforms promoted by the Radicals. The Bonino List had no clear political advantage in quickly developing an alliance with either the centre-left or centre-right coalitions; the party's appeal was based, in part, on a rejection of the traditional parties and by keeping an equidistant position from both electoral coalitions it preserved its potential bargaining power.

The European Dimension

While the post-election analysis of the results focused primarily on their importance for domestic politics, the European dimension was also significant. The nineteen Italian lists which won seats in the European elections dispersed to each of the seven party groups in the European Parliament. As Table 5.3 shows, membership of the party groups in the Parliament is often inconsistent with party alliances in the domestic political arena; for example, Forza Italia, the principal party of opposition in national politics, sits in the same group as a number of the small parties which form part of the centre-left governing coalition in Italy.

These anomalies reflect the fluid nature of political alignments in Italy, particularly in the centre of the political spectrum where a plethora of small parties are located. In their competition to occupy distinctive political space, Italian parties view membership of the European Parliament's party groups as a means to cement their political identity in the domestic political arena. For example, in the late 1980s the 'Euroleft' strategy followed by the *Partito comunista italiano* (Italian Communist Party: PCI) emphasised the party's links with European socialist parties in an attempt to project a new political identity and to enhance its domestic political legitimacy.

Table 5.3 *Membership of Party Groups in the European Parliament*

EP Party Group	Italian Parties/Lists	Seats
Group of the EPP	FI	22
(Christian Democrats)	PPI	4
and European Democrats	CDU	2
	CCD	2
	SVP	1
	Pensioner's Party	1
	UDEUR	1
	RI-Dini List	1
Union for a Europe of Nations Group	AN-Segni Pact	9
Confederal Group of the	PRC	4
European United Left/Nordic Green Left	PDCI	2
Group of the Party	DS	15
of European Socialists	SDI	2
Group of the European	Democrats	6
Liberal, Democrat and	LN	1
Reform Party	PRI-Lib-ELDR	1
Group of Greens/European Free Alliance	Greens	2
Non-attached	Bonino List	7
	LN	3
	MS-FT	1
Total		**87**

Source: European Parliament and the Ministry of the Interior

More recently, Forza Italia has joined the newly formed Group of the European People's Party (EPP) and European Democrats, thus locating itself in the mainstream of European centre-right parties. This is consistent with Berlusconi's domestic political strategy of moving Forza Italia to occupy the centre-right political space, formerly the domain of the DC.

In response to this political challenge, one of the leading parties descended from the DC, the left-leaning PPI, tried for many years to block Forza Italia's membership of the EPP. The parties opposed to Berlusconi's entry into the EPP argued that Berlusconi's party would shift the party group to the right, giving it a more conservative identity; that Forza Italia's alliance with the AN in domestic politics made it politically unacceptable; and that Forza Italia did not share the EPP's traditionally strong pro-Europeanism. However, with the support of the Spanish prime minister, Jose-Maria Aznar, and Helmut Kohl, Forza Italia was admitted to the party group in June 1998 and was finally granted full membership of the transnational party in early December 1999.[22] In a ballot of MEPs belonging to the party group, seventy-three voted in favour of Forza Italia's full membership, eighteen voted against and four abstained: of the Italian parties in the party group, *Il Centro cristiano democratico* (Christian Democratic Centre: CCD) and the CDU voted in favour while the PPI and *Rinnovamento italiano* (Italian Renewal: RI) voted against. As a result of Forza Italia's entry, the small centrist parties (the PPI, CDU, CCD, the German-language *Sudtiroler Volkspartei* [South Tyrol People's Party: SVP], the *Unione dei democratici europei* [Union of European Democrats: UDEUR], and RI) have seen a relative weakening of their positions within the EPP while Forza Italia has become the largest Italian representative in the party group. The leader of the PPI, the MEP Pierluigi Castagnetti, was particularly worried by Forza Italia's entry into the group, a decision which he regarded as a centrist stamp of approval that Berlusconi would be able to exploit in domestic politics in his efforts to encroach on the political space occupied by the small centre parties. Forza Italia's use of the European Parliament to bolster its image in domestic politics was clearly illustrated in September 1999 when the party made much of its willingness to put national interests above partisan divisions and voted in favour of the new Prodi Commission.

Forza Italia's centrality in the newly elected 1999 European Parliament, as a member of the Parliament's largest party group, contrasts with its marginalisation when it first entered the Parliament after the 1994 elections. Forza Italia's alliance in government at that time with the post-fascist AN coupled with the party's more eurosceptic approach, epitomised by Foreign Minister Antonio Martino, left the party without allies in the European Parliament and it was forced to create its own party group, Forza Europa.

The potential importance of European Parliament (EP) party group membership is also illustrated in the cases of the Democrats and the AN. Following the European elections, it was not immediately clear which party group Prodi's Democrats would adhere to. Given the political make-up and programme of the Democrats, the movement was a potential candidate for membership of either the EPP or the PES. Both these options, however, posed political difficulties for the Democrats' alliance strategy in the domestic political

arena and for the political identity it sought to project. The Democrats eventually joined the Group of the European Liberal, Democrat
and Reform Parties (ELDR), traditionally a party group leaning to
the centre-right although the Democrats' presence may shift its
political axis. Membership of the ELDR at European level was seen
by the Democrats as consistent with their attempts to develop a
bridging role between the centre and left at the national level.

Membership of an EP group has also presented problems for the
AN. Following the 1999 European elections, the AN had hoped to
join forces with the French Gaullists. The Gaullists, however,
joined the Group of the EPP and European Democrats while the
AN entered the Union for a Europe of Nations Group (UEN), a
choice which leaves it outside of the mainstream European right
and is potentially damaging to its efforts to cultivate a new political identity as a modern conservative party.

The potential impact of the European Parliament's party groups
on domestic politics was clearly illustrated in December 1999 when
the PES tried to persuade the leader of the *Socialisti democratici
italiani* (Italian Social Democrats: SDI), Enrico Boselli, to continue
his party's support of the D'Alema government. Enrique Baron Cre-
spo, president of the PES, openly criticised the behaviour of the
SDI, a member of the Socialist party group, in calling for the resignation of a government led by a party, the DS, belonging to the
same group in the European Parliament.[23] The SDI, however,
rejected this intervention, claiming that it was an illegitimate
encroachment on a party's autonomy in the national arena.

Conclusions

The 1999 European elections in Italy centred primarily on domestic politics rather than European issues. Most of the parties viewed
the elections as an opportunity to improve their standing in the
national political arena and the main focus of the electoral campaign was on domestic political issues and divisions. The results of
the elections were likewise interpreted by the parties primarily
from the standpoint of their impact on domestic politics.

The outcome of the elections confirmed the fluid state of party
politics in Italy. The hyper-proportional system used for European
elections permitted very small parties to gain representation and
exacerbated the fragmentation of the party system. The elections
produced significant successes for two 'new' formations, the
Democrats and the Bonino List, both of which reject traditional
party politics and favour a new majoritarian electoral law designed

to create a bipolar party system. The other major winner in the elections, Forza Italia, could also make some claim to novelty.

The results of the European elections produced some important internal changes in both the centre-right and centre-left electoral alliances. On the centre-right, Berlusconi's Forza Italia strengthened its position at the expense of the AN, while on the centre-left the success of the Democrats weakened the dominant position of the DS. The electoral breakthrough of the Bonino List brought an important 'new' player into national politics and one which both the centre-left and centre-right alliances hope to attract in future electoral contests.

The election results had no immediate impact on the governing coalition and prime minister D'Alema quickly dismissed calls for new parliamentary elections or a government reshuffle. In the longer term, however, the results of the European elections highlighted the inherent weaknesses of D'Alema's fragmented coalition and emphasised the need for a more cohesive centre-left alliance based around a renewal of the Olive Tree. The opponents of D'Alema on the centre-left viewed the elections as a confirmation that the electoral alliance could not win the next parliamentary elections with D'Alema, a former communist, as the prime ministerial candidate. More generally, the elections underlined the need for further electoral reform designed to simplify the party system and create more stable and cohesive electoral alliances.

The European dimension to the elections was also important. The Italian parties view membership of the European Parliament's party groups and the transnational European parties as important symbols in the construction of their own political identities. Given the fluidity of party identities and ideological positions in Italy's changing party system, this external belonging takes on an added significance. In the longer term, the EP's nascent party system has the potential to contribute to a realignment of Italian party politics in the direction of the more stable political alliances found in most other EU member states.

Notes

1. For an analysis of the collapse of the Prodi government and the formation of the D'Alema government, see S. Fabbrini, 'Dal governo Prodi al governo D'Alema: continuità o discontinuità', in *Politica in Italia: Edizione 99*, eds D. Hine and S. Vassallo, vol. 14, Bologna, 1999, 139–59.
2. A pre-election opinion survey by Ipsos-World Media Network found that 45 percent of Italians regarded the European elections as an opportunity to express an opinion on national issues, while 28 percent of respondents saw the elections as a vote on European issues; see *La Stampa*, 2 June 1999.

3. Just over one-tenth of the vote for the Bonino List came from electors who had abstained, spoiled or left blank their ballots in the 1996 national elections; see the data reported by Renato Mannheimer in *Il Corriere della Sera*, 15 June 1999.

4. In order to assess the relative standings of the parties it is more meaningful to compare the 1999 European elections with the 1996 legislative elections rather than with the 1994 European elections. In making such comparisons, however, it is important to bear in mind that voters are not choosing governments in European elections and that the electoral systems for the two elections are quite different.

5. For European Parliament elections Italy is divided into five multi-member constituencies with the 87 seats allocated on the basis of population: the North-west returns 23 MEPs, the North-east 16, the Centre 17, the South 21, and the Islands 10. The parties present lists of candidates in each constituency (up to a maximum of the number of seats available) and seats are allocated to the parties on the basis of proportional representation. Voters may also indicate preferences for a candidate or candidates on the list; the number of preference votes available to the voter varies according to the number of MEPs elected in each constituency.

6. Forza Italia had the most loyal electorate, comparing the 1996 national elections with the 1999 European elections; in addition, the party won significant votes from AN, LN and PPI. See *La Stampa*, 15 June 1999.

7. See *La Repubblica*, 15 June 1999.

8. See the figures reported by Stefano Draghi in *La Stampa*, 15 June 1999.

9. Fini's project is likely to have alienated some of the AN's traditional support. For an analysis of political attitudes and self-placement of party militants see S. Bertolino and F. Chiapponi, 'I militanti di Alleanza Nazionale: ancora "esuli in patria"'?, in *Quaderni di Scienza Politica*, no.2, 1999, 211–49.

10. Only an estimated 30 percent of the LN electorate stayed loyal to the party from the 1996 national elections to the 1999 European elections, with the biggest losses of votes to Forza Italia and the Bonino List; figures from Abacus reported in *La Repubblica*, 16 June 1999.

11. D'Alema enjoyed high public approval ratings over his handling of the Kosovo crisis in the weeks before the European elections. Renato Mannheimer suggests, however, that D'Alema's support for NATO intervention in Kosovo may have cost him votes on the left. See *La Repubblica*, 17 June 1999.

12. See the figures reported by Stefano Draghi in *La Stampa*, 15 June 1999.

13. See *La Repubblica*, 16 June 1999 and *Il Corriere della Sera*, 18 June 1999.

14. Arturo Parisi, installed as leader of the Democrats shortly after the European elections, claimed that 51 percent of the Democrats' vote had come from outside the centre-left; 21 percent from abstainers and 30 percent from the Liberty Pole and the LN (see *Corriere della Sera*, 18 June 1999). These figures, however, were contradicted by those of Explorer which indicated that 80 percent of the Democrats' votes came from the centre-left (see *La Stampa*, 15 June 1999); similar findings were reported by the Abacus agency (see *La Repubblica*, 16 June 1999).

15. See R. Mannheimer, *Il Corriere della sera*, 15 June 1999 and *La Stampa*, 15 June 1999.

16. It was estimated that 26 percent of PPI voters switched to the Democrats; see *La Stampa*, 15 June 1999.

17. The precarious nature of these arithmetical summations was clearly illustrated when the CDU switched from the centre-left alliance to the Liberty Pole shortly after the European elections; on the basis of the European election results, this move by the CDU tilted the balance in favour of the Liberty Pole alliance.

18. On the reshaping of the Italian party system see R. D'Alimonte and S. Bartolini, 'Electoral Transition and Party System Change in Italy', in *Crisis And Transition*

in Italian Politics, eds M. Bull and M. Rhodes, London, 1997, 110–34: P. Daniels, 'Italy: Rupture or Regeneration?', in *Changing Party Systems in Western Europe*, eds D. Broughton and M. Donovan, London, 1999, 71–95.

19. See the interview with D'Alema in *La Stampa*, 17 June 1999.

20. See *La Stampa*, 18 June 1999. The PPI also rejected D'Alema's proposal, preferring to give priority to the strengthening of the centre within the centre-left alliance (see *Il Corriere della Sera*, 19 June 1999). Walter Veltroni, the leader of the DS, said he would prefer the creation of a single centre-left party but recognised that it was unrealistic to expect the various parties to renounce their separate identities; see the interview with Veltroni in *La Repubblica*, 16 June 1999.

21. Press speculation suggested that Prodi favoured the renomination of Mario Monti rather than Bonino.

22. As a condition for entry, Berlusconi was required to declare that the alliance with the AN is programmatic and due to the existing electoral law but does not constitute an essential component of Forza Italia's own identity; see *La Stampa*, 3 December 1999.

23. Rudolf Scharping, the President of the Party of European Socialists and German defence minister, also intervened; in a letter to D'Alema he wrote, 'The process of reform and modernisation of Italy should be strengthened and not hindered, particularly by a member of our European political family' (author's translation). See *Il Corriere della Sera*, 18 December 1999.

6

The election of Carlo Azeglio Ciampi to the Presidency of the Republic

Gianfranco Pasquino

At 13.04 on Thursday, 13 May 1999, on the first ballot, a joint session of parliament elected the seventy-nine-year-old Treasury Minister, Carlo Azeglio Ciampi, to the office of the ninth President of the Italian Republic (tenth if the 'provisional' President Enrico De Nicola, in office from 1946 to approval of the Constitution, is included in the list). This was only the second time in the history of the Italian presidential elections[1] that a candidate had been elected on the first ballot. On the single previous occasion (1985) – following adroit negotiations by the secretary of the *Democrazia cristiana* (Christian Democrats: DC), Ciriaco De Mita – the choice had fallen on the then President of the Senate, Francesco Cossiga, ex-Prime Minister, and Minister of the Interior at the time of the Aldo Moro kidnapping. The 707 votes gained by Ciampi (representing 71.4 percent of those entitled to vote) suggest a substantial majority, (albeit one not much over the quorum of 674 votes) in favour of the centre-left candidate. Yet the 183 votes lacking from the theoretical majority which should have sustained Ciampi from the first round of voting suggest that there were those who would have preferred matters to be much less clear-cut. There were some, that is to say, who counted on the possibility that, if the two-thirds threshold was not achieved on the first ballot, Parliament would see the onset of horse-trading of the kind conducted by the Christian Democrats on at least three previous occasions – the elections of Giovanni Gronchi

(1955), of Giovanni Leone (1971), and of Oscar Luigi Scalfaro (1992) – with unpredictable consequences for the candidate, for the solidity of the majority, and for Parliament. Indeed one can plausibly claim, given the importance assumed by the presidential election, that the duration of the legislature itself was in question.

Even taking account of the votes against Ciampi – explicitly declared only by the *Lega Nord* (Northern League: LN), which voted for its 'flag' candidate, Senator Luciano Gasperini (seventy-two votes), and by *Rifondazione Comunista* (Communist Refoundation: PRC), which cast the majority of its votes for the elderly Communist leader Pietro Ingrao (twenty-one votes) – there were still some 185 defectors. Some of these 'snipers' evidently voted against the instructions of their party leaders, choosing other candidates in the majority coalition such as, for example, Rosa Russo Iervolino (sixteen votes) of the *Partito Popolare* (Italian Popular Party: PPI), Giulio Andreotti (ten votes), the President of the Senate Nicola Mancino (six votes), the ex-secretary of the PPI, Mino Martinazzoli, (four votes), the governor of the Bank of Italy Antonio Fazio (four votes), and the former President of the Republic Francesco Cossiga (three votes). Although these votes were presumably cast by members of the PPI, and hence by the Christian Democrat diaspora, they were certainly not untargeted. Rather, they served a distinct purpose and should be interpreted not as a signal of persisting dissent but as an attempt to keep the presidential election open.

There were at least three reasons why this attempt was not entirely impracticable. Firstly, reaching consensus on Ciampi had by no means been straightforward, and it was achieved only on the evening before voting was due to start. Secondly, although the secretary of the PPI, Franco Marini, was out manoeuvred at the meeting held by the majority leadership that evening, he certainly did not give up the struggle. Thirdly, not even the *Polo per le libertà* (Liberty Pole), which had entertained the idea of testing the cohesion of the majority coalition on the first ballot before voting for Ciampi, could have long supported a candidate who had lost his official legitimacy following devastating defections from within his majority. That nothing actually happened can be taken to be an excellent and encouraging outcome on several counts. It is encouraging firstly as regards the general political relationships between the centre-left majority, i.e. what is left of the *Ulivo*, on the one hand, and the *Polo* on the other. The second and correlated reason is that it prompts optimism as to the resumption of institutional reform, not least because of the view attributed to Ciampi that a majoritarian and bipolar party system is necessary in order to enhance Italy's role in Europe. The third reason, this too correlated with the former two, is that Ciampi's election bodes well for the stability of the Italian political situation and for the completion – following significant electoral, institutional and constitutional reforms – of the country's long and incomplete transition.

The Strategy followed by the Popular Party

In each of these respects, all the other main political actors correctly located the actual and/or perceived position of the PPI on the side of institutional and constitutional conservatism. The secretary of the PPI, Franco Marini, must have realised that he was at a disadvantage from the outset. In fact, in order to make up lost ground and move his party, and himself, to the forefront of the race for the presidency, he devised a strategy intended to show that the PPI could boast numerous suitable candidates for the Quirinale. In order to persuade both his centre-left allies and at least part of the *Polo* opposition alliance – or conversely the Polo's allies and some of the opponents of renewal in the majority coalition – Marini deployed a combination of old and new arguments. For some time, in fact, not only Marini but the majority of the PPI had believed that they could use Italy's incomplete transition to repropose the outgoing President Oscar Luigi Scalfaro as candidate for the Quirinale, and with good chances of success. The most convincing argument was that Scalfaro had ensured – albeit amid perhaps inevitable controversy – the continuity of transition over the past seven tormented years, and that he had facilitated the achievement of several important outcomes (six governments formed and supported by multiple majorities; two dissolutions of parliament).[2] He therefore deserved to continue his work until the transition had been completed. To this end, the idea was circulated among the parties that, with the *Bicamerale* (Bicameral Commission on Institutional Reform) having failed, it was sufficient to extend Scalfaro's presidential mandate, perhaps for a couple of years, for the noble and specific purpose of resuming and promulgating reform.[3] The idea was superficially attractive, not least because it seemed to rescue the chestnuts from the political fire while confirming the power of the politicians.

Constitutionally, however, any extension of Scalfaro's mandate was highly dubious, as well as being disruptive, because it would have required a constitutional amendment, something extremely difficult to accomplish in the short run. Politically, the proposal was defeated by the opposition raised by the *Polo*, especially by the leader of the ex-fascist *Alleanza nazionale* (National Alliance: AN) Gianfranco Fini, but also – as far as one can tell from their somewhat wayward pronouncements – by Umberto Bossi, the leader of the separatist *Lega Nord* (Northern League: LN). Fini's opposition did not stem from a unreasoning hostility *ad personam*. On the contrary, it was deeply rooted in his strongly critical assessment of the performance of the Scalfaro Presidency both as an institution and as the exercise of power (see below).

Slowly but surely, Scalfaro's recandidature for a full seven-year term, or a two-year extension of his mandate, faded into the background. For that matter, Scalfaro was not a candidate whose election Marini could claim to be his own work. If Scalfaro had managed to remain at the Quirinale, it would have been because of his own personal merits, while Marini urgently needed the election of a candidate who would demonstrate that the secretary of the *Popolari* wielded effective power and who would emphasise the crucial role that the *Popolari* – despite their reduced and, according to some, still declining electoral support – had acquired and were now exercising.

Of course, no argument of this kind (pivoting as it did on the power and visibility of the PPI) could be presented and justified in public. Marini consequently resorted to two other arguments that could lay claim to greater dignity. In truth, the first of them – the attempt to restore equilibrium within the centre-left majority – revealed that Marini's political thinking still tenaciously clung to the tradition of the First Republic. Indeed, one of the criteria most frequently and successfully used in screening presidential candidates during the First Republic had been the need to alternate the Quirinale between the Christian Democrats and their 'lay' (i.e. non-Catholic) partners. Naturally, there were some exceptions – the Christian Democrat Antonio Segni succeeded the Christian Democrat Gronchi in 1962, and likewise the Christian Democrat Scalfaro succeeded the Christian Democrat Cossiga – but these were exceptions justified by the circumstances. Gronchi was not the official Christian Democrat candidate in 1955 (he was elected thanks to deciding votes cast by the left), and Segni's election was justifiable in that it restored the balance both within the DC, reassuring the nervous right wing of the party, and in the relationships between the DC and the Socialists at the beginning of the centre-left period.

The election of Oscar Luigi Scalfaro, however, occurred when all previous arrangements and precedents no longer applied.[4] From the outset, in fact, the Scalfaro presidential election was influenced and characterised by criteria decidedly different from those of the past. Having suffered a heavy defeat in the general elections of 5–6 April 1992, the main concern of the Christian Democrats and the Socialists, together with the Liberals and the Social Democrats, was to redeem that defeat. At the same time, however, the three leaders of the CAF (Craxi, Andreotti and Forlani) found themselves caught up in a damaging and highly suspect struggle for only two offices: the Presidency of the Republic and the Premiership. The problem could not be solved by applying the criterion of the Christian Democrat/lay alternation in the Quirinale, firstly because Craxi seemed to prefer his own return to Palazzo Chigi (the Prime Minister's residence), and secondly because Andreotti, and to a lesser extent Forlani, now ageing and at the end of their careers, both seemed to prefer the Quirinale. Given that following the unexpected resignation of President Cossiga some months before the expiry of his mandate, it would be the new President of the Republic who nominated the Prime Minister, Craxi preferred to see Forlani elected, having less trust in Andreotti (whom he had once warned with the jibe that 'sooner or later all foxes end up as fur coats'). However, Forlani's election proved extremely difficult, and after a protracted series of ballots, thirteen in all, he withdrew. It should be noted that Scalfaro's election was brought about by an event as unforeseeable as it was traumatic: the Mafia bomb attack which took the lives of judge Giovanni Falcone, his wife and his escort.

Having just been elected President of the Chamber of Deputies, Scalfaro had never seriously been a candidate for the Quirinale, but when parliamentarians experienced an outbreak of conscience in the wake of the attack on Falcone, he had two distinct advantages, Firstly, his impartiality had already been acknowledged by his election to the Presidency of the Chamber, a position which in the past had often been a useful springboard to the Presidency of the Republic (Gronchi, Leone and Pertini had all been Presidents of the Chamber of Deputies, and Cossiga of the Senate). His second and best advantage was his reputation as a 'defender' of Parliament and of its prerogatives. By virtue of this reputation, the leader of the Radicals, Marco Pannella, proposed Scalfaro as a candidate for the Quirinale in open opposition to Cossiga, who was more or less correctly described as 'presidentialist'.

There are two features that should be borne in mind when seeking to understand how the political establishment squared off for the election of the President in May 1999. Firstly, although not elected as such, Scalfaro belonged to the cultural tradition and political history of the Christian Democrats. Consequently, another President from the ranks of the *Popolari* (as members of the PPI are known) would have prolonged the Christian Democrats' grip upon the Quirinale to twenty-one years, which was too long by any reasonable standard. Although nobody would have applied such a narrow numerical calculation to unexceptionable *Popolari* candidates, it had an importance that Marini seems to have entirely underestimated.

As to Scalfaro's second advantage, his 'parliamentarism', it is an irony of history that he was involved in a transition that compelled him to behave as a 'presidentialist', or almost. I shall develop this important point later. To return to Marini, his revival of the Christian Democrat/lay criterion was somewhat curious, for he applied it to the distribution of offices among the leaders of the centre-left. Since the prime minister at that time was Massimo D'Alema of the Democrats of the Left, Marini declared that the office of President of the Republic should be conferred, by way of a highly unusual trade-off, on the PPI, which was the second largest party in the governing coalition. Anybody who knew anything about the way Italian politics works – the entire political class in the broadest sense of the term, journalists included – regarded the exchange as improper and unfair unless it had been an unspoken agreement of the government crisis of October 1998 which brought D'Alema to Palazzo Chigi in the place of Prodi. In fact, barring unpredictable and traumatic events, Presidents of the Italian Republic remain in office for seven years. Barring equally unpredictable, though much less traumatic, events Italian prime ministers last for approximately ten-and-a-half months. Hence not even the most optimistic prime minister could expect to remain in office, even with interruptions, for the full seven years (only De Gasperi had ever managed to do so).

Of course, behind Marini's demand lay the ill-concealed threat of provoking a government crisis should the secretary of the Democrats of the Left, Walter Veltroni, who was brokering the negotiations for the nomination of the President, not accede to the demands of the PPI. Moreover, with a leap of political logic that is difficult to justify, Marini argued that a *Popolari* candidate for the Quirinale would have restored the balance not only within the centre-left coalition but also between the centre-left and the centre-right, between the governing majority and the *Polo* opposition alliance. Marini's idiosyncratic geometry seriously alarmed Veltroni and the DS, who feared that Marini might attempt to put together a broad Christian Democrat centre alliance by reaching an understanding with Berlusconi and Forza Italia on the PPI's candidate for the Presidency, who might even have been Marini himself.

Other positions, other criteria

For a while the president of Forza Italia, Silvio Berlusconi, entertained the idea of driving a wedge between the centre-left by supporting Marini. His ally Fini rejected any such suggestion from the outset, however, both because it would have marginalised the AN and because it would have reinvigorated the centrist parties, thereby encouraging a return to the broadly consociational and proportion-alist style of politics so long practised by the DC. Thus, throughout the run-up to the presidential election, Fini continued to insist on a candidate who would come out in favour of a majoritarian and bipo-lar system and who was not declaredly hostile to presidentialism.[5]

Incidentally, these principles were largely shared by Veltroni, although he had to deal with the conspicuous institutional conser-vatism of the centre-left, which was embraced, not particularly covertly, even within the ranks of the Democrats of the Left. Implicit in Fini's insistence was a sharp criticism of President Scalfaro, a criticism which Forza Italia and Berlusconi could only endorse because it referred in particular to the so-called *ribaltone* (literally 'overturning' of the parliamentary majority) caused by the LN's defection from the Berlusconi government coalition in December 1994–January 1995 and which had led to formation of the Dini gov-ernment. At the time, both Berlusconi and Fini had called stridently, but ultimately unsuccessfully, for new elections after their political-parliamentary-governmental betrayal by Bossi's *leghisti*.[6]

In the meantime, there had been two dramatic new developments, one concerning the candidates, the other concerning methods. With an off-hand remark, Giuliano Amato – much interviewed by the media and closely listened to by politicians – hinted at the possibility of a woman candidate for the Quirinale, the first in history. A broad-based committee which contained few representatives of the political class, but a far wider and prominent cast of journalists, actors, busi-nessmen and super-models, came together to support the candidacy, not just of a woman, but of the European Commissioner Emma Bonino. First a deputy for the Radicals and then a Euro-MP, at the forefront of the Italian battles for contraception, divorce and abortion, vigorously committed to human and women's rights, most recently involved in the creation of the International Tribunal of Human Rights, Emma Bonino accepted the candidature offered her by the 'Emma for President' Committee only on 7 March 1999, although her provocative slogan 'The right man for the Quirinale', which empha-sised that ability, not gender, was the key to her campaign, had already been in circulation for some months. The impact on public opinion was forceful and extremely positive. A poll conducted by UNICAB in February showed that 67 percent of Italians thought that the parties should declare the names of their candidates for the Pres-idency; that 81 percent thought that the candidatures should be pub-licly debated; that 88 percent thought that the various political alignments should describe "the programme and characteristics of their candidates for the Presidency of the Republic".[7]

Thus, the overwhelming majority of the respondents were critical of the secrecy that surrounds the selection of candidates for the Presidency, greatly preferring open public debate on the merits and shortcomings of candidates. The process of electing the President of the Italian Republic is notoriously opaque. There are no declared candidates; indeed, anyone who might be a candidate carefully avoids being mentioned for fear of being 'burnt off'. It is a common strategy to propose someone else as a candidate with the deliberate purpose of eliminating him/her by instigating criticism, reservations and alternative proposals. The years have seen so many smear campaigns, so much scandal mongering and blackmail that no historian of the Presidency of the Republic or constitutionalist would dare to claim that the best candidate, the one most prominent or most representative of his time and of Italian politics, has ever been elected (not even Luigi Einaudi or Sandro Pertini, in very different periods, could be described as the best candidates at their elections). Consequently, the innovative way in which Bonino presented her candidacy was attractive and much appreciated. Her campaign was transparent, presented her merits, encouraged open discussion of her qualities, and finally, in a letter to parliamentarians just prior to the vote, even published her programme, which featured a closely argued constitutional criticism of the outgoing President and his over-frequent and often biased public pronouncements.

The more that Emma Bonino's candidature caught the attention of the media (usually loath to 'cover' events that have not been created by themselves or by their political cronies[8]) the more the method of innuendo, intimidation and deal-fixing stubbornly clung to by Marini appeared outmoded and foolish. It was at this point that Walter Veltroni realised that the situation was unsustainable. Inevitable comparisons were being drawn between Marini's roster of undeclared candidates (evergreen figures whose chief qualifications were a past in the old DC and a decidedly flexible attitude to the composition of the parliamentary majority necessary to elect one of them) and Emma Bonino, whose record as a European Commissioner had been widely eulogised in the German press, as well as in the much more demanding British press.

Ciampi's candidature

Having rejected the *Polo*'s request for a roster of names, Veltroni set himself the arduous task of finding the centre-left's candidate. He declared that the majority coalition would propose its candidate to the *Polo* as well in the hope of gaining its consent. Although the

Polo objected that this 'take it or leave it' procedure was too rigid, and indeed amounted to an imposition, Veltroni's greatest difficulty lay with the governing majority. The Polo took prompt advantage by suggesting the name of Giuliano Amato, who belonged to neither the DS nor the PPI, as a candidate for whom it would be willing to vote. Veltroni was therefore now compelled to counter both the flourishing candidature of Emma Bonino and the nascent one of Giuliano Amato. Marini's continuing strategy of proposing a roster of *Popolari* candidates seems incomprehensible, unless he himself was aspiring to the Quirinale and was only waiting until his candidates were rejected and someone, namely the Democrats of the Left but better still Berlusconi, offered him a candidature that he could not refuse. Indeed, he would have graciously accepted it for seemingly reasonable motives: out of a sense of duty, in order to avert a head-on clash between the centre-left and the Polo, and because, in his idiosyncratic view, the PPI were entitled to the Presidency of the Republic in any case.

It thus came about that Veltroni decided to launch the candidature of Carlo Azeglio Ciampi, and he did so by acting in a manner which was entirely at odds with the former system, for various reasons. Firstly, Veltroni made the explicit and timely announcement of an individual who might well have risked being 'burnt off' under the former system. Secondly, he chose a non-politician who consequently represented none of the parties. Thirdly, he not only announced Ciampi's name, but drew up a list of the criteria and therefore the qualities that had led him to choose Ciampi as the best candidate possible.[9]

From that moment on, anyone wishing to oppose Ciampi would have to follow suit by stating the qualities and achievements of their own candidate. Of course, according to these criteria, Emma Bonino's candidature was still well on course. But objectively, as well as being substantially unacceptable to the ex-Christian Democrats now part of the centre-left and, even more numerous still, in the Polo, Bonino was probably also objectionable to a large proportion of the centre-left, given that she had been elected a deputy within the ranks of the Polo at the fateful elections of 1994. In the meantime, although overshadowed by NATO's military action against Serbia, until the last week of the electoral campaign, the referendum on the abolition of the remaining PR element in the electoral system provoked further conflict between the PPI and the DS and became a factor in the selection of the presidential candidate. The split was particularly apparent between Marini and Veltroni, who stuck to the official party line of supporting a majoritarian and bipolar system, while both sides in the referendum campaign (but more the supporters of the 'Yes' vote) improperly regarded the outcome as a factor to be given serious consideration when the time came to elect the President of the Republic.

More specifically, the 'Yes' supporters, prematurely convinced of their success, asked the voters to return a result that would strengthen the majoritarian character of the electoral system and favour the election to the presidency of someone who, as the slogan put it, was assuredly 'majoritarian and bipolar': in other words, a person whose political record guaranteed that s/he would ensure conversion of the referendum result into a truly majoritarian electoral law and steer the political system towards genuine bipolarity. Of course, none of the PPI's candidates – by history, culture or commitment – could fulfil these criteria. The only exception was the President of the Senate, Nicola Mancino, who (precisely because of his qualities) had never officially figured among the names proposed by Marini except at the end, when it was too late, whereupon he commendably ruled himself out of consideration, announcing that he did not wish to create divisions in the majority.

The meaning of the Presidency

The somewhat low-key referendum campaign introduced into the political and constitutional debate the alternative – obstinately resisted by the majority of leftist constitutionalists – between a 'continuist' and 'reformist' interpretation of the Constitution. Oddly enough, most of the conservative-leaning institutional and constitutional jurists belonged to the political left. Almost all of them had for years underestimated the weight of the long-drawn-out Italian transition on any interpretation of the Constitution that failed to take it into account. The majority did no more than call for an evidently unlikely 'return' to the Constitution, thereby contradicting their own assertion that the constitutional set-up and the workings of the political-constitutional system were constructed and predicated on a proportional electoral system. With the elimination of the proportional system, even the more conservative jurists ought to have regarded undertaking a careful reform both of the parliamentary system and of the President/Parliament/Government 'circuit' as imperative since both had been distorted by the new electoral law, as indeed the whole Scalfaro presidency – value judgements aside – had shown all too clearly.

Under this legitimate interpretation, a positive outcome of the referendum would have intensified both political pressures and the juridical need to update the Constitution and reform the institutions. Of course there was no guarantee that the current members of parliament – as always resistant to reform – would have accepted this interpretation of the referendum result and set about making the necessary changes. In any event, the problem never arose and consequently no counter-proof is forthcoming. In fact, rather surprisingly, the electoral referendum narrowly failed to achieve the necessary quorum of votes.[10] Whereupon, flushed by what he considered to be his victory, having always been explicitly against the referendum, Marini committed the reverse error to that of the promoters of the referendum. He thought that the result could be used to turn the clock back and secure the election to the Presidency of a candidate who was neither majoritarian nor bipolar: his preference being for one of the *Popolari* candidates that he had nominated (and, naturally, for himself). More precisely, on realising that the campaign in favour of Emma Bonino had left its mark even on his own party – which was anything but in favour of greater representation for women – Marini proposed Rosa Russo Iervolino, the incumbent Minister of the Interior, and, as a back-stop, Sergio Mattarella, Deputy Prime Minister and author of the controversial electoral law that had survived the referendum.

Yet the reality of the political and parliamentary situation was not as Marini imagined. Although the electoral reformers had lost, this did not mean that the institutional conservatives and the electoral restorationists enjoyed a majority in the country and in Parliament, still less that the failure of the referendum would raise a conservative wind of such intensity that it would sweep a candidate backed by the PPI into the Quirinale. There was too little support in Parliament and no particular sign that public opinion was favourable either. In the meantime, moreover, Berlusconi's determination to split the centre-left majority by supporting a *Popolari* candidate, rather than the one preferred by the DS, began to falter. Faced with the uncompromising stand taken by Fini, who insisted on a 'majoritarian and bipolar candidate not hostile to presidentialism', Berlusconi decided not to risk creating a cleavage within the *Polo* or, even worse, finding himself excluded from voting for the successful candidate. With unity restored to the Polo, it was apparently a last-minute intervention by Prime Minister D'Alema that settled the centre-left's choice of Ciampi.

One can only hypothesise that D'Alema, on receiving Berlusconi's reassurances of support (Fini had never shifted his position), was able to call the bluff of a government crisis that the secretary of the PPI was certainly reluctant to play. It would in fact have been extremely difficult, though not impossible, for Marini to justify a government crisis on the ground that the centre-left, with the Polo's

approval, was proposing not a member of the DS, but the Minister
of the Treasury for the Presidency of the Republic. It was at this junc-
ture that the personality of the candidate made all the difference.

Neither the centre-left nor the Polo could deny Ciampi's merits,
which are by now a matter of historical record. Governor of the Bank
of Italy after the crisis provoked by Andreotti's attempt to undermine
the independence of the Bank in 1979; Prime Minister from April
1993 to the elections of March 1994, and therefore the overseer of the
approval of the electoral law imposed by the April 1993 referendum
on electoral reform; and then, after a two-year political sabbatical,
Minister of the Treasury in the Prodi government, Ciampi had (has)
an extraordinary curriculum which has combined (and still com-
bines) considerable technical expertise with proven political skills.
Curiously, the two architects of Italy's unexpected entry into European monetary union, Romano Prodi and Carlo Azeglio Ciampi, have
been rewarded as rarely happens in politics (and even more rarely in
Italian politics). With the highly fortunate – because it was made possible by the unexpected resignation of the entire European Commission headed by Santer –appointment of Prodi to Presidency of the
European Commission, and with Ciampi's election to the Presidency
of the Italian Republic, a period of Italian political history as positive
as it is (almost) virtuous has come to a close. And another period has
now begun in which the Ciampi Presidency can and will have to
exercise the powers with which that high office is endowed.

The future of the reforms

That said, nobody truly believes that the method used to reach
agreement between the centre-left and the Polo on Ciampi's election
can be automatically extended to Italy's controversial institutional
reforms. An election, which can be resolved at a stroke, is quite a different matter from a set of decisions with respect to which the
minorities in both alignments may make repeated use of their power
of veto, in both the special Commissions and the Chambers. Moreover, institutional recipes and constitutional models provoke far
more controversy and conflict in the Italian Parliament and among
jurists and political scientists than does the generic objective of con-
structing a majoritarian and bipolar political system. Finally, now
that the phase of constitutional rhetoric has passed, no-one believes
that the constitutional reforms can be steered, still less achieved, by
the Quirinale (though their passage might be eased). Those who
want a majoritarian and bipolar outcome to the Italian transition will
be relieved that the occupant of the Quirinale has no party affilia-

tions to represent and favour; an occupant whose past as a militant in the *Partito d'Azione* is essentially European and therefore bipolar.

Nevertheless, precisely because President Ciampi's deepest values were formed during the resistance in this short-lived, non-confessional, liberal and progressive political organisation, his conduct in office will adhere closely to the rules and will respect the limits of his power. Paradoxically, however, what counts most among the Italian President's attributes are his twin powers to nominate the Prime Minister and to dissolve Parliament, and given the seven-year duration of Ciampi's mandate he is bound to be confronted by both problems. In this regard, it will be sufficient if Ciampi ensures that no hasty 'outburst' prejudices his exercise of these two powers to make the political establishment much more responsible in its behaviour. For example, if those who provoke a government crisis know that the President is willing on principle to dissolve Parliament during a crisis, they will take very careful consideration of the President's position. So too will those who do not oppose the crisis in the hope of exploiting it to their own advantage, up to and including higher office in the event of a government reshuffle: a strategy as practicable and constitutional as it is deleterious to the building of a majoritarian and bipolar democracy.[11] Unfortunately, Ciampi did not apply this healthy principle in the crisis experienced by D'Alema's government just before Christmas 1999.

One may plausibly argue that if the Scalfaro Presidency, with its positive and negative aspects, can be judged satisfactory, this is essentially because Scalfaro prevented Italy's political and institutional transition from lapsing into a crisis of the democratic system. Since May 1999 the Ciampi Presidency (1999–2006) has been faced by an even more elevated, complicated and ambitious task: the truly historic endeavour of accomplishing Italy's transition by means of constitutional reform and a recasting of the party system. Not only is it legitimate to expect commitment by the Quirinale to this undertaking, but certain jurists maintain that it is precisely this that should be the most widely shared 'sense of constitutional unity'. Ciampi has already begun by appealing to political leaders and parliamentarians, declaring that transition can be successfully brought to conclusion. Thanks to his authoritativeness and his admirable intention – as he himself has declared – to 'put his soul' into what he does, President Ciampi appears perfectly positioned – to use Giuliano Amato's metaphor – to play all the notes of the 'accordion of presidential powers'.[12] However, it is by no means certain that parties and coalitions, on the right, on the left, and at the centre, have any intention of dancing to that music.

Translated by Adrian Belton

Notes

This chapter is a revised and extended version of my article 'The Election of the Tenth President of the Italian Republic' published in the *Journal of Modern Political Studies*, vol. 4, no. 3 (Fall 1999), 405–15.

1. For useful analysis of these elections see A. Baldassarre and C. Mezzanotte, *Gli uomini del Quirinale. Da De Nicola a Pertini*, Roma-Bari, 1992.
2. Specifically, the following governments: Amato (June 1992–April 1993), Ciampi (April 1993–May 1994); Berlusconi (May 1994–January 1995); Dini (January 1995–May 1996); Prodi (May 1996–October 1998); D'Alema (October 1998 –).
3. I show why this argument was based on serious misunderstandings of the outcome of the *Bicamerale* in my 'Post-mortem of the Bicamerale' in *Politics in Italy: The Return of Politics*, eds David Hine and Salvatore Vassallo, Bologna, 2000, 101–20.
4. I analysed this election in my 'Electing the President of the Republic', in *The End of Post-war Politics in Italy*, eds Gianfranco Pasquino and Patrick McCarthy, Boulder, 1993, 121–40.
5. Fini's words were: 'a President who believes in bipolarism and is not hostile to presidentialism', quoted *La Repubblica*, 8 May 1999.
6. Opinions differ significantly on this point. I have argued that *ribaltoni* are possible, but only in certain circumstances and with 'parliamentarist' consequences, in my *Mandato popolare e governo*, Bologna, 1995. A substantially positive judgement of Scalfaro's presidency is D. Hine and E. Poli, 'La Presidenza Scalfaro nel 1996: Il difficile ritorno alla normalità', in *Politica in Italia. Edizione 97*, eds R. D'Alimonte and D. Nelkin, Bologna, 1998, 203–21. By contrast, C. Fusaro, *Le radici del semipresidenzialismo*, Soveria Mannelli, 1998, is decidedly critical (see especially 148ff.). Considerable far-sightedness for the time was shown by Vincent Della Sala, 'The Cossiga legacy and Scalfaro's elections in the Shadow of Presidentialism?' in *Italian Politics: A Review*, eds S. Hellman and G. Pasquino, London, 1993, 34–49.
7. UNICAB survey, *Elezione del presidente della Repubblica*, February 1999.
8. Worth mentioning is the position taken up by *La Repubblica*: substantial silence by its editor Ezio Mauro; a swingeing attack by Eugenio Scalfari on Emma Bonino, which can only be explained by his enmity for Marco Pannella: in fact, the only real reservation concerning Bonino's candidacy was that she might become Pannella's stooge; criticisms by Miriam Mafai; and support by Mario Pirani, who rated Ciampi and Amato equally, but which was in any case a great boost for Bonino. By contrast, serious consideration was made of Bonino's candidacy by the editors of *Il Corriere della Sera* and, in general, *Il Sole 24 Ore*.
9. Interview with Veltroni, *La Repubblica*, 13 March 1999, with a listing of Ciampi's merits: 'First: Ciampi is committed to bipolarism. Second: he is not a party member. Third: he is not even a member of parliament. Fourth: he can guarantee that the transition will continue and the reforms will be made. Fifth: he is a supporter of the Euro. Sixth: he enjoys great international prestige. Seventh: he is a layman in politics, although personally he is a Catholic'.
10. See the analysis by M. Donovan in this volume.
11. Unfortunately, Ciampi could do nothing to prevent the somewhat bizarre government crisis that developed just before Christmas 1999, though he did actively contribute to resolving it.

12. I have developed this only apparently musical conception of presidential powers, aptly suggested by Giuliano Amato, in my essay 'La fisarmonica del Presidente', *La Rivista dei libri*, March 1992, 8–10. More generally, on the role and powers of the Italian President see S. Merlini, 'I presidenti della Repubblica', in *La politica italiana. Dizionario critico 1945–95*, ed. Gianfranco Pasquino, Rome-Bari, 1995, 93–119.

7

HISTORY IN THE COURTS: ANDREOTTI'S TWO ACQUITTALS

Jean-Louis Briquet

Twice in just one month – on 24 September by the court in Perugia and on 23 October by the one in Palermo – Giulio Andreotti was cleared of charges that had hung over him since the first allegations by *pentiti* (repentant mafiosi) of his involvement with the Mafia. The first of these charges was that he had commissioned the mafia killing of the journalist Mino Pecorelli, who had threatened Andreotti and members of his entourage that he would reveal compromising facts concerning the political and financial *Italcasse* scandal of the late 1970s. The second accusation – less serious from the criminal point of view but certainly more significant from the political one – was that since the 1960s Andreotti had established a 'pact' with Cosa Nostra, either directly or through his political allies in Sicily. In both cases, the verdict rekindled the controversy on the political 'activism' of certain public prosecutors' offices, and on the role played by the investigating magistrates in the collapse of the so-called First Republic. The verdict, in fact, has been hailed as Andreotti's political absolution and, more generally, as rehabilitating the *Democrazia cristiana* (Christian Democrats: DC) and the 'regime' with which he has been identified for almost fifty years. The sentence has also been used to accuse certain magistrates of using criminal investigations for political ends, and of trying to impose a simplistically 'criminal' view of Italy's recent history.

The political significance attributed to Andreotti's two acquittals therefore extends well beyond their purely judicial implications.

This 'extension' has been possible because Andreotti's trials have been interpreted as issues which concern not only his personal responsibility for the specific crimes of which he stood accused, but also his political role. Thus judicial decisions determined solely by procedural criteria have been exploited to validate (or invalidate) political positions beyond the remit of the judiciary. They have been transformed into value-judgements on the history of the First Republic and paradoxically they have helped dispel its 'shadow areas', which Andreotti's career was considered to symbolise.

The 'Trial of the Century'

When, on 27 March 1993, the Palermo Prosecutors' Office asked the Senate for authorisation to begin proceedings against Andreotti on charges of collaboration with the Mafia, the news caused a public sensation. This was mainly because of the status of the person accused: seven times Prime Minister, more than thirty times Secretary of State, and a minister between 1947 and 1992, Andreotti was one of the most powerful leaders of the DC and a figure emblematic of the First Republic now collapsing – at precisely the moment when the charges were brought against Andreotti – under the blows delivered by the investigations into political corruption and, shortly thereafter, the referendums. Andreotti personified the 'old system' denounced by the proponents of moral renewal in Italian politics. His defenders insisted on his stature as a statesman of international fame; his adversaries instead pointed to him as the symbol of the 'duplicity' so often considered distinctive of the exercise of power in Italy: Giorgio Bocca, for example, writing in *La Repubblica* of 28 March 1993, described him as 'the black soul of the republic'. The same critics highlighted his ambiguous role in the numerous *affaires* that had marked the recent history of Italy and the Christian Democrats (the Sindona affair, the murder of General Dalla Chiesa, and also the Moro kidnapping).[1] This identification of Andreotti with the First Republic, therefore, was a constant feature of the trials. Commentators repeatedly claimed that 'the history of Italy is at stake', while Andreotti's supporters violently accused the judges of engaging in a 'global manoeuvre' against the DC and everything it stood for. His opponents, by contrast, saw the accusations as bearing out their criticisms of a 'power system' personified by Andreotti above all others. As a consequence, the Andreotti trials came to symbolise the collapse of the First Republic and the disgrace into which its leading elites had fallen.

To be sure, the magistrates in the Palermo Prosecutors' Office – and after them those of the Perugia Prosecutors' Office[2] – constantly defended themselves against accusations of staging a political show trial (and even more, against putting Italy's history in the dock), claiming that their sole purpose was to bring criminal proceedings against a particular individual suspected of specific offences. Moreover, they claimed, since the judiciary is duty bound by the Constitution to enforce the law, the proceedings were justified by the obligation of action incumbent upon them. The Chief Public Prosecutor of Palermo, Giancarlo Caselli, had constantly argued this position since Andreotti's committal for trial on 2 March 1995: for example, in August 1997, he declared: 'This [the Andreotti trial] is not a political trial. It is the trial of a specific person who was by profession a politician and concerning specific facts which relate solely to that person. ... Politics and the history of Italy have nothing to do with these specific facts concerning a particular individual'.[3] In the aftermath of the sentence, Caselli reiterated – as did his successor as head of the Palermo Prosecutors' Office, Pietro Grasso – the point: not only were criminal proceedings against Andreotti mandatory following allegations by the *pentiti* that he had links with the Mafia, but the trial had been made possible (and the action of the prosecutors in some way ratified) first by the Senate and then by the judge responsible for the preliminary investigations, who had decided that Andreotti should stand trial. In bringing charges against him, the Palermo Prosecutors' Office had acted in accordance with its institutional prerogatives: Andreotti had been indicted, tried and acquitted for acts defined as criminal under the law, and in no wise for his political activity.

Nevertheless, these facts concerned issues with a pronounced political connotation – especially the question of the relationship between the Mafia and politics – and which implied a general judgement on Italy's recent history. Andreotti had been put on trial for his alleged links with the Mafia. In Palermo, he was accused of being the national 'political referent' of Cosa Nostra and of having 'made the power structure of his political faction available to it, in the awareness that by so doing he was contributing to the activities of that association on a stable basis'.[4] In Perugia, he was accused of using Cosa Nostra to rid himself of a journalist who possessed information which, if published, would have severely damaged his political career.[5] Verification of these facts would assuredly have proved Andreotti's guilt, but it would also have borne out a series of more general political accusations concerning the exercise of power by the DC and the political use of violence (by the Mafia or other criminal organisations associated with political forces).

These accusations had been frequently voiced and had long been debated within the left, and especially the *Partito comunista italiano* (Communist party: PCI). As Pietro Folena has pointed out: 'The notice of indictment [against Andreotti] confirms the analysis always made by the PCI concerning the pact between the Mafia and a part of the national ruling class'.[6] In fact, the Palermo trial did not only address the question of the crimes with which Andreotti was charged, it also concerned his political allies in Sicily. With the importance given to Salvo Lima,[7] the most powerful of those allies, and examination of the links between Andreotti's faction in Sicily and Cosa Nostra, the trial reconstructed the system of political/mafia collusion denounced as early as the mid-1970s by adversaries of the DC (and also internally to the DC), and documented since those years by the reports of the parliamentary anti-Mafia commissions.[8] Given the matters examined, therefore, the trial was part of a broader historical and political debate often polemically directed against the DC; a debate which centred on the ties between part of the political system and the Mafia, and on the consequences of such complicity on the workings of the country's democratic institutions.

The prosecution of Andreotti also tended more generally to vindicate 'criminal' versions of recent Italian history, of which the denunciation of political/mafia collusion was only one element. As the editor of *MicroMega*, Paolo Flores d'Arcais wrote, for example,

> If ... we are convinced of the soundness of the indictment drawn up by the Palermo Prosecutors' Office, we are forced to admit that the history, perhaps not of politics in general, but at least of Italian politics since the war, has been a history of criminality ... It is evident that Italian politics since the war is not the history of a criminal gang. But it is also evident that a much more complex and intricate reality displays the black thread of a constant relationship between the governing classes and every form of illegality.[9]

The uncovering of an 'underground' political world was all the more sensational because the trial examined some of the most obscure and controversial episodes of recent Italian history (the Sindona case, the Moro affair, the murder of General Dalla Chiesa); episodes which now could be examined afresh in the light of Andreotti's alleged relationships with the Mafia. The trial therefore provided a means to investigate (and to officialise) the covert features of Italian democracy and to denounce the criminal and secret activities that had come to permeate the official power structure.[10]

The judicial proceedings against Andreotti were also part of the broader process of legitimating the endeavour of political renewal that had begun with the ousting of numerous representatives of the old political class for illegal conduct. The judiciary played a decisive role in this process, for by enforcing the law it had actively participated in the renewal of the Italian political elite between 1992 and 1994. The criminal action brought against Andreotti – like the judicial proceedings against other political leaders for corruption or links with criminal organisations – therefore merged with one of the most acute and controversial political questions in Italy since 1992: the role of the judiciary. The debate on this issue shifted ground in the course of the Andreotti affair. Initially, the action of the judiciary enjoyed broad consensus among the public and a ruling class which – within the already-existing parties and the new political formations that arose in the crisis period of 1992/94 – saw judicial action as a way to build enduring political capital. After 1994, the legitimacy of the judiciary's intervention in the political arena was increasingly contested, especially when some of the new actors on the political stage – Silvio Berlusconi and other leaders of *Forza Italia* – were incriminated. The prosecutors' offices most actively engaged in uncovering corruption were violently criticised, on the grounds that their actions were discretionary and therefore 'politicised' and that they were making illegal use of certain methods of investigation (in particular, the use of *pentiti* in Mafia trials). Numerous attempts were made to restrict the judiciary's capacity for action.[11] The Andreotti trials were interpreted on the basis of precisely these criticisms. And by means of them, the legitimacy of the judiciary's intervention in the political arena was put to the test, and so too was the validity of using *pentiti* in anti-Mafia investigations, with the consequence that the trials served to focus conflicts within the political parties on the 'justice question'.

The alleged links between Andreotti and the Mafia were therefore not the only matters at issue in the Andreotti trials – particularly that of Palermo. They were certainly at the centre of the judicial debate, but once the Andreotti affair moved onto the political agenda it could not be confined to the penal arena alone. Transformed into public issues, the Andreotti trials were immediately 'politicised', in the sense that they were interpreted and evaluated in political and ideological clashes that went far beyond the judicial dimension.

The Logic of Judicial Action

The trials, unlike the political battle waged outside the courtroom, were instead conducted in a non-politicised manner, and in accordance with the autonomous logic of a criminal prosecution. The sole purpose of a trial is to establish the guilt of the defendant as regards facts defined according to their penal significance. Although some of these facts (or more often the circumstances that permit interpretation of them) may have explicitly political significance, it is not on those grounds that they are evaluated.

The charge brought against Andreotti in Palermo was that of *'partecipazione ad associazione mafiosa'* (membership of a mafia association). Introduced into the criminal code in 1982, this crime has the distinctive feature that, like all conspiracy crimes, it carries punishment only for offences committed as a member of a criminal organisation. According to Italian case law, the conduct liable to prosecution on this ground is voluntary, effective and continuing contribution to a criminal association, membership of such an association, and 'realisation of its criminal programme'.[12] The prosecution therefore sought to demonstrate the existence of a continuous and voluntarily established connection between Andreotti and Cosa Nostra; a tie which bolstered the power of the organisation and favoured its criminal activities. For the Prosecutors' Office, the discussions held in Palermo between 26 September 1995 and the end of 1998 confirmed the existence of this relationship,[13] the purpose of which was 'for the defendant, personal advantage consisting in an exponential growth of his power within the party and consequently of his power *tout court'*, since this would have made him party to the 'clientelistic allocation of positions of power throughout the institutional system'. Cosa Nostra for its part had benefited by gaining a 'permanent and structural advantage consisting in access to a power structure articulated nation-wide and ramifying through all the main institutions, thereby to fulfil the organisation's various interests, which encompass every sector of the political and administrative system'.

The pact involved an exchange of services. For Andreotti, the prosecution alleged, the trade-off brought mafia-ensured electoral support for his political allies in Sicily, as well as the availability of criminals to get rid of political adversaries.[14] For Cosa Nostra it guaranteed direct intervention by Andreotti in defence of its interests, both financial (as witness his attempts 'to rescue Michele Sindona's bank, the depository of Cosa Nostra's proceeds from drug trafficking'), and judicial (through mobilisation of his network of relations in the institutional apparatus to 'fix' trials, the maxi-trial in particular [15]). According to the prosecution, Andreotti also made a more general contribution to defending Cosa Nostra's interests by 'placing himself at the disposal of Cosa Nostra' and transforming 'the Andreotti faction into a service catering to Cosa Nostra', enabling it to infiltrate every level of Sicily's public administration and 'to assert its sovereignty as an illegal state with substantial impunity', or in other words to assert its legitimacy outside the law and on part of the political system.

Establishing the existence of this pact required twofold proof: on the one hand, the prosecutors had to demonstrate collusion between Cosa Nostra and the Andreotti faction in Sicily; on the other, they had to prove that Andreotti deliberately encouraged such collusion and directly helped to maintain and strengthen it. The prosecutors' reconstruction of the ties between Cosa Nostra and the Sicilian political machine was central to this proof. In order to understand the reasons that induced Andreotti – again according to the prosecution – to enter into a 'pact' with the Mafia, one must go back to the 1960s and the transformation of the rural Mafia into an urban Mafia whose interests were increasingly bound up in the construction industry, markets and public financing. This transformation forced Cosa Nostra to 'enter the great game of politics, infiltrating the institutional system and those power machines which …became the factions of the government parties'. The accumulation of resources in the public institutions due to their domination by the parties explains why, from the 1950s onwards, the Mafia sought to penetrate political and administrative bodies. For this purpose it established close ties with the politicians then building their careers at the expense of Sicily's old notability, and profiting from the island's urbanisation and economic and social modernisation. Lima was one of those politicians. His career, according to the prosecution, had been followed and encouraged by Cosa Nostra, which had thereby accumulated considerable political and electoral weight in Sicily.

In the same period, the prosecution alleged, Andreotti had sought to increase his influence within the DC and to give greater weight to his faction. The stakes were high because the changes then taking place in the party meant that control of a faction was indispensable for participation in the 'share-out' of positions of power, both nationally and locally. This was the origin of the 'fatal and inseparable embrace between Cosa Nostra and Andreotti' which began in 1969 when Lima – formerly tied to Gioia and the Fanfani group – joined the Andreotti faction. 'As his dowry for Andreotti he brought what had hitherto been his strategic resource and which thereafter became one of the levers of power manipulated by his faction leader: the Mafia's enormous and ubiquitous ability to mobilise consensus, its force of intimidation, and its military power'. Henceforth, the trade-off between Andreotti and the Mafia became a permanent arrangement, as evidenced by his supposed meetings with leading members of Cosa Nostra.[16] The 'pact' continued after the seizure of power by the Corleonesi in the mafia 'cupola', which was followed, from the end of the 1970s onwards, by the progressive elimination of the 'traditionalist' mafia groups that had been Andreotti's first allies in Sicily. The pact gave rise to a 'hybridisation' of legal and criminal power and the growth of a 'politico-mafioso' power system based on violence (directed against politicians and institutions which sought to free themselves of mafia influence[17]) which breached the rules of democracy and subjugated the public institutions to the interests of criminal groups and their political allies.

The failure of attempts to 'fix' the maxi-trial marked the end of the politico-mafioso pact. According to the account of events offered by the Palermo prosecutors, Andreotti and his Sicilian allies had promised Cosa Nostra that they would secure the 'happy out-come' of the maxi-trial, or, in other words, annulment by the Court of Cassation of the sentences inflicted by the appeal court on the mafia bosses and invalidation of the 'Buscetta theorem'.[18] But on 30 January 1992, the Court of Cassation – Judge Carnevale having been suspended in the meantime – instead confirmed the sentences and with them the collective guilt of the members of the cupola. The prosecution alleged (see note 13 for full citation):

> Cosa Nostra accused Andreotti of failing to keep his promise ... and the period of score-settling began. Andreotti and Lima were judged and found guilty by Cosa Nostra. On 12 March 1992 ... the first sentence was carried out with the execution of Lima, a murder intended to strike at the heart of Andreotti's power in the island and which reawakened in public opinion the suspicions of collusion between Andreotti and the Mafia that had haunted it in the past, and at precisely the moment when Andreotti entered the race for the presidency of the Republic.

Another of the presumed intermediaries between Andreotti and the Sicilian Mafia, the mafia-linked businessman Ignazio Salvo, was murdered on 17 September 1992. The Andreotti faction was destroyed and Andreotti's political career came definitively to an end.

The prosecution therefore combined a historical reconstruction of the relations between Cosa Nostra and certain political circles in Sicily – a reconstruction very similar to the one proposed by the parliamentary anti-Mafia commissions – with the arraignment of Andreotti for a specific crime: that of criminal conspiracy. However, the charge could not be supported by circumstantial evidence alone; the prosecution had to furnish material proof that Andreotti had voluntarily entered into his pact with the Mafia. The allegations that Andreotti had met the mafia bosses, that he was personally acquainted with the Salvo cousins and with Judge Carnevale, and that he had effectively provided services for Cosa Nostra therefore became of crucial importance in the trial.

It was on these allegations that the defence focused in order to rebut the charges against Andreotti.[19] The defence's main argument – beside its constant mention of the measures introduced by Andreotti and his government in the second half of the 1980s to strengthen the fight against the Mafia – was that there was no independent corroboration of the episodes cited by the prosecution to establish Andreotti's guilt. According to the defence, the prosecution had not been able to produce material evidence to support the allegations of the *pentiti* (above all concerning Andreotti's meetings with the mafia bosses) or to demonstrate that Andreotti and members of Cosa Nostra had exchanged favours (in the 'fixing' of trials in particular). In this regard, one of the defence lawyers, Franco Coppo, declared during the hearing of 8 June 1999: 'This is a criminal trial, and in a criminal trial every statement must be backed with proof; that is, it must be corroborated by the facts. Therefore every statement must be anchored in fact. If it does not have this anchoring in fact, it may be considered a conjecture, it may be considered an opinion, it may be the fruit of personal inference, but it cannot constitute proof'. The defence constantly emphasised the weakness of the evidence adduced by the prosecution, pointing out that most of the allegations by the *pentiti* were hearsay (based on 'rumours' from an 'environment that cannot be checked'[20]); that many of them had appeared contradictory during the debate (especially those concerning Andreotti's meetings with mafia bosses, or his relationships with Salvo and Carnevale); and finally that the prosecution had been unable to provide evidence of Andreotti's direct involvement in the defence of mafia interests (for example, evidence of his direct commitment to 'fix' trials). The defence also sought to deny the evidential value of the testimony provided by the *pentiti*, disputing its authenticity (pointing out that certain cases of 'repentance' may have been motivated by financial considerations, or contrived in order to obtain immunity[21]), and especially by declaring that such testimony should be confirmed by the facts (and not 'crosswise' by the declarations of other *pentiti*).

The defence thus produced an image of Andreotti that was the direct opposite of the portrait of him painted by the prosecution: the image of a statesman extraneous to local politics – in Sicily as elsewhere – whose career had been entirely devoted to the 'grand politics' of the nation and its government. Another of the defence lawyers, Gioacchino Sbacchi, in his summing-up of 19 May 1999, described Andreotti as 'a prestigious representative of the Christian Democratic Party', a leader of great standing who 'has worked in absolute detachment from local situations' and who has 'always had a broad vision of the problems of politics' without lowering himself to 'the petty contingent problems of his party's local activities'.[22] Thus the defence not only sought to contradict the prosecution's contention that Andreotti had entered the 'pact' in order to safeguard his political interests through the increased power of his faction (because, according to the defence, his stature as a national politician was already assured when Lima joined his faction, and the latter had never been 'a mainstay of his power'), it also endeavoured to confute the thesis that the links between Cosa Nostra and the leaders of the Andreotti faction in Sicily (whether or not they actually existed) constituted proof of Andreotti's guilt. Defence lawyer Sbacchi declared on 2 June 1999: 'We have refuted the hypothesis that one can in some way attribute ... to Senator Andreotti ... all the relationships that the public prosecutor has alleged of his entourage'. The defence therefore claimed that, because the prosecution's arguments lacked objective corroboration, they were to be rejected, while also describing the prosecution's case as based on a 'theorem': 'We, in short, have something of the impression that once [the public prosecutors] had become convinced that Andreotti must be a member of Cosa Nostra, their conviction thereafter entirely conditioned reconstruction of the facts and evaluation of the facts in pursuit of an objective more postulated than proven'.[23]

The trial therefore 'judicialised' political facts. These facts were constituted in accordance with the logic of judicial action and existed only as 'conditions for a value judgement' defined by law. They were selected according to the probative strategies of the parties present (prosecution and defence), which acted on the principle of the imputation of personal responsibility, and they were consequently assessed according to categories or methods which sought to prove (or to disprove) that a crime had been committed.[24] This autonomous logic of judicial argument explains why facts with a political significance (most importantly, the politico-mafioso collusion that went on within the Sicilian DC) could not be considered in themselves, but rather in relation to the crime with which Andreotti was charged. The verdict was valid only in that context. There is no need to know the reasons[25] for the verdict to state that the Court decided solely on this basis: that is to say, on the basis of the relationships between the facts adduced during the trial and the crime of which Andreotti was charged, not on those facts in and of themselves.[26]

Penal Verdict and Political Verdict

Yet the verdicts in Palermo and Perugia were hailed as Andreotti's political absolution, as the rehabilitation of the First Republic, as a rebuff to the magistrates who had helped bring about the latter's collapse by revealing its widespread corruption, and as a condemnation of the 'drift' by judicial action away from its proper purposes in the Italy of *Tangentopoli*. In short, the sentences were given a political significance which they did not possess (and did not claim to possess).

In the aftermath of the verdicts, therefore, most reactions emphasised the political significance of the acquittals. The former Christian Democrats regained their lost unity to applaud the 'rehabilitation' of their party, the end of their 'persecution' by certain judges, the refutation of the 'falsified versions' of their party's history propounded by certain procurators' offices. The opposition (Silvio Berlusconi especially) celebrated the end of the 'judicial revolution' and rejoiced that 'politicised' magistrates could no longer interfere in the political contest, 'unjustly' incriminating certain of its protagonists (*imprimis* Berlusconi himself). Among those that had most overtly supported the judicial investigations, the *Democratici di sinistra* (Democrats of the Left: DS) in particular, reactions were muted, it being merely noted that the magistracy had demonstrated its independence and that a judicial sentence should be accepted as an expression of that independence, together with more or less explicit agreement that it was time to put an end to judicial interventionism and find an enduring solution for the 'justice question'.[27]

This merging of judicial and political verdicts came about because the Andreotti trials had raised political issues which went beyond their specifically judicial content. It was for this reason that the verdicts could be used for political ends and exploited to accredit opinions which the acquittals were not intended to express. From a legal point of view, Andreotti's two acquittals in no wise amounted to his political absolution; even less did they amount to a rebuttal of critical assessment of the DC's record in Sicily, of certain sections of the country's ruling groups, and of the ruling class of the First Republic. Nevertheless, this equivalence became firmly established in public opinion, firstly because a part of the political system exploited certain judicial decisions in its campaign to delegitimate the judiciary, and secondly because the judiciary's intervention in the political arena – through the use of criminal prosecutions (both for corruption and politico-mafioso collusion) – contained an inherent contradiction: by transposing political issues to the judicial field, it 'collapsed' the political and penal verdicts together, thereby causing confusion between the two.

By so doing, the judicial investigation of political facts led to a simplification of historical reality – which tended to be reduced to its criminal aspects alone[28] – and it also carried the risk that what had been revealed about that historical reality by the work of the judiciary would be erased. Salvatore Lupo has written as follows about Italy's recent political history:

> the cross-contamination between the political and judicial spheres does not derive either from manoeuvres or from the twisting of facts or from particular interpretations of them, but rather from the evolution of the facts themselves. Politics shifted outside or beneath itself into the judiciary's sphere of action, in a situation where illegality (as regards business, terrorism or the mafia) was not just an instrument of power but one of the areas in which power itself was exercised.[29]

This is why the judiciary, in uncovering the criminal aspects of the exercise of power in Italy, became a key actor in the political struggle. Yet its investigations turned criminal responsibility into a mechanism supplementary to political responsibility, a mechanism which – as the Andreotti case exemplifies – may have paradoxically justified the collective rejection of exactly what the judiciary had helped to reveal.

The existence of enduring and structured relationships between the Mafia and a part of the political system, particularly in Sicily, was one of these revelations. But the judiciary was not alone in exposing those relationships. Rather, it was thanks to the anti-Mafia commissions (which, moreover, frequently drew on judicial sources) that the links between Mafia and politics were documented and their existence recognised. The Andreotti trials (the one in Palermo especially) moved the problem of politico-mafioso collusion into the judicial arena. They used the information available about such collusion (particularly that published by the anti-Mafia commissions) as contextual items with which to reconstruct Andreotti's alleged ties with Cosa Nostra. They also provided a great deal of evidence on the existence of those ties and specified their form (by reconstructing the continual contacts between members of the Andreotti faction in Sicily and mafia groups). Of course, this information was not considered sufficient to establish Andreotti's guilt. Moreover, his committal to trial enabled Andreotti to avoid the issue of his political responsibilities, since he could address facts susceptible to political judgement solely in terms of their penal significance. For example, he refused to answer questions about his support for Lima on the grounds that the latter had never been convicted in a court of law (as his defence had constantly argued) and that his own guilt could not be deduced from that – also presumed – of his political allies.

However, Andreotti's twofold acquittal does not prevent examination of the facts debated during the trials in the light of their historical and political significance, independently of judicial considerations. Accordingly, interpretation of the Andreotti trials does not stop with the final verdicts. When a judge deliberates on the facts, he or she does so according to the relationship between these facts and a crime attributed to a particular individual. The historian and the political scientist behave differently. Since it is not their purpose to establish responsibility, they can combine these facts into an account broader than that imposed by the need to define an act in legal terms. Moreover, since it is not their intention to pass normative judgement on individual behaviour, they may resort to conjecture (the 'historically determined possibilities'[30]) in order to account for that behaviour and to recreate the context in which it came about. The truth that they seek does not have the character of a final verdict; instead, it responds to their obligation to describe and explain – methodically, of course, but always by hypothesis – a complex reality irreducible to judgements at law. This reality (or the relationships between the Mafia and politics) has not been erased by Andreotti's acquittals. On the contrary, it must continue to be the object of the quest for truth by historians and political scientists.

Notes

1. This identification between Andreotti and an exercise of power based on duplicity, cunning and deceit existed long before the trials: as confirmed, for example, by his biography: M. Franco, *Andreotti visto da vicino*, Milan, 1989. The trials reinforced this impression, which became emblematic of Andreotti and his public image.

2. After the investigations by the Palermo Prosecutors' Office investigations into Andreotti's relations with Cosa Nostra, several *pentiti* (most notably Tommaso Buscetta) accused Andreotti of involvement in the murder of Mino Pecorelli. These allegations gave rise to further judicial proceedings, first by the Rome Prosecutors' Office and then by that of Perugia. The Perugia trial began on 11 April 1996 and concluded on 24 September 1999 with acquittal of all the defendants, for whom on 28 April 1999 the Prosecutors' Office had requested life sentences.

3. *Il Corriere della Sera*, 12 August 1997.

4. According to the indictment drawn up by the Palermo Prosecutors' Office reproduced in S. Montanaro and S. Ruotolo eds, *La vera storia d'Italia*, Naples, 1995, 885. On the case for the prosecution see. P. Allum, 'Statista o padrino ? I processi Andreotti', in *Politica in Italia. Edizione 1997*, eds R. D'Alimonte and D. Nelken, Bologna, 1997, 265–80 and P. Arlacchi, *Il processo*, Milan, 1995.

5. According to the prosecution, this information concerned the part played by Andreotti and members of his entourage (one of whom was the senator Claudio Vitalone) in the Italcasse scandal. Pecorelli had threatened to publish this information in his magazine, *Osservatorio politico* (Op). He had also allegedly come into possession of missing papers from Moro's statement to the Red Brigades which, again according to the prosecution, accused Andreotti of involvement in the Italcasse scandal and, more generally, violently attacked his political role. Cf. A. Silj, *Malpaese. Criminalità, corruzione e politica nell'Italia della prima Repubblica (1943–1994)*, Roma, 1994, especially chapter ten.

6. *Il Corriere della Sera*, 28 March 1993.

7. Salvo Lima had been murdered in Palermo on 12 March 1992. It was the investigations into his murder that bred the further investigations into the links between Andreotti and the Mafia.

8. Political-mafioso collusion was denounced by the final report of the first Anti-Mafia Commission of 1976 (N. Tranfaglia (ed.), *Mafia, politica e affari (1943–1991)*, Bari, 1992), but it is described in most detail in the report by the commission led by Luciano Violante (Commissione parlamentare antimafia, *Mafia e politica*, Bari, 1993). In this report, which reiterated the findings of previous commissions in more trenchant terms, Salvo Lima is directly accused of Mafia involvement (p. 117ff.) and Andreotti is cited by name when the commissioners point to the 'possible political responsibility of Senator Andreotti deriving from his relationship with Salvo Lima', the latter being described as 'the leader in Sicily of the faction of the Christian Democratic Party headed by Giulio Andreotti' (p. 123).

9. P. Flores d'Arcais, contribution to the round table 'Il caso Andreotti e la storia d'Italia', *Meridiana*, no. 25, 1996, 118.

10. On images of Italian politics from the point of view of its secret and undergound aspects see F. De Felice, 'Doppia lealtà e doppio Stato', *Studi storici*, no. 3, 1989, 493–563; and for a critique of these images as 'myths', G. Sabbatucci, 'Il golpe in agguato e il doppio Stato', in *Miti e storia dell'Italia unita*, Bologna, Il Mulino, 1999, 203–16.

11. The debate on the Bicamerale Committee on institutional reform shows that the desire to resolve the 'justice question' by reducing the judges' capacity for action gradually came to be shared by most of the political class. Cf. M.L. Volcansek, 'La giustizia come spettacolo: la magistratura nel 1997', in *Politica in Italia. Edizione 98*, eds L. Bardi and M. Rhodes, Bologna, 1998, 157–74, and G. Pasquino, 'Autopsia della bicamerale', in *Politica in Italia. Edizione 99*, eds D. Hine and S. Vassallo, Bologna, 1999, 117–38.

12. G. Turone, *Il delitto di associazione mafiosa*, Milan, 1995.

13. The quotations that follow are taken from the prosecutor's summing-up, the introduction and conclusion of which have been printed in *Segno*, no. 26, June 1999, 79–100.

14. As demonstrated, for the prosecution, by the Pecorelli killing but also, it seems, by the murder of Dalla Chiesa. The appointment of the latter as prefect of Palermo was a threat to the Andreotti faction in Sicily (which the general had described as 'the most tainted political family of the place' and which he had declared would be investigated). But, according to the prosecution, Dalla Chiesa was also in possession of the unpublished parts of Moro's statement to the Red Brigades, which Andreotti would stop at nothing to prevent from being made public.

15. Apart from the involvement of numerous mafia bosses, the maxi-trial was important for Cosa Nostra because it constituted legal recognition of the existence of the Mafia as an organised and hierarchised structure (the so-called

'Buscetta theorem'). Such recognition enabled the incrimination of the leaders of Cosa Nostra (the members of the 'Commission') for numerous mafia crimes.On the maxi-trial see R. Catanzaro, 'Il maxiprocesso di Palermo. Può essere sconfitta la Mafia?', in *Politica in Italia. Edizione 86*, eds P. Corbetta and R. Leonardi, Bologna, 1986. See also for a historical analysis of the Sicilian Mafia since 1950, S. Lupo, *Storia della Mafia dalle origini ai giorni nostri*, Rome, 1996.

16. According to the prosecution – in this case relying on statements made by *pentiti* – Andreotti had personally met such leading mafiosi as Frank Coppola (in 1971), Stefano Bontate (in 1976, 1979 and 1980, on the last two occasions to discuss the attempts by Piersanti Mattarella to rid the Sicilian DC of its mafia links and to arrange for his murder), Michele Greco (in 1980) and Toto Riina (in 1987, to discuss 'fixing' the maxi-trial: it was during this meeting that the famous episode of the 'kiss' between Riina and Andreotti allegedly occurred).

17. Of these 'excellent murders', that of the President of the Sicily Region, Piersanti Mattarella, on 6 January 1980, was a key element in the prosecution's case. The murder, in fact, exemplified the strategy of frontal attack on the institutions pursued by Cosa Nostra in the 1980s and which Andreotti, by maintaining his ties to the latter, was in some way alleged to have promoted.

18. The existence of a close relationship between Andreotti and Corrado Carnevale (who presided over the first penal section of the Court of Cassation between 1985 and 1992, known as the 'sentence-buster' judge because of his frequent anullments of sentences, very often on technicalities) had enabled Andreotti, according to the prosecution, to 'guarantee' the 'happy outcome' of the maxi-trial. This thesis led to Carnevale's committal for trial requested by the Palermo Prosecutors' Office and granted in April 1998 for 'external association with a mafia organisation'.

19. On Andreotti's defence see his statements made to the Palermo court in October and November 1998 and published in G. Andreotti, *A non domanda rispondo*, Milan, Rizzoli, 1999, and the defence's summing-up reproduced in its entirety on the Radio Radicale website (http://www.radioradicale.it/giustizia/andreotti).

20. The expression was used by Coppi during the hearing of 8 June 1999.

21. The most notorious case was Baldassare Di Maggio, the only direct witness of the meeting between Andreotti and Riina in 1987. The fact that Di Maggio had received large sums of money from the state during his period of 'repentance', and above all that he had confessed to a murder committed after turning state's witness cast serious doubt on his allegations. More generally, the Di Maggio case was exploited to criticise the use of *pentiti* by the police and the procurators' offices and to discredit the *pentiti* themselves.

22. Hearing of 19 May 1999.

23. Hearing of 8 June 1999 (defence lawyer Coppi).

24. Y. Thomas, 'La vérité, le temps, le juge et l'historien', *Le Débat*, no.102, 1998, 17–36.

25. The grounds for both the Palermo and Perugia verdicts had not been published at the time when this article was written.

26. The same reasoning applies in the case of the Perugia trial, but less markedly so, given the more specific nature of the charge against Andreotti. That trial, too, mixed circumstantial elements (collusion between Andreotti's faction and Cosa Nostra) with a specific accusation (that Andreotti had commissioned a murder). The prosecution again relied largely on allegations by *pentiti*, and the defence again sought to deny the evidential value of such allegations, adopting arguments very similar to those employed in Palermo.

27. The search for this solution (after the failure of the *Bicamerale* Committee) pro-
    duced a first result at the end of 1999 with approval of a new law (proposed
    two years earlier) on the use of mafiosi who turn state's witness and the 'fair
    trial' reforms. The outcome of the Andreotti trials, and the reactions that fol-
    lowed, certainly helped to accelerate the parliamentary process which led to
    approval of those reforms.

28. This criticism is made most explicitly in the writings of the ex-communist
    leader Emanuele Macaluso: *Giulio Andreotti tra stato e Mafia*, Soveria Mannelli,
    1995 and *Mafia senza identità. Cosa nostra negli anni di Caselli*, Venice, 1999.
    For an interesting discussion of this thesis see G. Fiandaca, 'Il processo
    Andreotti tra politica e giustizia', *Segno*, no. 186, June 1997, 29–34.

29. S. Lupo, *Andreotti, la Mafia, la storia d'Italia*, Rome, 1996, 26.

30 The expression is from C. Ginzburg, *Il giudice e lo storico. Considerazioni in
    margine del processo Sofri*, Turin, 1991, 108.

8

THE FUNDING OF POLITICAL PARTIES AND CONTROL OF THE MEDIA: ANOTHER ITALIAN ANOMALY

Véronique Pujas

The debate in 1999 on how to finance the Italian party system centred on two aberrations from the European norm that are linked to the wider issue of the unfinished transition of the Italian political system. The first of these aberrations is that the Italian political class has yet to find a definitive remedy for the illegal funding of the country's political parties. Although public funding has been envisaged since the law of 1974,[1] subsequent legislation has always been determined by circumstances and has never addressed the real needs of parties. The second problem concerns the control of three television channels by the state, on the one hand, and of three further channels by a media entrepreneur and political leader, Silvio Berlusconi, on the other. In the opinion of many observers, this situation comprises an interweaving of interests harmful to democratic pluralism.

The issues provoked by these aberrations came to the boil in the parliamentary and public debate that marked the spring and summer of 1999. In effect, the campaign leading up to the European elections of June 1999, and the results of those elections, triggered fierce controversy on the problem – which is certainly not confined to Italy – of funding of 'cartel parties' and, more generally, of political communication. The economic power of the largest party in Italy, *Forza*

Italia, which obtained 25.2 percent of the votes in the European elections, was interpreted as deriving from the political marketing campaign mounted by Berlusconi's television channels. On this view, and in this post-electoral context, the problem of the so-called *par condicio*, (or legislation requiring equal access to the media by all parties during electoral campaigns) became one of extreme urgency. The importance assumed in Italy by the debate should be regarded as reflecting both the distinctive nature of the Italian political situation, as regards both the funding of the political parties (which gave rise to numerous scandals in the 1990s) and the anomalous and by now 'institutionalised' conflict of interests personified by Berlusconi.

This article first outlines the political context of the previous regulations on the funding of parties. Then, in view of the inadequacy of the legal framework, it examines the debate in Parliament prior to the vote on the law of March 1999. It concludes by showing how the outcome of the European elections shifted the debate on political party funding towards the issue of the control over political communication, which is symptomatic of the increasing importance assumed by this aspect of politics in the organisation of the Italian political parties.

The Regulation of Party Financing
from the 1993 Referendum to 1999

Retrospective examination of parliamentary debate on the issue of party financing shows that the political state of play is the key explanatory factor in the measures introduced. As a consequence, therefore, it is necessary to show how the legal provisions on political party funding prior to the law of 1999 were conceived.

A law regulating the public financing of the political parties had been on the statute books since 1974, in fact, but it never ensured sufficient funds for them. Although the sums allocated to the parties had been increased on several occasions, after 1992 the *Tangentopoli* scandal and subsequent investigations uncovered a generalised state of corruption that meant that an alternative to the system had perforce to be found. In 1992, the political system of the First Republic was collapsing under the combined effect of at least four factors: the disappearance of the communist threat (after the fall of the Berlin Wall) that had been a cornerstone of the Italian political system; the economic-financial crisis of the state; the revelations of the pool of Milan investigating magistrates, which discredited the entire political class; and the lack of a definite programme among past and present political actors for the renewal and reform of the political system.

The disintegration of the governing coalition became evident with the national elections of 5 and 6 April 1992. These elections, in fact, marked the demise of the system of government monopolised by *Democrazia Cristiana* (Christian Democracy: DC), whose electoral support slumped to below 30 percent. Judicial inquiries and poor electoral results had devastating effects, especially on the parties in the governing coalition, whose leaders had been under investigation since April 1993. All the political parties were now afflicted by a severe financial crisis provoked by various factors: a decline in their resources caused by cuts in electoral reimbursements and declining memberships, as well as the halt in their corrupt practices brought about by the incisive investigations of the magistrates. Most of the parties were forced to sell real estate and their 'intellectual' assets (periodicals and newspapers) in order to stave off bankruptcy.

The electors' desire for change became fully apparent in April 1993 with the proposal of eight referendums by various political movements which put themselves forward as the standard-bearers of renewal: the reform committee headed by Mario Segni, the Giannini Committee, the *Verdi* (Greens) and the *Partito Radicale* (Radicals), all of which hoped to curb the power of the parties. These referendums concerned reform of the electoral law, the elimination of certain ministries, the appointment of senior managers in the banking sector, and abolition of the public funding of political parties.

Debate within the *Bicamerale*, the parliamentary commission on electoral reform which also evaluated the proposed referendums, soon ranged the proponents of the referendums against the more traditional formations striving to preserve a substantial proportional component in the majoritarian system envisaged by the new electoral law. Constant wrangling among the members of the commission, and the resignation of eight of them when they came under investigation for corruption, highlighted the impotence of Parliament, which still sought to exercise its prerogatives in terms of self-reform. However, their fear of appearing to defend an utterly discredited system induced the traditional parties, the DC and the Socialists in particular, to give their support to the referendum, although their ulterior, and primary, purpose was to win back popular support.

Thus, aware that they could influence the reform of the system, Italians flocked to the polling stations (turnout was 77 percent), and 90.3 percent of them decided that the public financing of political parties was to be abolished. The result of the referendum of 18 April 1993 was interpreted by all commentators as an anti-party landslide.

The changes made to the electoral law represented the most important and positive effects upon the political system, whereas from the financial point of view the unusual situation was created in which the parties found themselves stripped of the economic resources previously paid to them out of state funds. Furthermore, and this seems to have been the true cause of the parties' financial crisis, they suddenly found themselves deprived of the 'source of financing' constituted by *tangenti* or kickbacks, as well as suffering, as a corollary to widespread anti-party sentiment, a steep decline in their memberships. Bribes were no longer forthcoming for two reasons: first the judicial investigations, and second the inability of companies to comply with inflated requests for pay-offs by politicians because of cutbacks in public spending (with the consequent shortage of public tenders, which had been the main source of corruption), which imposed more cautious financial behaviour on businesses.

Abolishing the 1974 law therefore dismantled a system of party funding which had been in place for twenty years and compelled Parliament to pass new legislation on the issue. On 10 December 1993, Parliament approved a law (no. 515) which introduced a new system, based on the direct reimbursement of electoral expenses to candidates, and did away with the subsidies previously paid to the parties. The new law also regulated access to the media and the use of opinion polls during run-ups to elections, restricted electoral spending and the use of private sources of funding, while also introducing new rules on the submission of party budgets for auditing by the *Corte dei Conti* (Court of Accounts), with sanctions for non-compliance with the rules.

The introduction of this new system obviously changed the behaviour of the party treasurers between 1995 and the national elections of 1996. In 1995 numerous infractions were detected: the limits on spending had been exceeded by almost all the parties, and numerous omissions were found in their declarations of sources of funding. Faced with bankruptcy, the majority of parties found it extremely difficult to find sufficient amounts of legal funding to ensure the proper functioning of their bureaucratic apparatuses.

In January 1997, a new form of public support was proposed (law no. 2) whereby taxpayers could allocate four lire in every thousand of their IRPEF (income tax) payments to party finances. Unfortunately, however, scant publicity was given to this provision, and little more than 12 percent of Italian taxpayers signed the relevant section on their tax returns. The substantial failure of the measure was a factor upon the Italian political scene until 1999.[2] Apart from the reimbursement of electoral expenses, the real sources of party financing during this period are unknown.

The Debate on the New Law

The bill on the new method for funding the parties began its passage through parliament on 12 January 1999, and it was finally approved on 12 March of the same year. During the two months of debate, divergences of opinion among the representatives of the various parties gave rise to unusual cross-alliances at odds with any logic of opposition against, or support for, the government. Indeed, the positions taken up by the leaders *vis-à-vis* the bill essentially reflected the financial situations of their parties.The new law abolished the voluntary contribution of four lire per thousand paid in tax, on the grounds that the measure had not achieved the hoped-for results. It had also aroused the ire of voters when it was disclosed that the parties had already awarded themselves advance payments of 110 billion lire per year, a figure that sharply varied from the amount actually devolved to them by the taxpayers. The new law substituted a reimbursement for electoral expenses calculated according to the percentage of votes received. Two alignments formed on the issue: on the one side were the parties which considered the reimbursement to be a camouflaged form of the public funding already abrogated by the referendum (among them *Alleanza Nazionale* (National Alliance: AN), which refused to vote for a law that would have authorised a further interim payment). On the other side were those parties which had defended the law because they urgently needed the reimbursements to fund their electoral campaigns for the European elections in June.

During the first session of the Senate's Constitutional Affairs Commission, on 12 January, there were stormy exchanges among the party treasurers on the provisions of the bill. The latter stipulated that all citizens, including children, should contribute 4,000 lire to reimburse the electoral expenses of parties gaining at least 1 percent of all votes. The money would be divided up – in proportions calculated according to votes received – after the national, administrative and European elections. The first instalment, equal to 40 percent of the total, was to be paid on 31 July, while the rest, around 250 billion lire per year, would be distributed in the course of the legislature, the only proviso being that if the Chamber were to be dissolved the parties would no longer be entitled to any reimbursement. The treasurer of the AN (Francesco Pontone) and Elio Vetri of *Italia dei Valori* (Italy of Values) contested the right of the parties to continue receiving advances under the new law until the figures on the funding allocated under the old law (the four-lire-in-every-thousand system) had been published. On 28 January 1999, the opposition coalition of the AN, Forza Italia and the Italy of Values (157 votes against) blocked the achievement of the 75 percent quorum necessary for approval of the fast-track procedure that would have accelerated parliamentary examination of the new law on party funding. Votes in favour (283) were cast by the groups in the majority coalition together with the *Lega Nord* (Northern League: LN), the *Partito dei Comunisti d'Italia* (Party of Italian Communists: PDCI) and the *Centro Cristiano Democratico* (Christian Democratic Centre: CCD), and there were four abstentions.

The fast-track procedure used for the party funding bill was criticised in particular by the former public prosecutor Antonio Di Pietro, who described it as immoral, denouncing the omission of the voluntary element from the new law and pointing out that the payments would exceed the ceiling imposed on the parties during electoral campaigns. The defection of the Di Pietro faction (who were accused of demagoguery) from the centre-left coalition provoked much controversy, while the Radicals denounced the 'return *sic and simpliciter* to the system of party funding rejected by the referendum of 1993'. On 3 March, the day before parliament voted on the bill, the Radicals staged a media event during which they returned two million lire in banknotes to passers-by in front of the parliament building.

By contrast, Carlo Giovanardi, vice-president of the CCD – unusually siding in this case with the government majority – declared that, 'Politics has a price. There are those who want to strike a pose for public opinion, while the "stokers", the administrative secretaries, are obliged to cope with parties that are penniless or sunk in debt'. On the side of the supporters of the new law, the PDCI described it as 'a law which guarantees the transparency of payments' and is therefore 'an act of civilization and democracy'.[3]

On 3 March, the Senate rejected an amendment proposed by Melchiorre Cirami of Cossiga's UDR (and supported by Forza Italia) which sought to decriminalise the offence of financing political parties out of public funds, while on the following day a first bill was rejected in Parliament. The bill had not been to the liking of Romano Prodi, leader of the *Democratici* (Democrats), who criticised it as a 'hybrid' because it promised such large reimbursements of electoral expenses that it was in reality a cash cow for the parties: an outcome, as Fini pointed out, that 31 million Italians had rejected with the referendum of 1993. Thus, together with Forza Italia, the Radicals and the AN, Prodi contrived to have the bill voted down.

After failure to reach agreement on a revised text of the bill, on 5 May the Chamber saw a violent exchange of accusations between the majority and the opposition. In this debate, broadcast live on television (at the request of AN and Forza Italia), those in favour of the new law – the *Democratici di Sinistra* (Democrats of the Left: DS), the *Partito Popolare Italiano* (Popular Party: PPI), the Northern League, the CCD – defended themselves and attempted to broker a last-minute deal with its opponents. Sergio Sabbatini (DS), the proposer of the bill, suggested that the advance of 110 billion lire should be cancelled. Romano Prodi announced that he was against, not the funding of parties as such, but funding in the form proposed by the majority and the LN. Antonio Di Pietro attacked the law as 'legalised theft' in that it envisaged the direct public funding of parties that the Italians had forcefully rejected in 1993.[4]

Finally, on 11 May, again during a live broadcast on the RaiTre television channel, the centre-left gave the go-ahead for the new law on party funding which, over the next three years, will distribute 663 billion lire in the form of electoral reimbursements and tax relief. An intra-party deal had thus been finally reached.

The new law on party funding

On 12 March 1999, the new law (no. 157) was approved and sent for examination by the Senate. The majority coalition (with the exception of the Democrats), together with *Rifondazione Comunista* (Communist Refoundation: PRC), the LN and the CCD, gained 300 votes, while votes against were cast by the AN, Prodi's Democrats and Forza Italia (Berlusconi came out in favour of a 'no' vote, although he added that he would not refuse the state contribution). On 24 March the law was also approved by the Senate's Constitutional Affairs Committee, without amendments to the text. On the same day as the vote in the Chamber, Gianfranco Fini announced that he would promote a referendum for its repeal, arousing protest by other deputies that a referendum would cost the state much more than the sums allocated by the new law to the parties. Fini was also charged with hypocrisy for having initially promised that AN's entire refund would be given to charity, but having then changed his mind and decided to keep two-thirds of it to finance his party.

Turning to analysis of the main provisions of the law, the key provision is that 'for each electoral campaign (Chamber, Senate, regional and European), a reimbursement of 4,000 lire shall be paid for every person entitled to vote. A reduced reimbursement of 3,400 lire shall be provided for the European elections of June 1999 only' (article 1). The parties thus will receive total electoral reimbursements for the 1999 European poll amounting to 166 billion lire, as opposed to the mere 45 billion that they had received five years before. From 2000 onwards, on the occasion of regional and national elections, the parties will have an extra 80 billion lire to spend on their electoral campaigns. The previous ceiling on electoral spending was 20 billion. Moreover, given that a party is entitled to reimbursement of its electoral expenses if it manages to exceed the (distinctly low) threshold of 1 percent of votes, a further fragmentation of the party system may come about at precisely the moment when part at least of the political class is striving to reinforce the majoritarian constraints that will lead to greater bipolarism.

To continue with analysis of the law, it is further noticeable that the reimbursements are to be paid in a single instalment for the European and regional elections of 1999 and 2000, while for the national elections they will be staggered over five years, with 40 percent of the sum paid in the first year, followed by 15 percent in each of the four subsequent ones (article 1). The advance payment of 110 billion lire that the parties originally intended to bestow upon themselves by virtue of the 4-lire-per-thousand tax mechanism has therefore been annulled, thanks to an amendment put forward by the Democrats. Also eliminated was a lengthy clause that would have permitted candidates to mail electoral publicity material at the bargain rate of 70 lire in the last month of an electoral campaign. Financial coverage for this latter proposal is in any case lacking.

The Chamber instead approved a bulky package of four types of tax relief on the management of real estate owned by the parties, on their national party conventions, and on all legal or notarial instruments connected with their activities. Specifically, tax exemption is granted for articles of association, statutes and any other declaration necessary for compliance with the provisions of law (article 5); an individual wishing to make a financial contribution to a political party is allowed to deduct 19 percent of the donation from his/her taxable income, up to a maximum of 200 million lire, though funding in any form by the state or by any publicly-owned body is prohibited (article 4); a reimbursement of 500 million lire is provided for every referendum promotion committee, provided that the quorum of votes is obtained, with a maximum ceiling of 5 billion lire per committee (article 4); in order to encourage political participation by women, each party must undertake initiatives to encourage women to enter politics (article 3).

Despite the result of the 1993 referendum, in its final form the new law effectively sanctions the public funding of political parties. Reintroduced surreptitiously in the guise of the reimbursement of electoral expenses, such funding is now calculated on the basis of the number of voters enrolled on the electoral registers, and it is distributed proportionally to the votes received by the parties. The inflation of the sums allocated for electoral campaigning and the raising of the spending threshold constitute, in fact, the outright funding of party organisations.

A New Aspect to the Problem of Political Party Funding on the Eve of 2000

The polemic surrounding the law on party funding exploded once again during the run-up to the European elections. Various problems came to the fore, and the debate rekindled in the summer of 1999 no longer concerned party funding, shifting instead to the connected issue of equal party access to the media.

What were the issues highlighted by the last electoral campaign and by the results of the European elections? The first and most evident of them were the levels of spending by the two lists that campaigned most vigorously: Forza Italia spent 6,273 million lire in the first one hundred days of electoral campaigning, and the Lista Bonino (associated with the Radicals) between 7 and 9 billion, sums which far outstripped those spent by the other parties. According to most reliable estimates, Forza Italia spent a total of around 10 billion lire. Therefore, considering the electoral results (25.2 percent), on the basis of the new electoral law in March (3,400 lire for every vote gained), it received a reimbursement of fully 44 billion lire – a profit of 400 percent. Likewise the Radicals pocketed a cheque for 14 billion lire. In the light of the number of votes obtained (8.5 percent), the sums spent on promoting the Radicals' electoral campaign on the private television channels owned by Mediaset and Tele Monte Carlo – according to Emma Bonino and Pannella the only networks that give their party media coverage – turned out to be excellent investments. Commentators subsequently wondered how many votes their opponents would have obtained had they mounted an equally massive television campaign.

This observation presupposes that political advertising has a substantial persuasive effect, which is doubted by the majority of specialists on the subject. But the crucial issue is that, with three television channels at his disposal, Berlusconi can always outspend anyone else on television propaganda, and in the event of electoral victory (which is not necessarily tied to the intensity of media advertising) he will receive such substantial amounts of reimbursement as to transform his political activity into a business. The billions invested in electoral advertising by Berlusconi as president of Forza Italia revert to him in his capacity as the owner of Mediaset. The situation of the DS or the PPI is profoundly different. In order to publicise themselves on Berlusconi's television channels, they are forced to finance the company of their main political adversary. Besides the paradoxical nature of this distinctive feature of the Italian political scene, such a confusion between economic and political interests raises the problem of defending the general interests of citizens.

Secondly, given the inadequacy and the overlapping of the rules introduced in an attempt to deal with the situation created by the Mammì Law on media ownership (no. 223 of 6 August 1990), there is no way out of the twofold problem of conflict of interests and of equal access to the media. The Mammì Law, approved by the so-called CAF (Craxi–Andreotti–Forlani) majority coalition in the face of objections (and the resignations) from five Christian Democrat ministers, did no more than acknowledge what was a *fait accompli*. The law's only positive aspect was that it prevented the formation of 'mega-conglomerates' in the media sector by prohibiting newspaper proprietors from simultaneously owning television networks. Berlusconi's entry into politics in 1994 was, for that matter, closely bound up with an attempt to modify the Mammì Law, since its repeal would have damaged the volume of business enjoyed by his media empire. The abrogation of the law in December 1994 by the Constitutional Court, and Berlusconi's resignation as prime minister, gave impetus to attempts to introduce arrangements commonly referred to as 'blind trusts' and 'anti-trusts'.

The anti-trust law of 31 July 1997 (no. 249), which took the name of the former minister Maccanico, stipulated that no television network may receive more than 30 percent of the total earnings in the sector. In actual fact, however, the law has never been respected: in 1998, out of a total of around 10,000 billion lire, Mediaset earned almost 4,000 billion from advertising and RAI just over 4,000 billion from licence fees (2,477) and advertising (2,169). Neither the private nor the public network, therefore, is respecting the law and both of them are exceeding the ceiling imposed by Parliament: Mediaset by 39.6 percent and RAI by fully 46.1 percent. Conflict of interest is regulated by article 2373 of the Civil Code, which states that business-owners must divest themselves of all corporate responsibilities, assigning them to other administrators, should they occupy public positions in which they are required to take decisions which involve both their private interests and their public ones. Various situations of conflict of interest can be observed in practice.[5]

In April 1998 a new law on conflict of interest was approved by the Chamber on its first reading. The text of the law requires that prime ministers, ministers or under-secretaries must 'separate' themselves from their assets in two cases: if the value of such assets exceed 15 billion lire, and if they consist of mass media in whatever form and regardless of their economic value. This 'separation' can occur in two ways: by selling the assets, either in part or entirely, or by assigning them to an 'independent administrator'. However, this administrator is obliged to keep the owner informed on matters concerning his or her company. Hence the relationship between the owner and the company persists and cannot be severed. The text of the law was approved almost unanimously in the Chamber, which prompted the assumption that it would receive rapid approval in the Senate as well. Instead, following the collapse of the most recent *Bicamerale* Committee, presided over by the current prime minister, Massimo D'Alema, the law languished in the Senate's Constitutional Affairs Commission, where the centre-left proposed amendments that the *Polo per le libertà* (Liberty Pole) found entirely unacceptable.

So far as current legislation on political communication is concerned,[6] the situation is somewhat confused because it is split among three layers at the national level: the Penal Code, the Mammí Law (law no. 223), and the regulations on advertising. Added to these are EU legislation on the matter and international agreements. Amid this regulative confusion regarding both conflict of interest and political communication, and given the urgency of enforcing the rules on political advertising, in the summer of 1999 the problem of media access arose.

In early March, RAI lodged a complaint with the Communications Authority against Mediaset, which it accused of giving greater coverage to a particular political area during the campaign for the European elections. The complaint, however, has been inconsequential because the Authority is unable to monitor media campaigning, an operation which is hugely expensive and requires specialised personnel. The main problem is that the leader of Forza Italia is a television impresario who produces information, culture, sport and entertainment, and thereby influences public opinion in various ways. He is able to broadcast indirect political propaganda throughout the year and with greater intensity during election campaigns. Given this situation, which the Mammì Law established '*de facto*', and the absence of sanctions imposed by the Authority, in August debate began on the *par condicio*, or on parity of media access among political parties during election campaigns. One of the first measures devised to deal with the problem was the imposition of restrictions on campaign expenditure, together with the obligation to provide cheap 'advertising' space for all political parties. After this initial proposal had been examined by the Council of Ministers, attention moved to devising measures to prohibit political commercials during the run-ups to elections. Severe and immediate sanctions will be applied to broadcasters found to be in breach of the law.

Only two months after presentation of the law, on 21 October 1999, the Senate approved, on its first reading (154 for, 69 against, and 7 abstentions), a bill on the *par condicio* which prohibited any form of political advertising on national television channels during electoral campaigns, allowing it only on local television stations. The only exception to this sweeping provision is that party-financed propaganda on national networks during electoral campaigns is permissible for committees campaigning for 'Yes' or 'No' votes in referendums. The text of the law was then submitted for examination by the Chamber of Deputies,[7] where Silvio Berlusconi, obviously, strenuously opposed it, aware that it would force him to cut back his investments in his own television channels and thus restrict his greater political profile.

Conclusions

In summary, the recent measures taken by the Italian Parliament in regard to the financing of political parties and the regulation of electoral campaigning are unsatisfactory in various respects. Firstly, they have increased the fragmentation of the political system, as became immediately apparent with the European elections,[8] when the low ceiling of 1 percent of votes required to qualify for reimbursement of electoral expenses prompted the presentation of fully twenty-six lists.

Secondly, as the particular instance of Berlusconi's conflict of interest demonstrates, these measures do not entirely ensure equal opportunity for political parties and electoral candidates. Although the law on *par condicio* now before parliament will restrict spending by prohibiting party political commercials during election campaigns, it does not solve the problem of Berlusconi's ability to exploit his dominant position (with respect to his political adversaries) in the Italian radio and television system.

Thirdly, it cannot be said that the spiralling of electoral costs has been curbed, given that the recent provisions instead set higher ceilings on spending. In particular, since the rules are breached (as in the case of Forza Italia's campaign for the European elections), an authority must be organised which has greater and broader powers.

As regards the merging of economic and political interests, Berlusconi's situation as the owner of half of Italy's largest media group would be incompatible with government office, should he gain election. And the situation is aggravated by two further factors: the lack of professionalism and political independence displayed by numerous Italian journalists[9] and, in the context of the ongoing fragmentation of the left, the absence of a party or politician with sufficient charisma to stand as an effective alternative to Berlusconi.

Finally, as in the case of the last but one provision (the four-per-thousand system), absolutely no account has been taken of the will of Italian citizens to abolish the public funding of political parties as expressed by the referendum of April 1993. When parties are publicly financed against the express desire of the population, the alienation of public opinion from politics grows apace, and civic participation is discouraged.[10]

Although the recent provisions are unsatisfactory, like those before them, the issue of party funding seems for the moment to have disappeared from the public agenda. In the 1990s, the problem arose because of the public disgust provoked by a series of scandals associated with the illegal funding of parties and political corruption. In the post-*Tangentopoli* political scenario, there are signs that an attempt is being made to rehabilitate the political class of the First Republic – precisely that class which organised the illegal funding of political parties. There are various symptoms of this rehabilitation: the trials of judges which began in 1997, and more recently the discovery of Moscow's large-scale funding of Italian Communism (at least until 1991), and the acquittals that concluded the Andreotti trials.

This climate of 'rehabilitation' probably explains why debate is no longer directly concerned with the issue of public funding, but has shifted to other issues less damaging to the political class, such as media access during electoral campaigns. However, the problem of financing the political system in Italy is still unsolved, and two further referendums to repeal the relative provisions of law, proposed by the AN and the Radicals, may jeopardise the law arising from hard-won consensus, providing further evidence that the Italian political class is incapable of resolving this fundamental problem in a definitive and satisfactory manner.

Translated by Adrian Belton

Notes

1. Law no. 195 of 2 May 1974 provides for the public funding of parties gaining more than 2 percent of votes in general elections. M. Rhodes, 'Financing Party Politics

in Italy: A Case of Systemic Corruption', *West European Politics*, vol. 20, January 1997, 54–80. See also: V.Pujas and M. Rhodes, 'Party Finance and Political Scandal in Italy, Spain and France', *West European Politics*, vol. 22, July 1999, 41–63.

2. During the parliamentary session of 20 January 1999, the Finance Minister, Vincenzo Visco, announced the figures on the number of Italians who had signed the relevant section in their tax forms: only 1 million out of 14 million taxpayers. This meant a shortfall of 50 billion lire which could have swelled the bank balances of the parties, and which amounted to only half the sum that they had already paid themselves on the basis of decidedly more optimistic forecasts.

3. Statements made to *La Repubblica*, 29 January 1999.

4. In a statement of 7 March made in London.

5. For example, Giorgio Fossa, leader of Confindustria, is simultaneously national president of the private employers' association and chairman of SEA (a publicly-owned service company which runs the Milan airports). In 1988, Cesare Romiti was the managing director of Agnelli's FIAT company, which owns the largest group of Italian daily newspapers, including *Corriere della Sera* and *La Stampa*.

6. F. Gobbo and F. Cazzola, 'Il sistema televisivo dopo i referendum e di fronte alla "rivoluzione multimediale"', in *Politica in Italia. Edizione 96*, eds M. Caciagli and D. Kertzer, Bologna, 1996, 257–79.

7. 'Disposizioni per la parità di accesso ai mezzi di informazione durante le campagne elettorali e referendarie e per la comunicazione politica', voted by the Senate, http://www.repubblica.it/cittadino.lex/...condicio/stato991021

8. V. Pujas, K. Talin, 'Culture européenne et enjeux nationaux : la paradoxe de l'Europe du Sud', *Revue Politique et Parlementaire*, July–August 1999, 70–85.

9. L. Ricoffi, 'Politics and the Mass Media in Italy', in Crisis and Transition in Italian Politics, eds M. Bull and M. Rhodes, London, 135–56.

10. M. Teodori, *Soldi e partiti*, Milano, 1999, 213.

9

Transformations in Italian Capitalism: an Analysis of Olivetti's Takeover of Telecom Italia

Dwayne Woods

Olivetti's successful takeover of Telecom Italia was an astounding feat that represents a significant change in Italian and European capitalism. As one observer put it, 'for Americans who have long since grown used to the dog-eat-dog world of hostile corporate takeovers, none of this sounds new. But for Europeans, the ground is shaking'.[1] The fact that Olivetti succeeded in such a flamboyant fashion in acquiring a firm seven times its size indicates that the structure of ownership in Italy is changing and that the Italian stock market has finally become a player in determining ownership and influencing the behaviour of management. In particular, the family-owned and tightly knit ownership patterns of the past are giving way to the influence of shareholders. It is becoming harder for a few shareholders with a limited amount of stock to control a company. Also, foreign investors, in particular, Americans and British, are demanding clearer accounting practices and the reporting of quarterly earnings.

As in the United States, maximising shareholder value is becoming the leitmotiv of European businesses. Globalisation and the single currency, the Euro, are the central factors behind the accelerated pace of change in Italy and other European countries. Both are contributing to changes in ownership and corporate governance across Western Europe in two important ways.[2]

First, globalisation has forced companies to compare their performances with other firms worldwide. Executives are now under
pressure to slash costs, combine overlapping operations, and
enhance shareholder value, even if they do not compete globally.
As Manfred Kets de Vries, a management specialist, says, 'there's
tremendous pressure from institutional investors who have seen
the positive effects of shareholder power in the U.S. and are
demanding similar moves in Europe'.[3]

Second, the advent of the Euro has further heightened competition by eliminating the currency risk for investors, contributing to
an investment and takeover boom. Statistics compiled by Securities
Data/Thomson Financial show that by the end of the first quarter
of 1999 merger activity involving European companies had
reached $345 billion, up from $145 billion in the same period last
year.[4] Over the last year in Italy, Unicredito, based in Milan,
launched a $16 billion bid to buy its northern rival Banca Com-
merciale Italiana. This bid was followed by a $9.7 billion offer by
San Paolo-IMI, the country's largest commercial bank from an earlier merger, for Banca di Roma.

It is within the context of globalisation and the impact of the
Euro that this chapter examines the implications of Olivetti's
takeover of Telecom Italia. It begins with a descriptive account of
Olivetti's bid for Telecom Italia. Then it provides an explanation as
to why Olivetti succeeded. Finally, the chapter explores the broader
implications concerning the structure of ownership and management in Italy.

David against Goliath

Olivetti, an information, technology and telecommunications company, accomplished two major feats in a limited span of time. First,
the group metamorphosed itself from a computer company losing
lots of money to a profitable telecommunications entity, with a
strong presence in the portable telephone market via its subsidiary
Omnitel. Then, it launched a takeover bid for Telecom Italia, with
the aim of transforming Olivetti into Italy's largest telecommunications firm. These two feats are quite remarkable considering that
less than three years ago Olivetti was on the verge of financial collapse. Although it was still heavily engaged in the computer and
information technology sector, the firm was no longer competitive
and lacked the financial resources to redress its position.

Efforts by Carlo De Benedetti, the president, to diversify the
company and give it a European dimension had failed. In light of

Olivetti's dire financial situation, De Benedetti stepped aside as president in 1996 and turned the running of the company over to Colaninno, a specialist in redressing firms in difficult shape.[5] Colaninno accelerated the company's exit from the computer sector and focused heavily on telecommunications. After losing '915 billion lire in 1996 when it was in deep financial trouble, the company posted a profit of 240 billion lire in 1998'. Further evidence of the company's successful transformation was the 553 percent (in dollar terms) rise in Olivetti's share price on the stock market.[6]

Colaninno benefited from the phenomenal expansion of Italy's portable telephone sector and the company's expansion into information servicing. His long-term strategic interests, however, were not limited to redressing Olivetti. Unbeknownst to most, Colaninno saw Olivetti as a means to creating a larger and even more diversified telecommunications firm. He thus took the 'world financial establishment by surprise by launching Europe's largest post-war hostile takeover bid for Telecom Italia,' last February.[7] Colaninno bid 53 billion Euros (10 Euros per share) – a combination of cash, shares and bonds – to gain control of Telecom Italia.

To support his bid, Colaninno indicated that Olivetti would sell its shares in two joint ventures to Mannesmann, its German partner, and thereby raise 8 billion Euros in cash to help finance the bid. Moreover, it would raise 4.1 billion from a bond issue, and look to a core of shareholders to provide 2.6 billion. Overall, the initial bid offered shareholders 10 Euros a share, of which six were in cash and the rest in shares and bonds issued by Tecnost, a lottery-making machine subsidiary of Olivetti. Colaninno opted to organise the bid through Tecnost because he wanted to 'offer stock to Telecom shareholders without diluting his control of Olivetti'.[8]

Goliath Reacts

Despite rumours and press reports in January 1999 that Colaninno was preparing a bid for Telecom Italia, Franco Bernabé, the company's recently hired chief executive, did not believe them. His naivety was such that when he met Colaninno at a conference on 13 January, he accepted Colaninno's assurance that such reports were 'totally absurd', and 'pure fantasy', adding that, 'I wouldn't worry about it'.[9] Thus, Bernabé was caught off guard when Colaninno launched his formal bid for Telecom Italia in early February.

In a disorganised and hesitant fashion, Bernabé and Telecom Italia responded in a number of different ways to the takeover bid. Initially, the company attempted to block Tecnost-Olivetti's bid by claiming that it was void, because it failed to meet the technical standards established by Consob – Italy's stock market regulator. Telecom's chairman Bernardino Libonati, a lawyer, argued that the bid was so vague and technically flawed that it would be declared legally invalid. As he predicted, on 22 February Consob announced that Colaninno's bid was void. The regulatory agency declared that the financial structure of Tecnost-Olivetti's bid was unclear and thus inadmissible. Consob's ruling thus freed Telecom Italia to prepare defensive countermeasures, since 'Italian law forbids doing so after a valid takeover bid has been launched'.[10] In hindsight, it is clear that Telecom Italia's leadership failed to seize the window of opportunity offered to them by Consob's ruling. Although Bernabé organised a consortium of bankers and investment houses to advise him on how to block Olivetti's bid, he did not immediately adopt any of the defensive options they proposed. For example, he resisted borrowing money to bid for outstanding shares of TIM, Telecom-Italia's mobile-phone company, or to pursue a counter-bid for Olivetti. His hesitancy arose, in part, because of dissent among members of the Board of Directors and his dislike in taking on debt. Some members of the board wanted to entertain the bid, while others, including Bernabé, wanted to adopt an aggressive strategy to block the takeover. Essentially, the company waited. Three days later, Olivetti proffered a new bid that met the technical standards of Consob. Nearly two weeks passed before Bernabé responded with specific countermeasures.

Company officials attempted to convince the market that it had a plan of its own to increase shareholder value. The President of Telecom Italia presented his plan as an effective strategy to 'increase the value of company'. On 10 March, the board of directors approved Bernabé's plan of action for Telecom Italia. In the plan, Bernabé promised to cut costs by $560 million a year, including a staff cut of 40,000 employees, nearly a third of the company's total, if shareholders rejected the Olivetti bid.

In addition, the plan focused on integrating the company's fixed-line service more closely with its portable telephone service. Such a convergence, company officials argued, would increase shareholder value. According to the plan, Telecom Italia would buy back at least 10 percent of its shares on the market for up to 15 Euros and would acquire the rest of TIM, the mobile phone company, for more than 20 billion Euros. Furthermore, it indicated that the company was developing a more coherent strategy concerning international alliances with other telecommunications firms.[11]

Bernabé stated that his plan of action should be judged only on the basis of whether or not it increased shareholder value. He noted that it was 'on this point and only on this point that his cred-ibility came into play because he did not play games with the mar-ket. All of the cards are on the table'.[12] Unfortunately for Bernabé, the market was not impressed with his plan of action for Telecom Italia's future. Following the release of the company's plan of action, Telecom Italia's shares did not rise. Essentially, sharehold-ers and investors gave a negative vote of confidence to Bernabé strategy. According to one interpretation, 'they did not like using Telecom – which they said was undervalued – to buy TIM stock, which they thought overpriced'. [13]

While Bernabé struggled to come up with an effective defensive strategy, Colaninno was putting into place the players that would ultimately help him succeed in his bid. Chase bank was given the lead in enlisting foreign banks and investors to support the takeover bid for Telecom Italia. As the following account shows, however, Colaninno was not having an easy time in raising the capital:

> The Olivetti team was trying to win over its own sceptics. Even with generous terms, Chase couldn't enlist the banks at the top of its list. UBS, Credit Suisse Group, JP Morgan, Citicorp and others declined because they were already working for Telecom or because Telecom threatened to blackball them if they helped Olivetti. Others said their policies forbade lending to highly leveraged hostile bids. Olivetti's own banks had pledged 10bn Euros and Mediobanca had enrolled Banca di Roma and Monte dei Paschi di Siena, but it was not enough. On 8 March, McCree, Chase's director of acquisition finance, flew to Milan to warn Colaninno that the loan was in trou-ble. Three days later, Colaninno boarded a chartered jet for a week-long blitz of 30 banks in London, Amsterdam, Paris, Brussels, Frankfurt and Madrid; 25 signed on.[14]

Despite the problems Colaninno had in convincing investors to back him, he succeeded in raising the money by 26 March.

By early April, it was evident to all that Colaninno had the advantage in the takeover battle. With few options left, Bernabé, in an act of desperation, announced a merger with Deutsche Telekom, Europe's largest telecommunications firm, on 21 April, 1999. The market was stunned by the announcement of the proposed merger between the two former state monopolies. Like Telecom Italia, Deutsche Telekom's transition from a state monopoly to a private sector firm had not been smooth. Deutsche Telekom's revenues, for example, had declined in 1999 and the previous year's profits had been flat.[15] The proposed merger was valued at $82–95 billion. If the merger had taken place, it would have resulted in Europe's largest telecommunications company in terms of market capitalisation at $172 billion, and the world's largest in terms of operating cash flow, at $31 billion. Most market analysts, however, were sceptical about the merits of such a merger. Both companies needed major restructuring and had under performed market expectations.

As with his other efforts, Bernabé's solicitation of a 'White Knight' to save Telecom Italia from Olivetti's hostile bid fizzled. On 22 May , shareholders of Telecom Italia showed that they preferred Olivetti's bid against the proposed merger of Telecom Italia and Deutsche Telekom. Although the all-stock deal proposed by Telecom Italia and Deutsche Telekom was worth more than Olivetti's bid on paper, shareholders doubted its viability. They opted instead for Olivetti's revised bid of 11.50 Euros ($11.93) per share.[16] Although Colaninno's strategic plans for Telecom Italia are not radically different from the ones proposed by Bernabé, his more aggressive style seemed to be more convincing to investors.

Victory and Consolidation

Now that David has taken over Goliath the hard work begins. Colaninno will have to bring down the debt Olivetti has acquired in its bid for Telecom Italia. This process has already begun with the sale of Olivetti's interests in Omnitel and Infostrada, its cellular telephone and fixed-line networks, to the German company Mannesman for an estimated $8 billion. Analysts assume that Colaninno will further reduce debt by selling off some of the ill-conceived foreign investments made by previous Telecom Italia managers in Latin America, by the selling of real-estate assets held by Telecom Italia, and by a sharp reduction in personnel.

The other major challenge that Colaninno faces is putting into place a management team capable of restructuring Telecom Italia – something previous management was unable to do – and making it a major player in Europe's newly competitive telecommunications market. It is interesting to note that soon after capturing 51 percent of Telecom Italia, Colaninno moved to consolidate his position by reorganising the holding structure that allowed for Tecnost -Olivetti's successful bid of Telecom Italia. Essentially, Colaninno had put together a consortium of thirty investors, consisting of individuals, investment funds and banks, to mobilise the capital and debt he needed to carry out the takeover. It is apparent from the restructuring that Colaninno intends to reduce the number of core investors in order to consolidate his position around a stable nucleus – *nucleo stabile* – led by Mediobanca.[17] In other words, he is making sure that a swashbuckling entrepreneur does not attempt to do to him what he succeeded in doing to Bernabé: that is, taking over a company by appealing to shareholders.

How David Beat Goliath

Colaninno won his bid for Telecom Italia for two main reasons. First, the Italian government ultimately preferred a hostile takeover by a national company rather than the absorption of a former public monopoly by a foreign entity. According to *The Economist*, 'the Italian government sank Telecom Italia's defensive plan for a merger with Deutsche Telekom, preferring a private-sector Italian company, albeit one with a shaky past, to a German giant'.[18] Second, analysts underestimated Colaninno's resolve. Colaninno showed his resolve by persisting in his bid after the initial reaction was largely negative and few believed he could pull it off. In fact, the biggest obstacle that Tecnost-Olivetti faced once it launched its bid for Telecom Italia was gaining credibility.

Few believed that Olivetti had the resources to acquire Telecom Italia. At the time of the bid, it was dismissed within and outside of Italy. Investors responded to the bid by dumping Olivetti's stock. After the bid was made public, Olivetti shares dropped almost 7 percent. Investors were sceptical for a number of reasons. Olivetti was seen as too small and lacking the capital and management resources needed to take over a national behemoth like Telecom Italia. To many, Colaninno's bid was nothing more than an attempt to get Telecom Italia to pay a handsome price to stop a takeover threat. Moreover, the bidding price was seen as too low to convince shareholders to sale. Finally, the bid was poorly drafted. According to experts, it lacked clarity and was bound to be rejected by stock market regulators.

While many of these things were correct, analysts underestimated Colaninno's determination to overcome them. For example, he raised the bid price; he succeeded in bringing together a consortium of banks and investment houses to support his bid. And he was able to take advantage of Telecom Italia's slow reaction to Consob's rejection of the first bid to put another one on the table several days later.

More significantly, Colaninno proved his doubters wrong because he understood something that they underestimated. That is, the significant changes in the Italian stock market brought about because of the single currency and the Draghi reforms discussed below. As indicated above, the introduction of a single currency has changed the character of capital markets across Europe. Specifically, it has made the raising of large sums of capital much easier. As one banker noted, 'for the right deal, previously unfathomable sums can be raised'.[19]

The other development was the Draghi reforms of Italy's capital markets. In 1996, the director general of the treasury, Mario Draghi, instituted a significant reform that changed the rules of stock market transactions and ultimately corporate governance in Italy. As Bortolotti and Siniscalco summarise the reforms:

> Draghi's reforms encompass many aspects of the future of capital markets, proposing a model of regulation that is more flexible for financial intermediaries (in itself a revolution for Italy), that disciplines the market (including stock market companies), by weakening cross-holding pacts, facilitating takeover bids and hence the possibility of changing management via the new threat of a hostile takeover.[20]

As a financial strategist, Colaninno realised that Draghi's reforms undermined the ownership structures that had traditionally governed the Italian market. In the past, a small number of shareholders were able basically to control a company and ignore the majority of shareholders. As Rossant noted, 'elaborate cross-shareholding schemes, in which tiny stakes guaranteed absolute control of vast enterprises, gave industrial dynasties like the Agnellis and Pirellis virtually unlimited access to capital and deals'.[21] Shareholder value had little meaning in this context. Draghi's reforms have made Italian capital markets more transparent and fluid. Thus, it is easier for an outsider to rely on the market for capital and as a way to gain control of a company's outstanding shares.

In addition to the reforms introduced by Draghi and the decline in the role of the state in the economy, low inflation and interest rates have changed the logic of smallholder and institutional investment in Italy. The traditional pattern of purchasing government bonds and maintaining a high savings rate has given way to increased levels of investment in capital markets. Italians, like their Anglo-Saxon counterparts, now expect good returns on their investments in the market. All of these factors are making capital markets in Italy more central in the determination of ownership of assets and who manages them.

A Troubled Privatisation

Beyond Colaninno's resolve and changes in the rules of the market, Olivetti succeeded because of the uneasy transition of Telecom Italia from a public monopoly to a private entity. STET, later renamed Telecom Italia, was privatised in 1997. It was sold off only after a great deal of confusion over how it should be done; over what type of regulatory authority should oversee the telecommunications sector; and, whether or not it should be reorganised before going public. Its privatisation followed that of other state-owned enterprises controlled by *Istituto per la Ricostruzione Industriale* (IRI); however, it was the first public monopoly to be privatised. Unlike the state-owned oil and gas company – *Ente Nazionale Idrocarburi* (ENI) – which was rehabilitated, ironically, under the leadership of Franco Benarbé, the privatisation of STET went ahead without any major restructuring.

Telecom Italia's shares were offered to the public with the aim of attracting a broad shareholder base. Thus, they were sold at a discount. In October 1997 when Telecom Italia shares were offered at 10,908 lire per share, over two million shares had been purchased. The government, however, kept 3.4 percent of the shares, referred to as 'golden shares', as a way to maintain a veto right over major decisions. Also, 9 percent of the shares went to what the government termed a hardcore group of shareholders, including the Agnelli family and a few public banks.

From the time of its flotation on the Milan stock market until its takeover, Telecom Italia's market valuation was volatile. Less than a year after its privatisation, its shares had reached a low of 8,824 lire before recovering to around 12,000. The reasons for the volatility were unsteady management and unclear strategic plans. Management turmoil has been the company's biggest problem. Since its privatisation, five different management teams have tried to run the firm.

Leading up to its privatisation, the company was governed by two men, Biagio Agnes and Ernesto Pascale, who symbolised the political patronage system that had dominated state-run enterprises in postwar Italy. As one observer put it:

> Biagio Agnes (Chairman, 1990–97) Chairman of Telecom Italia's state-run predecessor, STET, considered the ultimate symbol of the political patronage system that ran telecoms in postwar Italy. Like every STET chairman after 1945, he was drawn from the ranks of the ruling Christian Democrat Party. (To balance this, the boss of its SIP division came from among the Socialists.) Ernesto Pascale (CEO, 1994–97) Known as the 'Iron Man' of Italian telecoms, Pascale was appointed to streamline the cumbersome management structure in preparation for the company's conversion from monopoly to competitive culture. But he continued to run it like a state fiefdom, with managers appointed according to political rather than professional qualifications.[22]

Agnes and Pascale were followed by Guido Rossi (Chairman, 1997–8), a respected lawyer, who navigated Telecom Italia through the privatisation process. He resigned after several months in office because his demands for changes in the company's corporate governance structure, including a more powerful role as chairman, were thwarted by his chief executive officer, Tomaso Tommasi di Vignano. Rossi was followed by the short but tumultuous reign of Gian Mario Rossignolo. Although Rossignolo had no experience in telecommunications, the Telecom board picked him because of his purported 'compromising management style'. He quickly moved to consolidate his power by turning himself into a powerful executive chairman. He succeeded in forcing Tommasi di Vignano, a longtime Telecom manager, out.

Under the leadership of Rossignolo, Telecom Italia floundered. The company became embroiled in incessant managerial conflicts and abrupt changes in foreign alliances and policies. Before he was forced to resign himself, Rossignolo presided over the haemorrhaging of much of the company's top management. He 'reorganised Telecom Italia's management structure to undermine his enemies, even dissolving the old CEO position to remove his rival, Tomaso Tommasi di Vignano; he has also sacked no fewer than 11 out-of-favour bosses'.[23] The company was essentially paralysed by the internal squabbling and managerial conflicts. Rossingolo soon lost the support of the board of directors and Telecom Italia's shareholders. Consequently, the company's stock declined.

The final straw came in October after false financial results were leaked implying strong company earnings. Rossingolo was forced to resign.[24] Franco Bernabé replaced him. Bernabé had taken over ENI in the early 1990s and succeeded in turning around Italy's major energy company after years of mismanagement and corruption.[25] Bernabé was viewed as the right person to introduce dynamic leadership to Telecom Italia and modernise its operation. Unfortunately for Bernabé, the twenty-two months of management turmoil and a low stock price had exposed the company to an outside takeover. Although it was the largest private company listed on the Italian stock market, with assets amounting to 100,000 billion lire, it was not in very good shape. It was a giant with feet of clay.

Daniel Liefgreen of the *Herald Tribune* summed up the troubled privatisation of Telecom Italia nicely, when he stated that:

> The government has itself only to blame for the failure of what it once described as 'the mother of all privatisations.' Telecom Italia … was dragged, kicking and screaming, into the new liberalised era. As early as 1994, Chairman Ernesto Pascale was given *carte*

blanche to streamline the company's management structure. Instead, just as STET chairmen had been drawn from the rank and file of the ruling Christian Democrats for five decades, so some managers continued to be appointed according to political not professional qualifications. The make-up of the hardcore group of shareholders, which committed itself to nine percent of the share capital when the company was privatised, similarly brought little sign of a fresh start. With the immensely powerful Agnelli family's holding company IFIL, owning a 0.6 percent share and a series of public banks taking much of the remainder, Telecom Italia resembles Italian capitalism at its worst – small cliques running corporate empires with relatively little financial outlay.[26]

Underlying Telecom Italia's failed transition from public monopoly to private enterprise and the epic battle that ended in its takeover by Tecnost-Olivetti are issues of ownership and corporate governance.

Ownership and Corporate Governance in Italy and Europe

Since the early 1990s, a debate over the structure of Italian capitalism has been taking place. The debate has focused on ways to modernise and make Italian firms more accountable to shareholders and the market. Postwar Italian capitalism has been an odd admixture of three types of ownership structures.[27] First, there was the extensive state ownership of a large range of industrial, banking, and retail assets that had largely been inherited from the fascist period. Many of these assets were controlled by the state holding company IRI. Until the wave of privatisation in the mid-1990s, Italy had one of the largest state-controlled sectors in the Western industrialised world.

Second, there were a small number of oliogopolistic firms dominated by prominent families such as the Agnellis and Pirellis. These firms often had a dominant position in specific segments of the Italian market. In many instances, their shares were open to the public but the companies remained under the control of the families that had founded them. They had established close working relations with certain banks, sometimes state-owned ones, and controlled the stock market with limited capitalisation. As an OECD report noted, 'corporate ownership was much more concentrated in Italy than in other major OECD countries. Single majority stakes account for about 60 percent of total stock market capitalisation, while the largest shareholders hold on average nearly 90 percent of outstanding shares of listed companies, compared with 25 percent in the United States and just over 40 percent in Germany'.[28] Thirdly, Italy has been characterised by a myriad of small to medium sized family owned businesses. These kinds of firms have not relied heavily on capital markets.

Globalisation and European integration are changing the tripartite structure of ownership in Italy. Privatisation has drastically reduced the state's role in the economy. Market reforms are now leading to changes in the private sector, at least among the large family-owned firms. Acceptance of the idea of the public company has gained support in Italy.[29] The idea of the public company is generally associated with the Anglo-Saxon model of ownership and capitalism. Within this model, industry is largely controlled by anonymous and a broad number of shareholders. Shareholders are individuals, pension funds or insurance companies that exist primarily to protect the interests of their constituents. Managers are judged on the basis of their performance and the value they deliver to shareholders.

Advocates of the public company argue that it makes management more accountable to shareholders. More importantly, it shifts ownership to the stock market and way from families or a small élite. Colaninno claimed that his successful bid for Telecom Italia was largely due to the increased role of the market in determining ownership in Italy. He noted that 'Italian business has been dominated by a lot of small and medium-sized companies managed and controlled by families or by the entrepreneurs who started the companies. Then, you have several big family-controlled industrial groups, like Fiat, controlled by the Agnellis, and Pirelli and Mediaset. What I think I have demonstrated to Italian investors is that companies can and will be fought over'.[30] He added that his successful takeover of Telecom Italia was proof that 'investors, not linked to specific family dynasties, are ready to support management and when necessary to change managers when needed'.[31]

Thus, for many, the takeover battle represents changes in the structure of capitalism in Italy. Such a view, however, needs to be tempered since the takeover battle for Telecom Italia showed signs of both change and continuity. On the one hand, the fact that Colaninno succeeded in bringing together a consortium of domestic and foreign investors to launch his bid for the company indicates that Italian capital markets are becoming more open. Also, the fact that the government allowed the hostile bid to go forward indicates an important shift in state-business dynamics in Italy.[32]

On the other hand, the fact that Mediobanca played such a pivotal role in Colaninno's bid suggest that not much has changed. For decades, Mediobanca has been at the centre of 'la Galassia', or the Galaxy, as Northern Italy's vibrant but clannish capitalism economy is called.[33] It organised most of the complex ownership structures that allowed certain prominent families to dominate broad sectors of the Italian economy and the capital markets.

Before the Telecom Italia bid, some analysts had believed that Mediobanca's power had waned. Mediobanca's failure to gain control over Milan's Banca Commerciale and Rome's Banca di Roma in 1998 seemed to indicate that Mediobanca's honorary chairman – Enrico Cuccia – had lost his legendary ability to control the flow and direction of Italian capitalism. Rossant argued that Mediobanca's failure in the bank deal 'shows that fresh air is sweeping through Italian capitalism'. Cuccia's attempt to merge the two banks was blocked by management and minority shareholders. However, Rossant's bold statement that 'the new attitude toward corporate governance makes Mediobanca an anachronism' is premature.[34]

The obtuse ownership structure set up by Colaninno to control Telecom Italia appears to reflect the old ways of Mediobanca. While the shares are not cross-listed, they are held in a cascading fashion. At the heart of the ownership arrangement is Bell, a Luxembourg holding company, controlled by Colaninno and a few industrialists and banks in northern Italy and foreign investment houses. Bell, in turn, holds shares in Tecnost-Olivetti. Then, Tecnost-Olivetti shares are held by Mannesmann and Schroeders investment management and a diffused number of public shareholders.[35]

The most startling example of Mediobanca's continued influence and the difficulty that Italian capitalists have in changing their ways is the proposal made by Colaninno in late September. Colaninno presented what he termed an industrial reorganization of Telecom Italia that entailed Tecnost absorbing the cash producing Telecom Italia Mobile (TIM) – Telecom Italia's mobile phone unit – in exchange for Tecnost shares. That meant that Telecom Italia's minority shareholders 'would receive between 1.5 and 1.65 Tecnost shares for of their own shares in payment for TIM'.[36] The market reacted quickly to Colaninno's proposal by abandoning Telecom Italia shares. The *Financial Times* said that the proposal was nothing short of a swindle of minority shareholders. To most observers what Colaninno termed a industrial restructuring was nothing more than a naked attempt to grab TIM's cash flow to help pay down the debt acquired by Tecnost in the takeover of Telecom Italia.

Colaninno's plan was attacked from all sides. Luigi Spaventa, president of Consob, the stock exchange watchdog, directed the first salvo against Colaninno. He said that the announced plan violated the integrity of the market. He indicated that Consob might have to intervene if more details and clarifications were not forthcoming.[37] Prime Minister D'Alema stated that the government had not signed off on the proposed restructuring plan and that it could exercise its golden share option if he deemed that the interest of minority shareholders was being violated. More importantly, the market responded strongly. Telecom Italia's shares dropped sharply on 29 September.[38]

The tempest over Colaninno's restructuring plan forced him to retreat and distance himself from Mediobanca. He announced on 5 October that the plan would be substantially revised, stating that the Tecnost-TIM share swap had only been a hypothesis. Essentially, Colaninno was forced to back down. Unlike in the past, when Mediobanca was able to engineer complex deals that ignored minority shareholder interest, changes in Italian capitalism and the market have now made such tactics nearly impossible.

What the storm over Colaninno's plan indicates is that changes in corporate governance in Italy will continue for the reasons already outlined in this chapter. Globalisation and European integration have altered the context in which Italian capitalism functions. Domestic and foreign shareholders are not going to allow Colaninno to manage Telecom Italia as his personal fiefdom. If he does not produce results, investors will express their dissatisfaction by dumping Telecom shares. With the heavy debt incurred in the takeover battle, Colaninno cannot afford to alienate shareholders. In this sense, Mediobanca is no longer capable of directing the affairs of 'la Galassia' as it had done in the past.

Overall, I believe that Colaninno's successful takeover of Telecom Italia was as much, if not more, about the failure of a public enterprise to make the transition from a state-owned monopoly to a private enterprise, as about the emergence of a new form of swashbuckling entrepreneurship in Italy. Colaninno realised that:

> [Telecom Italia] was a tempting target, one with 80 percent of Italy's $28 billion market for fixed and mobile phone services. It had too many workers, generated 8 billion Euros in cash annually and suffered from bad managers and restless shareholders. Turmoil in the executive suite had reduced Telecom's share price by 44 percent in the 11 weeks to 9 October, making it attractive to a would-be raider. In October, the stock traded for five times cash flow per share, half the ratio of AT&T or British Telecommunications. And Telecom had 7.9 billion Euros in debt, just 14 percent of its total capitalisation.[39]

Thus, the poorly managed Telecom Italia was ripe for a leveraged buy-out (LBO) – a takeover in which the acquirer borrows money and uses the target company's own cash flow to repay it. In the future, Italy is likely to witness an increasing number of takeovers. This is particularly the case because more family-owned businesses are turning to the market to raise capital.

Notes

1. *Business Week*, 7 June 1999.
2. Phillipe Ricard, *Le Monde*, 4 July 1996; Carl Christian von Weizsacker, *Frankfurter Allgemeine Zeitung*, 27 June 1998; David Owen, *Financial Times*, 10–11 July 1999.
3. *Business Week*, 7 June 1999.
4. Ibid.
5. *The Economist*, 29 May 1999.
6. *Financial Times*, 18 June 1999.
7. *Financial Times*, 9 June 1999.
8. *Independent on Sunday*, 4 July 1999:
9. Ibid.
10. Ibid.
11. Ibid.
12. Ibid.
13. Ibid.
14. Ibid.
15. *New York Times*, 22 April 1999.
16. *International Herald Tribune*, 5–6 June 1999.
17. *Corriere della Sera*, 22 May 1999.
18. *The Economist*, 29 May 1999.
19. *Independent on Sunday*, 4 July1999.
20. Bernardo Bortolotti and Domenico Siniscalco, *Corporate Governance, una rivoluzione nel capitalismo, Il Mulino*, no.2, 1998, 266.
21. *Business Week*, 22 June 1998.
22. The *European*, 22 June 1998.
23. Ibid.
24. *La Repubblica*, 22 October 1998.
25. *The Economist*, 24 April 1999.
26. *International Herald Tribune*, 11–14 December 1998.
27. Fabrizio Barca, *Imprese in cerca di padrone: Proprietà e controllo nel capitalismo italiano*, Roma-Bari, 1994, 170–96.
28. OECD, *Economic Surveys: Italy 1995–1996*, Parigi, 1995, 59–60.
29. Ferdinando Targetti, 'Il governo dell'Ulivo e l'evoluzione del capitalismo italiano', *Il Mulino*, no. 6, 1998, 1047.
30. Ibid.
31. *La Repubblica*, 22 June 1999.
32. Targetti, 'Il governo del Ulivo', *Il Mulino*, no.6, 1998, 1038–1039.
33. *Business Week*, 22 June 1998.
34. Ibid.
35. Marie-Noelle Terrisse, *Le Monde*, 11 June 1999.
36. John Tagliabue, *New York Times*, 29 September 1999.
37. *La Repubblica*, 28 September 1999.
38. *La Repubblica*, 30 September 1999.
39. *Independent on Sunday*, 4 July 1999.

10

Italy's December 1998 'Social Pact for Development and Employment': Towards a New Political Economy for a 'Normal Country'?

Michael Contarino

On 22 December 1998, the centre-left Italian government and thirty-two social partners signed the *Patto Sociale per lo sviluppo e l'occupazione*, a complex agreement with the stated objective of boosting economic growth and employment, especially in Italy's South. This agreement, signed officially on 1 February 1999, was the last of three national accords of the 1990s which have explicitly embraced a model of economic governance based upon concertation among the so-called 'social partners'. The previous two agreements, the September 1996 accord on labour market reform and the July 1993 agreement on collective bargaining and incomes policy, had both embodied the concertational approach, and the 1993 accord in particular had been of undeniable importance to Italy's successful effort to reduce inflation and meet the Maastricht treaty's convergence criteria.

The new Pact went beyond these two earlier agreements in two significant ways. First, negotiation of the 1998 Pact was more broadly based than the previous agreements, as it included representatives of all the economic sectors, including large and small industry, commerce, services, artisans and the cooperatives. Furthermore, there was a rhetorical emphasis on the need for active involvement of actors at the local, provincial and regional levels: a 'Protocol concerning the participation of regional, provincial and municipal governments in the implementation of the Social Pact for Development and Employment' was signed with the Pact, calling for the extension of concertation to these levels, and emphasising the roles of governments and social partners below the national level in promoting growth and job creation. Second, the 1998 Pact committed the government not only to a broad array of specific policy commitments, but also to an implementation timetable, and biannual 'review sessions' to assess the progress of implementation. These sessions were to coincide with the government's springtime economic forecast, and the autumnal budget.

As with previous national agreements, the chief advocate had been the government. Negotiations for the Pact had begun in late summer, 1998, when the Prodi government, the unions and employers agreed that a new Social Pact should seek a trade-off between labour flexibility and increased investment. On 1 October, then Treasury Minister Carlo Azeglio Ciampi, in the context of presenting to the Chamber the 1999 budget, announced the government's proposal for a new Social Pact to build upon the accomplishments of the July 1993 agreement. Embracing concertation as the way forward for reform, Ciampi told Parliament: 'There needs to be a free choice by both unions and business to reduce certain labour market rigidities and to reinforce a new cycle of investment that will broaden the productive base.'[1]

The collapse of the Prodi government on 9 October did not interrupt the movement towards a Social Pact, and indeed the new government of Massimo D'Alema and employment minister Antonio Bassolino embraced the idea enthusiastically, with both D'Alema and Bassolino announcing immediately upon taking power on 21 October that the Social Pact would be central to the new government's strategy. The new employment minister stated further that the Pact should emphasise economic development in the South in order to boost employment. On 31 October, D'Alema indicated his view of a Social Pact based upon the broadest possible social base: 'The government's first commitment will be to open negotiations to renew the 1993 accord and to enrich the Social pact with new employment and development objectives while broadening it to embrace new participants'.[2]

The government pushed the social partners to complete an agreement by Christmas, and then presented the new Pact to Parliament for debate and approval (which was granted 16 January 1999, giving the Pact's provisions full statutory backing). This search by the government for a sort of *de facto* (and not legally required) 'confidence vote' on the concertational national economic strategy it was pursuing, together with the government's energetic pursuit of the Pact in the preceding weeks, suggests just how central concertation was to the new government's strategy.

This chapter will examine the Patto Sociale of 1998 and the status of its implementation after the second biannual review in September, 1999. It will consider both the ways in which the Christmas Pact of 1998 went beyond the agreements of 1993 and 1996, and the ways in which it did not, observing what the Pact's accomplishments and limitations may suggest for the prospects of concertation in the years ahead. It also will consider the ways in which this Pact is a bold step forward, and the ways in which it may be more style than substance. Finally, the chapter will consider the implications which the success or failure of the Pact to reduce unemployment in the months and years ahead may have for Italy's evolving political economy, and for the prospects for effective economic governance by coalitions of the centre-left.

The Christmas Pact of December 1998 in the Context of Earlier Agreements

The opening paragraph of the Pact explicitly endorsed the 1993 and 1996 agreements, their contributions to Italy's successful struggle against inflation and debt in the 1990s, and the concertational approach which they entailed:

> With [Italy's] entry into the single European currency, the significant reduction of inflationary forces within the economy and the restriction of public spending, the principal objectives of the Protocol on incomes policy and employment of 23.7.93 on wages and employment policy, on contractual agreements, on labour market policy and on support for the system of production were fully or partly achieved. Successively, the Labour Pact of September 1996 brought into being an agreement between the government and social partners that aimed at pursuing objectives of development and promotion that fulfilled the commitment to alter the legal framework for the labour market and the employment crisis in the direction of an active management of employment dynamics.[3]

The second paragraph of the Pact emphasised the importance of the collective bargaining framework of the 1993 accord, which, together with the abolition of the *scala mobile* wage indexation system, was crucial to the successful reduction of wage-push inflation. That agreement had stipulated four-year national sectoral contracts (with biannual renegotiation of wages only), supplemented by

company-level bargaining in which wage increases had to be be
linked to productivity and profitability :

> The model and the procedures laid down by the Protocol of 23 July
> 1993 have made possible stable and continuous relations between
> the government, labour unions and employers. The respect shown
> towards the Protocol's guidelines by the social actors has proved to
> be indispensable in guaranteeing the modernization of the nation
> and in determining Italy's passage to greater economic competitive-
> ness in the face of the challenge of globalization while at the same
> time maintaining adequate social conditions.[4]

The Pact then called for 'a new phase of concertation' to promote development and employment growth, through an incomes
policy and further institutionalisation of concertation 'at all levels'
(i.e. national, regional and local).[5] The earlier accords, which had
been negotiated by a smaller number of partners than the 1998
agreement, had been effective in reducing inflation, but not at
reducing unemployment. The July 1993 accord, signed by the government and CGIL, CISL, UIL, Confindustria, and several other
important labour and commercial organisations, was the more
important of the two, as it profoundly reshaped the 'rules of the
game' for industrial relations. The 1993 agreement lay the procedural bases for a non-inflationary incomes policy by specifying the
venue, timing and criteria for the negotiation of wage increases.
The more specific policy elements of that agreement, on youth
unemployment and the labour market, however, were not implemented. And while the 1996 'Pact for Jobs' called for a variety of
measures pertaining to vocational training, education, labour market reform and 'area contracts', it had failed to put a dent in unemployment, which was still officially over 22 percent in the South
when the 1998 Pact was being negotiated

The *Patto Sociale* of December 1998 committed the government
to several measures aimed at boosting growth and employment.
The main policy thrusts were to reduce labour costs and taxes,
encourage investment, improve training and labour flexibility, simplify and rationalise bureaucratic procedures, and focus development efforts in the South. These goals were to be sought within the
context of an incomes policy linking Italian price and wage
increases to the EU median inflation rate. This incomes policy, like
other aspects of the Pact, was to be pursued through coordinated
effort at the national, regional, provincial and communal level.

The Pact aimed to reduce labour costs by 3 percent over five
years, mainly through social insurance reforms and tax band
restructuring. In this regard, the government's most important

commitments were to pass legislation to: 1) reduce employer social security contributions, in order to promote working-hours reductions; 2) finance maternity benefits and family allowances out of general revenues in order to relieve employers of this tax; 3) rationalise and consolidate the social security system, and reduce employer contributions to the workers' compensation scheme; 4) expand the 'dual income tax', providing more tax breaks to encourage reinvestment of profits in worker development and new equipment and machinery; 5) reduce personal income tax rates and clamp down further on tax evasion. As this chapter was being written, the 27 percent income tax bracket was to be reduced to 26 percent, further income tax cuts were under consideration, and additional anti-tax-evasion measures had been adopted.

Pursuant to the Pact, the government would (and has) implemented a number of business-friendly administrative reforms, above all the *sportello unico* ('one-stop shop') to simplify bureaucratic procedures for businesses. The Pact also led to the creation, in January 1999, of the *Sviluppo Italia* development agency to coordinate programmes for the South and to seek to reduce the size of the underground economy. Legislation implementing Pact commitments also has led to increased funding for the national continuing vocational training fund, and to the requirement that all persons under eighteen not in school should participate in a training programme, an apprenticeship, or a vocational training scheme.

Significantly, the Pact established a timetable for the realisation of its commitments, and the government has met most, though not all, deadlines: of the seventy-six measures which were to have become law by 31 August, sixty-four (84 percent) had been implemented. As of 31 October, 1999, 134 measures had been realised. At the time of the second official review on 22 September 1999, 131 (56 percent) of all the specific measures called for in the Pact had become law.

Of the hundreds of laws, decrees and administrative acts which implement commitments under the Pact,[6] several of the most significant were contained in a maxi-decree of 9 March which extended the dual income tax, and which cut taxes on companies from 37 percent to 19 percent if profits were reinvested in plant, machinery or employee development. Funds amounting to 1,700 billion lire were also released from the employment fund to finance training. A *Collegato fiscale* to the 1999 budget, passed definitively by the Senate on 6 May, converted these into law, and contained important tax incentives, including 'Three-year tax reductions for those who provide new permanent additional employment in the South'. A *Collegato su lavoro e occupazione*, passed definitively on

11 May 1999, included incentives for new employment and reform provisions pertaining to the 'social shock absorbers' and the 'socially useful occupations'. Other measures of note reduced firms' social contributions for maternity benefits, while the government's four-year employment plan, approved 21 May, contained all the main provisions of the Pact as regards the implementation of flexible working measures, most notably those concerning part-time employment.

Despite the enthusiastic rhetoric about the Pact, not only by the government, but also by the social partners, and despite this flurry of legislative and administrative activity, it must be noted that many of these measures would have been taken anyway, and thus arguably should not really be attributed to the Pact at all. Notably, virtually all of the policies on employment and tax reform were already commitments of the Prodi government or contained in the previous Budget (which, for example, already contained measures to reduce labour costs by 0.82 percent).

Furthermore, the Pact failed to resolve a key question pertaining to collective wage bargaining, which had been at the top of both Confindustria's and the government's agendas. The government had advocated during the negotiations that the duration of all national contracts (including the pay element) be extended to four years, that all contracts should expire on 31 December, in order to concentrate collective bargaining at the end of the year, and that local and company-level bargaining be the focal points for negotiation of such issues as work organisation and flexibility. Confindustria would have eliminated the national agreements altogether, arguing that they remain impediments to flexibility and investment in poorer areas. Both the government and Confindustria argued that low inflation and EMU have rendered the national contract obsolete.

However, due to the resistance of CGIL (the CISL and UIL were more amenable), no reform of the two-tiered collective bargaining system was included in the Pact. Rather, the Pact reaffirmed the system inaugurated by the 1993 agreement, and spoke of 'decentred concertation', without however clearly indicating exactly what this meant – an ambiguity which remains. CGIL did, however, show some flexibility, proposing the introduction of a territorial-level agreement to replace the national contract, thereby ensuring that all workers would remain covered by a collective contract (only 40 percent of workers are currently covered by a company-level agreement). But failure of the social partners to agree on a reform meant that none took place.

Whether or not these shortcomings reduce the Pact, as some would argue, to *molto fumo, poco arrosto*, ('all smoke and no fire') is a matter of opinion, but certainly the argument can be made that beyond the fanfare, the government has proved unable to accomplish some very important things which would have been truly impressive and substantive. Most notable of all shortcomings, the Pact failed to address the welfare and pensions issues – the most important challenges facing the Italian political economy, and the matters with arguably the strongest relationship to the country's capacity to create new jobs and combat social exclusion. Together with the above-mentioned limitations, this failure shows not only the weakness of the present government, but also the limits of concertation in the present context.

Before assessing the possible long-term implications of the Christmas Pact, it will be useful to consider some recent thinking about how advanced industrial economies, in the EU and elsewhere, are responding to international economic realities, and how the Italian political economy has been perceived.

The Rise of Concertation in the 1990s: a Fundamental Change in the Nature of Italy's Political Economy?

Much recent literature has tended to divide the advanced capitalist economies into 'Liberal Market Economies' (LMEs), including the Anglo-Saxon and Irish economies, where there is relatively little non-market coordination among companies, and where labour is weak and the state relatively laissez-faire; and 'Coordinated Market Economies' (CMEs), typical of northern Europe, where firms engage in substantial direct and indirect non-market economic coordination, in which both the state and labour are involved.[7] Italy, in this view, has tended to be seen as a 'mixed case', characterised by a general lack of national-level coordination, but sharp regional and local differences, and a general pattern in the north and central regions resembling the CME model.[8]

The *Patto Sociale*, along with the 1993 and 1996 accords (as well as other nationally-negotiated agreements, such as the 1992 suspension of the *scala mobile*, and the 1995 pension reform accord reached under the Dini government) raises the question of whether Italy is evolving into a true CME. It is at least possible that these accords reveal a fundamental change in Italy's political economy, reflecting fundamentally changed national economic imperatives and political possibilities, in the era of the Euro and the Second Republic. It is also possible that they do not, and that we soon will look back on these accords as mere contingent departures from Italy's relatively uncoordinated system, to which Italy returned once the national emergencies of the 1990s were over. The next year or two will probably see either the substantially successful implementation of the *Patto Sociale*, or the breakdown of concertation in Italy. Whichever happens may reveal a great deal not only about the Second Republic's capacity for economic self-governance, but also about the structural and behavioural bases of sustained concertation as a political-economic phenomenon.

Italy's historic failure to establish systemic national-level concertational mechanisms sometimes has been explained in terms of the country's politicised and fragmented interest- group structure which, it has been suggested, prevents the resolution of collective action problems needed to sustain negotiated solutions to economic problems. However, recent comparative work has suggested that the roots of concertation may not lie in such structural factors, and that indeed concertation is possible even in the context of considerable interest-group pluralism. Regini,[9] for example, has argued that all countries, irrespective of their interest-group structures, need to strike a balance between public goods provision and flexibility, and hence may adopt concertational or deregulative solutions in different policy areas. He suggests that the placement of different nations along a flexibility-versus-public-goods spectrum in specific policy areas (rather than structural factors such as centralisation of interest groups, or the availability of resources to exchange) explain recent policy evolutions.[10] In this light, Italy's movement towards concertation across policy areas reflects above all that country's starting point at the flexibility end of the spectrum.

Furthermore, for a variety of reasons, Italian worker organisations and firms developed highly active 'micro-concertational' processes, and a culture of concertation, at the local and firm level in much of the North and Centre during the 1980s, when national concertation was impossible. The 1993 and 1996 accords can be seen as the extension of this lower-level concertation to the national level in changed economic and political contexts, which now permit such concertation. In this context, then, the *Patto Sociale* will be the test of whether Italy is becoming a CME, capable of sustaining concertational industrial relations not only during a national economic emergency, but also in more stable moments which lack dramatic exogenous threats such as the possibility of exclusion from EMU.

Efforts at national-level concertation among labour, management and the government have appeared, receded and appeared again in Italy in recent decades. After several turbulent years in the 1970s, the unions adopted a more moderate strategy (symbolised by the 'EUR' line of 1978) in which they sought to trade labour restraint for negotiated political and social reform. But national-level concerta-

tion declined in the 1980s, for a variety of reasons: (e.g. the organisational weakening of the confederal unions and their need to
recover waning support at the base; the need for more local- and
firm-based action in the context of post-Fordist restructuring; the
political weakening of the *Partito Comunista Italiano* (Communist
Party: PCI) and the aggressively anti-communist strategy of Craxi's
Socialists and *pentapartito* ('five-party') governments, which
heightened the salience of political divisions within the unions).

While pragmatic micro-concertation flourished at the local and
firm levels, at the national level, these factors – and above all the
political divisions among the unions – made accords extremely difficult.[11] Even the 1983 grand accord was at best a reluctant acceptance
by the Communists of the CGIL of an approach they disagreed with,
but which they saw as better than a rupture of the CGIL–CISL–UIL
unitary confederation. The 1983 accord did not lead to continued
national concertation, but rather was followed by increasingly unilateral moves by the Craxi government. As a consequence, the rupture of CGIL–CISL–UIL took place anyway (in 1984, over the *scala
mobile*) taking systemic national level concertation off the agenda
until the political climate changed dramatically in the 1990s.[12]

By the early 1990s, it was clear that inflation was undermining
Italy's international competitiveness in increasingly open European
and global markets. It was also clear that the unions were strong
enough to resist non-negotiated, market-based efforts to reduce
wage growth, but that a negotiated incomes policy was conceivable, especially after the birth of the *Partito democratico della sinistra* (Democratic Party of the Left: PDS) and the relative
depoliticisation of the CGIL. The Maastricht treaty then presented
Italy with the choice of exclusion from EMU (if it did not reduce its
inflation, deficit and debt), on the one hand, or the loss of devaluation as a means of restoring competitiveness, on the other. In
either case, a more effective anti-inflation policy was imperative.[13]

It was in this context that the old government alliance collapsed.
The Amato, Ciampi, Dini and Prodi governments then would work
with the social partners to achieve fiscal and other reforms needed to
reduce inflation, debt and the budget deficit, enabling Italy to meet
the Maastricht convergence criteria. The demise of the *Democrazia
cristiana* (Christian Democrats: DC) and of the Socialists, and the
movement of PDS closer to government significantly depoliticised
industrial relations, just as constituencies such as the self-employed,
which had been protected under the old regime, could be forced to
make sacrifices as well. As a result, technocratic and centre-left governments were able to reach negotiated agreements with the unions,
which could be presented to their members not as unilateral conces-

sions, but as contributions to national economic salvation, to which others also were contributing. It became possible for the unions to agree to suspend the *scala mobile*, and to start talks which then led to its abolishment a year later, and to the establishment of the 1993 accord's new mechanism for collective bargaining.

Italy's remarkable and unexpected success in reducing inflation and restoring national financial solvency in the 1990s would not have been possible without the 1993 accord and the ability of the social partners to work together towards shared goals through the decade. The near future will test whether the concertation which gave Italy so much in the 1990s reflected fundamentally changed structural factors, or just the contingencies of the run-up to EMU.

Implications for the Future

While, as mentioned above, the failure to go beyond the collective bargaining arrangements of the July 1993 accord might be seen as a sign of governmental weakness, the reaffirmation of those arrangements in the Pact should nevertheless be seen as a sign that Italy's system of labour relations is not backsliding into the poor institutionalisation and conflictuality of the past. The social partners have again embraced the negotiated incomes policy approach to boosting competitiveness and increasing employment, calling also for tripartitism at the local level, as well as stronger linkage between the national and local levels of wage bargaining. And while the Pact did not alter the collective bargaining framework established in the 1993 accord, the social partners may negotiate further contractual decentralisation, and the prime minister went so far as to express the view before Parliament that national wage contracts should be replaced by lower level agreements. That the prime minister should pronounce in Parliament his views on the institutional structure of collective bargaining – a matter traditionally left to the social partners themselves – is indicative of just how far Italy has already come in the 1990s in terms of tripartitism as a mechanism of national economic governance.

The *Patto Sociale* had been energetically pursued by the centre-left government, and received the clear endorsement of the social partners, most notably Confindustria and the CGIL, CISL and UIL.[14] This broad support of the Pact, by the government and by the major representatives of both labour and capital, reflected in part the success of the 1993 and 1996 agreements at stabilising the Italian economy, and enabling Italy to meet the Maastricht convergence criteria. While the past year has seen a predictable round of

polemics among the social partners pertaining to the implementation of the Pact, neither the unions nor the employer confederations are calling for an end to the concertational approach.

This broad support among the social partners for concertation
as the central mechanism for economic management, raises the
possibility that something fundamental for the future of Italy's
political economy may be happening here: the Social Pact is now
the third major national agreement marking Italy's movement
towards a formally institutionalised system of national political-
economic governance based upon regular and systemic concertation among the social partners at all levels.[15] If the *Patto Sociale*
succeeds, it is likely to consolidate further the coordinated system
of labour relations which has been in the making at the national
level since the early 1990s (and which had emerged informally at
the local level during the 1980s). Such a consolidation would represent a fundamental change in the traditionally informal and
weakly institutionalised nature of Italy's political economy.

Should the Pact succeed at keeping Italy on the path of tripartite
and relatively successful economic management, the political
implications also could be profound: the centre-left will have
demonstrated its credibility – most crucially among the business
classes – as the political alliance most capable of governing today's
economy. Accordingly, Prime Minister D'Alema's efforts may do
more than just move Italy further along in the direction of becoming the 'normal country'[16] he wants Italy to be: should the Pact
succeed, it could go a long way towards consolidating the centre-
left's hold on power. The political neutrality of Confindustria in
recent elections is testimony to the appeal to Italian businesses of
a centre-left government in Rome capable of delivering negotiated
solutions to economic problems facing firms. If tripartitism can
deliver sufficient benefits not only to businesses, but also to the
unions and the leftist electorate (above all, jobs), the possibility
emerges not just for greater institutionalisation of concertation, but
also for a more or less stable centre-left political hegemony.

The failed attempt of the centre-right Berlusconi government of
1994 to put Italy on a neoliberal track of economic and financial
renewal – based upon reforms and budget cuts made without the
consent of the unions – helped induce first the technocratic Dini
government and then the centre-left governments of Prodi and
D'Alema to seek reforms through concertation. The successes of
these recent governments resulted largely from their credibility
with and ties to all the major political tendencies within CGIL,
CISL and UIL – something no Italian government of the *pentapartito* years had ever enjoyed. The unions showed in 1994 that

they could prevent a centre-right government from undertaking urgently needed fiscal and other reforms. Since then, and in the 1992 and 1993 agreements as well, they have shown that they can cooperate – at least in a crisis situation – with friendlier governments to negotiate precisely such reforms.

The *Patto Sociale* will be a crucial test (along with pension reform) of whether the concertational model can continue to work without the immediate threat of exclusion from EMU which the 1996 and 1993 accords enjoyed. In a real sense, it is thus a test of whether or not the Second Republic will be a 'normal country'. Clearly the economic costs to the nation of failure of the Social Pact would be high. Indeed, precisely because of EMU, currency devaluation is no longer an option, making control of costs and improvements in productivity essential to competitiveness. Furthermore, the political costs of failure would be very high for both the government and for those tendencies within the unions with the greatest stake in tripartitism, and the closest ties to the political left. Accordingly, the prospect of failure will concentrate minds on the search for negotiated solutions to outstanding difficulties. But the various partners are also answerable to their respective constituencies, and with EMU having been achieved, the sense of national emergency, which was such a powerful incentive for compromise and cooperation, is gone.

The possibility of a breakdown of concertation cannot be discounted. Both business and labour leaders have at times criticised the government for slowness in implementation of the Pact, and the government and CISL clashed seriously in 1999, particularly over pensions – where the positions taken by this union with the weakest ties to the government suggest that uncompensated moderation will not be forthcoming. The still relatively strong political ties between the DS (*Democratici di Sinistra*) and CGIL have been a resource to the government, but even CGIL's ability to swallow sacrifice is limited, as the issue of contractual decentralisation showed. As Italy confronts delicate questions pertaining to welfare and pensions, CGIL must find a difficult balance between its dual needs to both support a 'friendly' government, and to maintain both the support of its members and collabourative relations with the other confederations.[17]

Will the government and the partners now be able to continue to sustain the levels of public dialogue and real sacrifice which national concertation entails in the months ahead? And will national concertation deliver the goods that the economy needs to grow and create jobs?[18] The answers to these two questions are related: to the extent that concertation delivers competitiveness and lower unemployment, it will be easier to sell to the constituencies which must support it. The Italian political economy is walking across a tightrope, in which success in the next year or two could produce more success – and a further institutionalisation of concertation, which could endure into the future. The consequences of breakdown and failure could be just as far-reaching. In particular, pension and welfare reform risk inflaming to breaking point the political divisions within the union movement. Further deterioration of inter-union relations could undermine Italy's capacity to continue along the concertational path.

As this chapter goes to press, relations among the social partners who signed the Pact are under strain, but a breakdown of dialogue has not occurred. While finger-pointing abounds among the partners, each accusing the others of not doing their respective part to realise the objectives of the Pact[19] (and tensions rise whenever the government broaches the issue of pension reform), there does not appear to be a credible neoliberal alternative to negotiated reform, and the most important initiatives of the Social Pact have already become law. Whatever the posturing and harsh words, so far the social partners still seem to really believe that concertation is needed for Italy to succeed in today's economy. Accordingly, given the strength of organised labour, and the ties of its strongest confederation to the centre-left, the prospects for continued concertation are still fairly good, and as a result the existing coalition or something like it remains a credible pretender to power in the years ahead.

Conclusion

In a recent contribution, Ida Regalia and Marino Regini wrote:

> Despite its importance, the tripartite accord of 1993 was an agreement on the rules, not a social Pact committing the parties to a shared vision of economic development and priorities. Indeed, even agreement on rules may soon deteriorate if it is not injected with new content. By a 'shared vision of economic development' we do not mean the old exchange between employment and productivity, but instead a conception of the competitiveness of the national economy based on a partially shared programme for the development of human resources. Despite the importance of recent events, the relationships among employers, unions and state in Italy are still a long way from achieving this goal.[20]

Indeed, many obstacles remain on the path to a shared model of development, as the struggle over pensions, for example, reveals. However, the 'Social Pact' of December 1998 has the potential to mark an important step on the way towards a 'shared vision of economic development'. Despite the doubts and problems and ongoing polemics, the Pact does express a substantially shared conception of how to develop the Italian economy. The state, the major unions, and employer organisations are in substantial agreement on what is needed to promote development, albeit not upon who must sacrifice the most and the least to make the model work. The Pact stresses above all the need for boosting productivity and job-creation through labour-cost containment, bureaucratic efficiency and more investment in both physical and human capital in a competitive open economy in which currency devaluation is no longer an option. The link between productivity, flexibility and labour costs on investment and growth is generally understood, despite differences of emphasis among the various partners.

While this does not guarantee that Italy will consolidate a fully institutionalised and concertational system of labour relations, it does suggest that such an outcome is at least possible. That it has become so reflects not only the changed European and global economic context, but also the changed political context in Italy, in which political parties linked to all three trade union confederations, most importantly CGIL, are in the government. In sharp contrast to the situation of the 1980s, when the largest of the confederations was linked to the opposition, today the unions and the government face 'friendly', if not always chummy, interlocutors, and parts of the business community are convinced that they can get results from centre-left governments that they could not get from centre-right governments. All the most powerful actors (Confindustria, CGIL, CISL, UIL, the DS and most of their allies in government) have a stake in making concertation work. Whether they can do so without undermining their respective strategic positions (a particular problem for CISL) and/or losing control of their respective bases of support is the question. It was one thing to pull together in the 'national emergency' of the early and mid-1990s, when the cost of failure was exclusion from Europe. It is something else altogether to create and maintain a fully integrated and fully institutionalised system of concertational labour relations, capable of handling the more mundane challenges of a more 'normal country' in more normal times.

Notes

1. Http:www.palazzochigi.it/patto_sociale/cronologia.html. The original Italian is:'Deve essere una libera scelta da parte di imprese e sindacati per far venire meno alcune rigidita' sul mercato del lavoro e rafforzare un nuovo ciclo di investimenti che allarghi la base produttiva'.

2. Http:wgww.palazzochigi.it/patto_sociale/cronologia.html. The original Italian was: 'Il primo impegno del governo e' quello di aprire la trattativa per rinnovare l'accordo del '93 e contestualmente arrichire il patto sociale di nuovi obiettivi, in termini di occupazione e di sviluppo, ma anche allargarlo coinvolgendo piu' soggetti'.

3. *Patto sociale per lo sviluppo e l'occupazione.* (Henceforth *'Patto sociale'*). (http://www.cgil.it_extranet/dirgen/pattoSOCIALE/patto.htm). The original Italian was: 'Con la piena adesione all'Unione Economica e Monetaria Europea, la significativa riduzione delle dinamiche inflazionistiche ed il contenimento della spesa pubblica, gli obiettivi principali del Protocollo sulla politica dei redditi e dell'occupazione, sugli assetti contrattuali, sulle politiche del lavoro e sul sostegno al sistema produttivo del 23 luglio 1993 sono stati in tutto o in parte consequiti. Successsivamente, con il Patto del Lavoro del settembre 1996 si è raggiunto un accordo tra Governo e parti sociale volto al perseguimento di obiettivi di sviluppo ed di promozione adempiendo all'impegno di modificare il quadro normativo in materia di gestione del mercato del lavoro e crisi occupazionali, in direzione di un governo attivo delle dinamiche dell'occupazione'.

4. *Patto sociale.* (p.1) The original Italian was 'Il modello ed le procedure messi in atto dal Protocollo del 23 luglio 1993 hanno reso stabile e continuo il confronto tra Governo, organizzazioni sindacali e associazioni datoriali. La responsabilità dei comportamenti degli attori sociali derivata dal Protocollo si è rivelata una condizione essenziale per garantire la modernizzazione del Paese e per determinare il passaggio verso una condizione economica che pone oggi l'Italia in condizione di maggiore competitività nella sfida della globalizzazione, garentendo il mantenimento di condizioni sociali adeguate.'

5. *Patto sociale.* (p.1).

6. For a comprehensive list of actions taken pursuant to the Pact, including legislation and specific legislative provisions, see http://www.palazzochigi.it/patto_sociale/monitoraggio/index.html

7. David Soskice, 'Divergent production regimes: coordinated and uncoordinated market economies in the 1980's and 1990s', in *Continuity and Change in Contemporary Capitalism*, eds H. Kitschelt et al, Cambridge, 1999. Variations within each of these groups have been observed, and the French 'state-business-élite CME' is seen as a third model altogether.

8. Soskice, 'Divergent production regimes'. See also Marino Regini, *Uncertain Boundaries: The Social and Political Construction of European Economies*, New York, 1995, and Richard Locke, *Remaking the Italian Economy*, Ithaca, 1995.

9. Marino Regini, 'Between de-regulation and social pacts: the responses of European economies to globalisation'. Istituto Juan March de Estudios e Investigaciones. Working paper 1999/133.

10. Considering national policy changes in different areas, Regini observes that 'there emerges an analytical alternative to the "deregulation" of the economy which can be called the alternative of "concertation". This no longer displays the typical features of the old neocorporatist systems, such as bargaining centralisation, close regulation of the labour market, and expansion of welfare benefits. Instead, the distinctive features are the search for greater wage coordination in order to counter-balance the effects of decentralisation, closer control on the selective and experimental character of flexibilisation processes, and the involvement of the social partners in welfare reform in order to render it compatible with competitiveness without endangering consensus'. Regini, 'Between deregulation and social pacts', 17.

11. It is worth noting, however, that despite low levels of institutionalisation of labour relations *per se*, and the rarity in the decade before July 1993 of peak-level

agreements, the Italian interest organisations for decades have been involved in broader areas (such as the implementation of public policies), and public institutions have been indirectly involved in labour relations. See Ida Regalia and Marino Regini, 'Italy: the dual character of industrial relations', *Changing Industrial Relations in Europe*, eds A. Ferner and R. Hyman.. Oxford, 1998.

12. For a clear and detailed account of these and subsequent developments, see Michael Braun, 'The confederated trade unions and the Dini government: the grand return to neocorporatism?', in *Italian Politics: The Stalled Transition*, eds M. Caciagli and D. Kertzer, Boulder, 1996.

13. For an interesting discussion of the failure of non-concertational monetarist efforts to control inflation in Italy, see Sofia Perez, 'The resurgence of national social bargaining in Europe: explaining the Italian and Spanish experiences'. Istituto Juan March de Estudios e Investigaciones. Working Paper 1999/130.

14. At the time of signing and during the parliamentary debate, numerous positive statements were made by all the signatories: See the interview with Georgio Fossa (Confindustria), *Adnkronos*, 14 January 1999; Sergio Cofferati (CGIL): 'Con questo patto, L'Italia sara' piu credibile nel sostenere a livello europeo la necessita' di politiche per lo sviluppo;' Sergio D'Antoni (CISL): 'Sara' un biglietto importante per l'Europa;' Silvano Larizza (UIL): 'Abbiamo creato le condizioni migliori d'Europa per investire.' La Stampa, 23 December, 1999.

15. See Regalia and Regini, 'The Dual Character', for a good overview of the structure of industrial relations in Italy, and its evolution in recent decades.

16. See Mark Gilbert, 'In search of normality: the political strategy of Massimo D'Alema', *Journal of Modern Italian Studies*, 3 (no.3) 307–17, for a succinct discussion of this topic.

17. The difficult position of the CGIL was evident in comments made by CGIL Secretary Sergio Cofferati in a televised discussion at the 1999 Festa dell'Unita' in Rome last July: 'Io e D'Alema siamo iscritti allo stesso partito, ma possiamo avere opinioni diverse. Discutere pacatamente serve per mettersi d'accordo, ma puo' non bastare. E' il merito che prevale su tutto e l'autonomia e' fondamentale per l'esercizio del mio mestiere.'

18. Critics of the concertational approach have argued that, while it may have served its purpose during the national emergency of the early-mid 1990s, today it imposes unnecessary, and inflationary, rigidities. See, for example, Renato Brunetta, *Il Giornale*, 29 December 1999. These critics have not, however, clearly outlined how non-concertational reform can take place in the Italian context.

19. After the second review in September 1999, both Confindustria Vice-President Carlo Callieri, and the chief union leaders, urged monitoring of inflation and urged the government to do more in the area of tax relief and assistance to low-income families. *Sole 24 Ore On Line*, 20 September 1999.
(Http://www.ilsole24ore.it.pattosociale)

20. Regalia and Regini, 'The dual character', 497.

11

THE NEW SOUTH IN THE NEW EUROPE: THE CASE OF SVILUPPO ITALIA

Vincent Della Sala

On 1 January 1999, Italy was amongst the group of initial countries forming the euro zone; on 9 January, just a few days later, the Comitato Interministeriale per la Programmazione Economica (CIPE) gave final approval to a motion to set up a new agency to promote regional economic development, primarily in the South, called *Sviluppo Italia* ('Development Italy'). While there is a tendency to look to European economic and monetary integration as the source of most economic, political and social developments in Italy in the 1990s, the two January developments were not totally unrelated. It may seem strange that the creation of yet another agency would qualify as an important highlight in an eventful year in Italian politics. However, the creation of Sviluppo Italia is an illustrative case study for a number of important political and economic trends of the last few years that came to the surface in 1999. These include economic development in the South in an integrated Europe, regional and industrial policy in an era of an increasingly neoliberal macroeconomic policy regime, and the question of how to address major social demands while state authority and capacity are being 'hollowed out' in an increasingly global economy.

Moreover, the story of Sviluppo Italia is part of a process that has seen the return to the forefront of the political agenda of the question of regional development, and particularly, the growth rate, income and employment differences between Northern and

Southern regions. The 1992 referendum that abolished the *Cassa per il Mezzogiorno* (Southern Italy Development Agency) and extraordinary intervention in the South, along with the political crisis of the first half of the decade, created a policy vacuum for regional development. The drive to meet the convergence criteria for entry into the single currency ensured that the over riding concern until entry was secured was with controlling public finances at the expense of other policy objectives. This chapter will argue that a new approach to regional policy emerged in the mid-1990s, shaped by the perceived demands of an integrated Europe; and that the creation of the new agency was seen as one of a range of instruments to deal with the 'new' South. The discussion will be divided into two sections. The first will provide a brief overview of the new approach to regional development; the second section will address the creation of Sviluppo Italia in 1999.

The Return of the South

There are a number of common themes that have run throughout the history of unified Italy. However, none have had the salience and durability of the question of the divide between the North and the South of the country. The issue has been defined and addressed in different ways at various points in time, reflecting political and social pressures that were able to shape the terms of debate. The 1990s have seen discussion of the South wane in the first half, and then re-emerge in the second half, especially after Italy's entry into the single currency seemed safe. A combination of external and domestic factors ensured that perennial issues, such as the disparity of income and unemployment rates between the South and the rest of the country, received less attention. The primacy given to meeting the convergence criteria for entry into the single currency seemed to be the only issue on the policy and political agenda for the period from 1992 to 1998. It was inevitable that, in a period where the emphasis was on austerity, rigour and discipline, policy areas whose basis was using the state to redistribute resources would have difficulty finding an audience. Moreover, there was a growing perception that the demands of a global economy required a more 'competitive' society.[1] The objectives of the 1950s to the 1980s of using state power to redress regional imbalances was increasingly seen to be at odds with the attempt to introduce individual initiative and agency in a competitive society, especially in the South.

However, while the external constraint imposed by European commitments was important, it was complemented by domestic developments. First, the meteoric rise of the Lega Nord was partly responsible for highlighting the fact that vast amounts of money had been transferred to the South with few concrete results. At the height of the Lega Nord's popularity, few political leaders would have risked speaking loudly of questions related to economic and regional development. Second, the 1993 referendum demonstrated that there was an overwhelming desire to put an end to extraordinary intervention in the South. Few were willing to step forward in the years that followed to propose an alternative strategy. Finally, the political crisis that shook the First Republic in the middle of the decade discredited an approach to politics that many saw as based on political exchange in the South.

The Southern question, then, slipped off the political map but issues such as unemployment and economic development remained. Indeed, with the single market and currency, a European Commission ever more vigilant about state aid to firms and greater economic liberalisation, there was reason to believe that the plight of some parts of the South was cause for concern. For instance, the figures in Table 11.1 reveal that the South, as a whole, continued the trend that began in the early 1980s of not keeping pace with economic growth in the Centre-North. The table reveals some of the changing dynamics in the relative wealth of different regions. The 1990s confirmed the primacy of the North-east regions especially with respect to the traditional industrial areas of the North-west. Moreover, the figures illustrate some of the consequences of two of most important economic developments of the decade: some of the effects of the withdrawal from the EMS in 1992 and the devaluation of the lira, and the recession of the first half of the decade. The result seemed to be somewhat of a paradoxical outcome. On the one hand, devaluation contributed largely to a record export boom; increases in exports are not unexpected with a currency devaluation. On the other hand, devaluation usually shields uncompetitive firms and industries in the short term, and allows them to put off choosing to restructure. However, in the 1990s, we have devaluation with an export boom along with retrenchment and downsizing. Clearly, the creation of the single market and the objective of the single currency forced firms and industries to look beyond devaluation to remain competitive. But a closer look at the figures in Table 11.1 might explain the presence of devaluation and retrenchment as regionally differentiated. The North-east, the basis of the 'third Italy' model, was able to exploit a weaker lira to have steady rates of growth and to achieve rates of close to full employment. In the meantime, some other regions paid the price for a tight monetary policy and industrial restructuring.

Table 11.1 *GDP per capita (as percentage of Centre-North regions)*

	1980	1983	1989	1990	1991	1992	1993	1994	1995	1996
Piemonte	100.8	98.8	99.1	98.1	96.4	95.9	94.9	96.1	96.4	96.4
Valle d'Aosta	112.7	112.4	112.2	111.0	109.5	111.9	111.6	110.1	110.2	109.5
Lombardia	111.1	110.7	111.7	110.7	109.7	108.2	107.4	108.4	108.8	108.2
Trentino A.A.	101.0	101.8	102.2	103.3	105.0	106.1	106.1	106.5	104.5	105.2
Veneto	93.9	94.5	97.3	97.0	97.4	98.7	100.7	100.7	101.2	101.4
Friuli V.G.	97.4	93.9	98.6	99.2	99.5	99.9	100.2	102.3	103.0	102.8
Liguria	95.7	93.3	95.1	96.6	98.4	97.8	97.6	97.5	97.2	96.8
Emilia										
Romagna	111.5	108.5	106.2	106.2	106.5	107.7	108.1	107.9	107.6	108.0
Toscana	93.5	95.1	90.8	90.4	91.4	91.0	91.9	90.6	90.6	90.8
Umbria	85.8	94.9	80.3	80.3	81.7	82.5	82.1	80.5	80.1	79.6
Marche	91.8	90.6	87.5	87.4	87.4	88.5	88.0	87.1	86.7	87.0
Lazio	86.7	91.8	92.4	94.4	95.6	96.1	95.9	94.3	93.7	94.0
Abruzzo	71.9	74.0	73.7	74.6	75.9	76.6	74.7	74.0	74.7	74.9
Molise	61.7	61.0	63.0	62.8	63.9	64.1	62.3	62.8	62.1	61.9
Campania	56.1	59.6	56.4	56.7	56.4	55.6	55.2	54.1	52.7	52.0
Puglia	60.8	60.6	59.9	59.4	60.9	59.9	58.8	58.4	56.6	56.0
Basilicata	57.8	54.6	51.1	51.8	51.6	52.1	53.1	52.9	52.8	52.8
Calabria	48.8	52.7	49.2	47.3	49.4	48.7	49.6	48.2	48.7	48.7
Sicilia	56.1	59.2	54.4	55.6	57.1	56.5	56.8	54.2	52.8	52.6
Sardegna	61.6	63.6	61.4	62.5	65.4	65.8	66.1	63.9	61.5	61.4
Mezzogiorno	57.8	60.0	57.2	57.5	58.6	58.0	57.8	56.4	55.2	54.9
Centro-Nord	100.0	100.0	100.0	100.0	100.0	100.0	100.0	100.0	100.0	100.0
-Nord-Ovest	106.3	105.2	106.2	105.5	104.6	103.5	102.7	103.7	103.9	103.6
-Nord-Est	101.6	100.5	101.2	101.4	101.7	102.9	103.9	104.1	104.1	104.4
-Centro	89.6	92.2	90.3	91.1	92.1	92.5	92.5	91.1	90.8	91.0
Italia	85.1	85.7	84.3	84.4	84.8	84.6	84.5	83.9	83.5	83.3

Source: SVIMEZ, *Rapporto 1997 sull'economia del Mezzogiorno*, Bologna:
Il Mulino, 1997, Table A6.

These different trajectories become even more apparent when
looking at unemployment rates. It becomes quite clear that Italy
has a number of different labour markets across its territory, and
that the question of unemployment in the South became an urgent
matter by the mid-1990s. In 1996, the unemployment rate in the
South was 21.7 percent, while it was only 7.7 percent in the Centre-North. It was even lower, at 5.6 percent, in the North-East. The
picture of the labour market is even more stark if we look at unemployment rates for males, with only 3.3 percent unemployed in the
North-east compared to over 20 percent in Campania and Calabria.[2] There may be some debate as to whether the large differences in unemployment rates, especially its high concentration

amongst youth and in particular areas, could lead to social tension.[3] However, there was little doubt that they contributed to the growing perception that there was a potential for social and political instability on many fronts. The fear was not only that an integrated Europe would entrench and aggravate regional differences, but that they would hamper Italy's competitiveness in a single market and economy.

It was within this context that discussion about addressing issues related to economic growth in the South occupied a growing importance within the Prodi government. Gradually, the policy void that had been left after the 1992 referendum, and the political crisis of the first part of the decade, began to be filled by a series of measures that traced the outlines of a new approach to regional policy. Moreover, this new framework would emphasise a different role for the state, a more enhanced role for parts of civil society and new relationships between centre and periphery.

One important element of the new approach was a series of instruments born largely in the wake of the rejection of extraordinary intervention, and known collectively as 'negotiated planning'.[4] The so-called *accordo di programma* ('planning agreement') was already used under the old regime for extraordinary intervention but is included in the new policy era because of its emphasis on public-private partnerships. It is an agreement that is based largely on an initiative of a central department or agency, and has a specific project as its focus. It brings together local authorities as well as private investors and firms. Perhaps the most famous example of a successful 'planning agreement' is the revitalisation of the port at Gioia Tauro. A second mechanism that was used was the 'planning programme' (which can be part of an *accordo di programma*) between a central department and a large firm or consortium of smaller firms. It is aimed at a specific investment or infrastructure project, such as the Fiat plant at Melfi. As in the case of the *accordo*, it is a part of the central state that takes a lead role, and provides some form of extraordinary intervention. However, it does involve consultation with parts of civil society and regional and local authorities.

The two instruments that received the most attention, and perhaps in which the centre-left governments placed the greatest expectations, were the so-called 'territorial pacts' and the 'area contracts'. The two were used to address the long-standing problem of Italy not accessing the structural funds allocated to it in Brussels. The pacts, which were endorsed at the European level at the Essen Summit, are based on local initiatives brought forward by local authorities and private sector actors, including mostly small and medium-sized firms, financial institutions, trade unions and associations. A deliberation by the CIPE stated that the general objectives of the pacts included the promotion of interregional cooperation, support for small and medium sized enterprises, job creation and use of EU funds.[5] More specifically, a limit was put on public funds at 100 billion lire for each project as well as on infrastructure investment; the private sector investment in the project must not be below 30 percent of the total; and the investment for each job created cannot exceed 500 million lire.[6] The pacts had a complex approval and monitoring process that began with an initiative from the social partners at the local level, an important role for the CNEL in facilitating concertation at the local level and final approval by the CIPE. The experience of the pacts has been generally regarded as a positive one by most of the social actors, and over fifty had been approved by mid-1999 with over 12, 000 new jobs being created.[7] The pacts were not exclusive to the South but the vast majority approved, and resources allocated, did go to the Southern regions.[8]

The 'area contracts' scheme has proven to be more difficult to implement. It is much broader in scope and the initiative rests with the central government, through the Task Force on Employment in the President of the Council of Ministers' office.[9] The aim is to identify areas where industrial decline and structural unemployment have been particularly acute, and to look for ways to simplify procedures so as to make the most of structural funds available. As this includes providing greater flexibility to labour markets and streamlining regulations and administrative procedures, concertation needs to take place with the social partners. The 'contract' does not have the specificity of the 'pacts', and this has helped contribute to the difficulties it has faced in being implemented. By the middle of 1999, no 'contract' had yet been realised and there were signals that the government and the social partners were not interested in promoting them further.

Although the different instruments may vary in their focus and may have produced different results, they do share a number of important features. They all involve an attempt at concertation, with the state playing the role of facilitator with the social partners. In addition, the state's role is presented as largely a technical one of providing support to local and regional authorities in preparing proposals, of coordinating the process and monitoring outcomes. The new policy regime is just as concerned with the process that places the emphasis on initiatives from civil society, as it is with the substance of policy. This is part of an attempt to bring about a change in attitudes about how economic growth is to be promoted in the South. Government ministers in recent years have spoken of ending a culture of dependency on state transfers and of fostering a sense of entrepreneurship.[10] It also reflects the fact that in an integrated Europe, the capacity for the state to use subsidies and fiscal incentives to attract investment is limited so that other means of mobilising existing resources must be found. Finally, the new policy regime implies state structures that have the technical and political capacity to make choices and to be selective amongst different proposals. Unlike the previous regime where transfers to individuals and firms and extraordinary intervention were seen to be more concerned with the undifferentiated diffusion of resources, there is now an emphasis on the capacity to choose amongst alternatives that are more likely to produce tangible results for which officials can be held accountable.

It is in this respect that the Ministry of the Treasury assumed the role of the central body within the national state that would take the lead in regional policy. An important development was the creation of the 'super' ministry when the Ministry for the Budget and Economic Planning was merged with the Treasury under the Prodi government.[11] The merger was the result of a gradual process in which the two ministries – one whose orientation was fiscal discipline and market based, and the other who had economic planning as one of its mandates – began to converge in their approach to macroeconomic policy. An important step was the abolition of extraordinary intervention in the South, and the subsequent search for a policy and a role for economic planning. The growing focus on finding ways to better utilise EU funds led to the creation of a *Cabina di regia*, ('control centre') within the Budgetary and Economic Planning Ministry in 1995. It was to act as a coordinating body for the various levels of government and parts of the central state that needed to be mobilised to gain access to EU funds. It was a recognition that an increasingly important role for the state was to facilitate the interaction between local and regional authorities, as well as parts of society and European institutions.[12]

An important part of the merger and the newly structured Ministry was the *Dipartimento per le Politiche di Sviluppo e di Coesione* (DPSC), which took over many of the functions of the old Budgetary ministry. It includes separate divisions that deal with: regional and territorial policies, the 'planning agreements', and EU structural funds. The importance of the DPSC to Treasury Minister Ciampi was highlighted by the fact that Fabrizio Barca, the head of research at the Bank of Italy, was appointed to head the department. Barca is one of the leading figures in a group of young economists who have gained prominence in the 1990s. His close links to

Ciampi and his reputation from his time at the Bank of Italy brought a significant measure of political and technical credibility to the DPSC.[13] It also signalled that the Prodi government was making a serious attempt to improve Italy's access to the EU structural funds allocated to it through mechanisms that involved a wide range of actors, with the primary role for the state that of coordination. The leaner state was also one where decision-making power continued to be centralised into fewer hands, with the Treasury and the Prime Minister's office becoming the epicentre for policy making.

The combination of an emphasis on new policy instruments and a central role for the DPSC was partly responsible for one of the most tangible successes of the Prodi and D'Alema governments. Italy's record on accessing allocated structural funds had reached significantly low levels. By 1996, only 12 percent of the funds set aside in Brussels had made their way to Italy. The principal reason was that local and regional governments had not come up with acceptable proposals to get the funds. This failure was a legacy of the long period of funds being transferred to the South with little regard for the viability of projects or their final outcomes. Under the old regime, there was little incentive to develop the technical capacity to draw up proposals that provided for monitoring of results and mobilising parts of civil society that would be required for the Commission. Clearly, the new instruments and the restructuring of ministries aimed to make regional and local authorities more accountable and responsible for shaping their economic futures. D'Alema was able to tell the Chamber of Deputies in January 1999 that the government had reached the objective of pushing the figure up to 55 percent in 1998.[14]

Discussion in the mid-1990s increasingly emphasised that the South was at a crossroads. On the one hand, a range of new instruments, policies, structures, ideas and a growing entrepreneurial class brought optimism that real progress could be made. The emphasis on clearly defined, sometimes modest, objectives with guarantees that there will be proper monitoring of outcomes has contributed to a sense that concrete results will be produced.[15] The evidence from some parts of the South, such as Basilicata and parts of Apulia which have shown significant rates of growth and strong export performances, supports this mild optimism. More generally, the positive view sees the economic restructuring that has resulted from economic and monetary integration as dislodging privileged and often unproductive forces; and providing space for new forms of entrepreneurship. But it also may result in a different future for the South.

The pessimistic view sees the South being left further behind as mobile capital will look to other parts of Italy and Europe that do not present the same number of obstacles. In addition to factors that might be found in the rest of Italy, such as taxation rates, investment in the South must contend with: areas poorly served by transportation and communication infrastructure, labour markets that may not match demand, organised crime and an inefficient and ineffective public sector.[16] These are obstacles that have often been invoked but an increasingly globalised economy in an integrated Europe is seen as providing few incentives and structures to address them without some form of endogenous change.[17] As national governments are increasingly losing the capacity to affect economic and social outcomes, they are beginning to look to ways in which to mobilise parts of civil society to respond to the changing economic and social landscape. The pessimistic view of the South in an integrated Europe essentially argues that the structural impediments to civil society will penalise it disproportionately.[18]

The centre-left governments' approach to regional development since 1996 has been based on both the optimistic and pessimistic visions of the South in an integrated Europe. Government ministers and senior policy makers have repeatedly emphasised the precariousness of the South in an integrated Europe. There was a lively debate and discussion in late 1998, with a meeting in Catania in December which produced a document from the DPSC called, 'One Hundred Ideas for Development'.[19] This was followed by a deliberation of the CIPE on 22 December 1998 that sought to lay out the timetable and parameters for preparing the six-year plan to present to the European Commission on Italy's plans for structural funds in the period 2000–06.[20] The 'Hundred Ideas' was a discussion document that provided the reference point for the negotiations between the central government and the regions. There were a number of issues that needed to be addressed in arriving at the new plan. These included the conditions for private sector financing of projects, methods for coordination amongst projects and different government departments and agencies, and a system for monitoring the proposal process and its outcomes.

The December meeting in Catania between the central agencies and the regions, and the CIPE deliberation, set the framework for a major government statement on regional policy in May 1999. The Orientamenti per il Programma di Sviluppo del Mezzogiorno 2000–2006 ('Towards a Development Programme for the South 2000–2006'), captures the view that regional development must be based on existing resources. Financial transfers from outside, whether from EU structural funds or the central state, are to be complementary and aimed at facilitating projects. There is no pretence that regional development is to involve redistribution of wealth or resources. For instance, the 'axes' for development in the Orientamenti are spelled out in separate sections on human, natural and cultural resources, cities and local systems of economic activity. It is clear that the guidelines are based on the view that the direct role of the state is limited, and centres primarily on facilitating or shaping the use of local resources. The Orientamenti are also interesting with respect to what is highlighted as indicators of effectiveness for the new policy regime. There is an emphasis on the amount of private sector investment drawn to natural and cultural resources, on innovation and use of new technologies, and on creating 'density' with new entrepreneurial activity. The state's role is primarily one of providing basic infrastructure, such as water, playing a repressive role in fighting crime and creating a 'secure' climate for economic activity, or in mobilising existing resources by creating networks and partnerships.

The guidelines and the programme that they formed for the use of structural funds both reflect and contribute to a new approach to the question of regional development, especially in the South. Despite the references to 'revolutionary' and 'negotiated' planning, which implies a highly interventionist state, the motor for development is market forces and reduced state intervention. Employment growth gets a great deal of attention in the renewed interest in the South, but the emphasis is on supply side factors in labour markets as well with fiscal and regulatory instruments. Even where there is to be direct state intervention, such as with infrastructure or education, it is to address issues of the supply of factors to improve productivity. There is little talk of using state spending as direct investment to secure employment, as was done in the past with nationalised industries, or of using transfers to individuals as a way of generating demand. Closing the gap between the South and the rest of the country will not come through redistributing resources but through the more accelerated rates of growth that are expected with the unleashing of market forces and investment in the Mezzogiorno.[21] The new South will be one with a new state: leaner, more efficient and one that has Europe and its markets as its reference points in determining policy.

Sviluppo Italia

It is within this context of uncertainty and promise for the South in an integrated Europe that the discussion and creation of the new agency, Sviluppo Italia (SI), took place in the period 1997–9. The legislative impetus for the creation of the new agency was the so-called 'Bassanini law' that laid out the framework for reorganising the public sector, from powers to be given to local governments to simplifying ministries and agencies.[22] More specifically, articles 11 and 14 of the law gave the government the power to issue *decreti legislativi* ('orders in council') that would rationalise government agencies. It is on the basis of this legislative provision that a concrete discussion began in May 1997 with investigative hearings by the Budget Committee of the Senate on the effectiveness and coordination of different policy instruments for depressed areas. The discussion continued throughout the summer of 1997, and the issue arose during the government crisis a few months later in October. The Prodi government, in an attempt to demonstrate to its Communist Refoundation (PRC) allies that it was an activist administration that was concerned not simply with fiscal austerity, highlighted its plans for the South. This included a reference to create a new agency that could, 'unify into a single public company all the diverse and uncoordinated activities that today are handled by the numerous industrial promotion agencies currently working in the field'.[23] Prodi also caused a stir by claiming that the new agency should rise from the 'ashes' of IRI, using what was best of the holding agency to develop the South. This led many to call the yet-to-be-proposed structure 'IRI-2'; a suggestion that was the source of some opposition.

There was, then, throughout 1998 a discussion about the new agency and what form it would take. Prodi's reference to creating something along the lines of IRI invoked images of a large agency of the central government that would be used for political purposes. This was a worry expressed not simply by some members of the opposition parties but especially by elected officials at the regional and local level.[24] The government's position on the nature and form of the agency began to take shape over the course of 1998, and all references to an 'IRI-2' began to be replaced by calls first for a 'South Agency' and then, eventually, Sviluppo Italia. Pierluigi Bersani, Minister of Industry, appearing before the Budget Committee of the Chamber of Deputies, spelled out the emerging government position on a new holding agency that brought together existing structures under a single management structure.[25] He claimed that the objectives for the agency were those for the government's policy for the South; namely, to stimulate private sector investment in industry and services to provide durable and stable employment and economic growth. Bersani argued that public funds were limited, and that the improved state of public finances and taming of inflation meant that capital that once was attracted to financing government debt was now looking for new sites to invest in. The role of the state was to ensure that this capital was directed to depressed areas without interfering with market forces.

The government's challenge was how to restructure some of its existing agencies that worked primarily on issues of regional development, especially in the South. These ranged from ENISUD which was controlled by ENI and was involved in a number of industrial conversion projects throughout Italy, to FINAGRA, which was controlled by the Ministry of Agriculture and was primarily a merchant bank specialising in agricultural enterprises. Bersani identified at least eleven agencies that carried out similar or complementary functions, and claimed that they created a cumbersome and often incoherent body of instruments. The government's plan was to create structures that were 'light', and which would mobilise local resources to create the conditions to draw private investment from Italy and abroad. In addition, the new structure would play an important part in providing technical assistance and securing financing for projects eligible for EU structural funds. Bersani summed up the government's vision of the new agency and policy in the South as, 'Doing it yourself, but not on your own'.[26] He captured the view that the new agency was meant to play a supplementary or complementary role for initiatives that came from the local and regional levels, and from civil society.

The legislative path for the new agency involved both chambers of Parliament in the spring and summer months of 1998. A joint meeting of the Senate's Budget and Industry committees produced a resolution in April that called for the creation of the kind of holding agency Bersani had mentioned, and whose aim was to attract investment and promote new forms of entrepreneurship.[27] The resolution was similar, in some ways, to a draft of a government order-in-council approved by the Council of Ministers on 1 October 1998. It was sent to Parliament for review and opinion, and it was dealt with in the appropriate committees in November and December. The final document was approved on 3 December 1998 by the Council of Ministers, and Sviluppo Italia came into being on 9 January with *decreto legislativo* 1/99.

Sviluppo Italia was created as a holding agency that would control the shares of eight public firms whose primary area of activity was in the South, or other depressed areas. It was organised into two main divisions, one dealing primarily with financial services and the second grouped the four firms whose primary focus was services aimed at technical assistance for firms and public authorities. The financial division included ITAINVEST, INSUD, RIBS and FINAGRA; while SPI, ENISUD, Imprenditorialita Giovanile (IG), and IPI formed the second division. A brief glance at who were some of the shareholders for these eight firms can provide an insight into the claim that there was a need for a single agency that could provide a unity of purpose and vision. The Treasury was the principal shareholder in INSUD, IG and ITAINVEST, while the industry ministry controlled IPI, Agriculture had both FINAGRA and RIBS, and SPI was part of the IRI group. When the range of activities and firms that each of these agencies had invested or worked in is reviewed, the case for Sviluppo Italia becomes even more compelling. The history of the eight agencies is that of state-held firms in Italy in the postwar period. They began with the best of intentions to address specific economic objectives and were targeted at particular areas. But as was often the case, they became involved in firms or industries that strayed from the original objectives, and began to address political or social objectives. For instance, SPI's main area of intervention was to help promote commercial activities, especially in areas where steel industries have declined. In addition to operating business innovation centres and agencies for economic development throughout Italy, it also had a stake in a range of firms from software development in Caserta to textiles in Taranto.

The directives to sort out the ownership and control issues were issued by the President of the Council of Ministers on 26 January 1999. The three ministries that had controlling interests in the firms that were now under Sviluppo Italia's control – Treasury, Industry and Agriculture – were to transfer their shares to the new agency. Sviluppo Italia itself would have the Treasury as its chief shareholder, strengthening its role as the central department that would now be responsible for regional development. It meant that the Treasury now had a division, the DPSC, whose focus would be on providing a broad policy framework for development policy, as well as guiding local and regional authorities through the range of instruments available at the national and European levels. This is complemented by Sviluppo Italia, which could make available financial and technical services to attract not only private investment but also EU structural funds. What remains to be seen is how the two different parts of the Treasury will work together, and to what extent the Treasury will intervene as major shareholder if there is ever a conflict between objectives and practices of Sviluppo Italia with that of the regional development unit. The Treasury's position was consolidated by a deliberation of CIPE on 22 January 1999 that allocated 35 billion lire for Sviluppo Italia's capital base, and established the Treasury's role as principal shareholder.[28]

The first article of the *decreto legislativo* and the directives issued by the government at the end of January 1999 set out the functions and responsibilities for the new agency.[29] These include the promotion of economic activities, new investment and initiatives for employment growth and new businesses. There were a number of important support roles assigned as well, including: support for innovation, to public authorities at all levels for financial and development planning, to local firms and to provide technical assistance to manage incentive programmes at the national and EU levels. The directives were more specific about the coordination activities to be carried out. It is quite clear that one of the roles for Sviluppo Italia is to help ensure that local and regional authorities, as well as local firms, can present proposals that are sure to be eligible for EU funds allocated to Italy as well as private investment. Sviluppo Italia is to be an important instrument to attract private investment to parts of Italy that have had not had a good record in drawing in private capital from other parts of Italy and abroad.

The creation of the new agency at the beginning of 1999 was met with great anticipation and broad support, but there was a widespread feeling that only time would tell what sort of instrument it would become. The appointment of Patrizio Bianchi as its first President addressed some of the fears about what sort of model of economic development might be pursued. There was a concern that Sviluppo Italia would be yet another central agency that would impose on the local level a model and instruments for economic development.[30] Bianchi, an economist, had gained a national reputation as a leading expert in industrial policy and economic development policies. As head of the economic and policy consulting firm, Nomisma, Bianchi had been one of the leading political economists that had challenged the dominant model for industrial and regional development policies pursued by Italian governments for much of the postwar period. Moreover, Bianchi has emphasised that economic development must be based on existing local resources and must be based on local initiatives.[31] The role of the state, and in particular agencies such as Sviluppo Italia, is to help attract private capital to those resources and initiatives.

The first few months of operation have concentrated primarily on the usual demands of dealing with reorganising existing agencies.[32] However, we can begin to identify what will be its main objectives and areas of activity. Nine sectors have been identified as 'motors' of development: biotechnology, agrofood, information technology, tourism, fashion, the environment, aerospace, female entrepreneurship and microsystem technologies.[33] The sectors combine some industries that have been conventionally associated with the Italian economy, such as fashion and agrofood, with new sectors such as information technologies and biotechnology. In the case of promoting female entrepreneurship, the objective is modernising Italian society and not simply ensuring economic development. Sviluppo Italia also has made much of the opportunities available for local authorities and businesses through territorial pacts, and of the services it can provide to prepare successful bids. An agreement with DPSC led to the creation of a working group within Sviluppo Italia, headed by the Confindustria Council official responsible for the Mezzogiorno, Antonio D'Amato. The aim of the group is to provide information and coordination across the forty-six territorial pacts that had been approved by the Treasury.[34]

In its first year of activity, Sviluppo Italia has not strayed too far from its stated objectives of being an agent to help attract investment; and it has stuck fairly closely to the policy areas listed earlier. The various agencies that are grouped into the two divisions have continued to be active in a range of activities. These include an emphasis on developing commercial skills through business innovation centres or on the financing of various projects such as the forty-two projects proposed by RIBS for the agrofood industry in June 1999. There has been an increase in the capital base from the original 35 billion lire to 2,442 billion, decided by a general assembly in September 1999. The Treasury consolidated its position holding 67 percent of shares, with the remaining third held by the Ministry of Agriculture.[35] Bianchi has continued to stress that the era of an increasingly global economy, and an integrated Europe, has meant that Italy, and especially the South, cannot afford to ignore the dynamics of competition. In this global marketplace, the initiative for regional development must come from the private sector in partnership with local authorities, with 'light' structures such as Sviluppo Italia acting as facilitators and mobilising existing resources.[36]

Conclusion

The debate in Italy on the single currency in the 1990s may be described as 'hopeful anxiety'. The hope is that the external pressure will lead to a modernisation of political, economic and social structures. The anxiety stems from the possible consequences if the modernisation does not take place. The risks include not creating political institutions that provide timely and accountable decisions in a rapidly changing environment; and not providing social and economic structures that can respond to the increasing demands of a global economy. Moreover, there is a concern that economic and social regulation based on market forces will lead to higher levels of social conflict. This tension between optimism and trepidation about the European future is most apparent when looking at the South. The risks are seen in regions that have lagged behind their Italian counterparts, falling further behind as Italian capital looks beyond the border for safer and higher rates of return.

Recent Italian governments have recognised that the economic future of not just the South but the entire country depends on new approaches to regional policy. The constraints of an integrated Europe have meant that many traditional instruments, such as direct subsidies or fiscal incentives, are much harder to use. The demands of an increasingly global economy are forcing government and its social partners to look more closely at the regulation of labour markets and ways in which to attract new investment. The creation of Sviluppo Italia has been consistent with the effort to find a way for a 'light' state to help promote regional development. It will be a valuable instrument in drawing in new capital and ensuring not only that the South is not left behind in an integrated Europe but also is an active part of it.

However, Sviluppo Italia and the 'light' state have few instruments to address some of the big issues facing the South. They can only help attract capital by mobilising local resources but they are limited in what they can do to further create and develop those local resources. Major problems, such as lack of infrastructure and the capacity of some local and regional administrations, have yet to be resolved. More importantly, the process of change is gradual but some of the immediate short-term consequences may be severe and cause social disruption. These will require a degree of political and institutional change that go well beyond the benefits that may be brought from an effective and efficient agency such as Sviluppo Italia.

Notes

1. See, Censis, *Inventare una Società Neocompetitiva*, Milan, 1994.
2. SVIMEZ, *Rapporto 1997 sull'economia del Mezzogiorno*, Bologna, 1997, Table A14.
3. For instance, Italy has a higher percentage of long-term unemployed than other EU members. However, this might be tempered by the fact that three-quarters are spouses or children; or by conditions in the supply of labour. One study found that if we exclude those who will work only in their place of residence or only in full-time work, and have carried out only one job search, then unemployment rates drop by as much as 5 percentage points. Sergio de Nardis and Giampaolo Galli, 'La disoccupazione italiana fra rigidità e cambiamenti globali', in *La disoccupazione italiana*, eds S. de Nardis and G. Galli, Bologna, 1997, 12–17.
4. For a useful summary of the various instruments, see, Censis, *La Situazione Sociale del Paese 1996, Note e Commenti*, no.10–11, October–November 1996, 82.
5. CNEL, *I Patti Territoriali: Dossier di Documentazione*, Roma, 1996, 73.
6. *Gazzetta Ufficiale*, 25 March 1997.

7. For a detailed examination of the patti, see the Ministero del Tesoro website: http://www.tesoro.it/ patti_territoriali.

8. By June 1999, 3,684 billion lire had been allocated for fifty-three 'pacts'; 2,958 billion of this total went to the South. Elysa Fazzino, *Il Sole – 24 Ore*, 22 June 1999.

9. Camera dei Deputati. XIII Legislatura. Servizi Studi. *I contratti d'area. Documentazione e ricerche*, June 1998, 3–5.

10. Camera dei Deputati. XIII Legislatura, *Atti Parlamentari. Quinta Commissione*, 26 February 1998, 281.

11. This was formalised with the *decreto legislativo* no. 430, 5 December 1997.

12. Ministero del Tesoro, del Bilancio e della Programmazione Economica. *Il dipartimento per le politiche di sviluppo e coesione sociale*, Roma, 1998, 12.

13. Barca resigned at the end of December 1999 and was substituted by Franco Passacantando, an ex-manager at the World Bank. No great policy changes are foreseen.

14. Camera dei deputati, *Atti parlamentari: Discussioni*, 13 January 1999, 41.

15. Alfredo Del Monte, 'La Nuova Politica per il Mezzogiorno: Dalla Centralizzazione allo Sviluppo Locale Incentivato', *Economia e political industriale* 25, no. 100, December 1998, 45–71.

16. 'Un sondaggio del Comitato Mezzogiorno Confindustria presso le Federazioni regionali,' *L'Imprenditore* 12 December 1997, 8–10.

17. Riccardo Varaldo, Nicola Bellini, et al., 'Le diversita' dell'industria italiana nella nuova integrazione economica internazionale,' *Economia e Politica Industriale* 25, no.100, December 1998, 33–4.

18. For a useful summary of the tensions and opportunities in the South, see the comments by the Under-Secretary to the Treasury responsible for regional development in the Prodi government, Isaia Sales, before the Budget Committee in: Camera dei Deputati, XIII Legislatura, *Atti Parlamentari. Quinta Commissione*, 26 February 1998, 281–86.

19. All the documents mentioned in this process produced by the Ministry of the Treasury may be found on its website: http://www.tesoro.it/index.

20. *Gazzetta Ufficiale*, 29 December 1998, 57.

21. The plan for the use of structural funds in 2000–06 projects that by the end of the period annual growth rates for GDP in the South will be double the expected national rate of 2.5–3.0 percent, and to rise from 0.4 percent to 6 percent. See Fabrizio Barca in: Camera dei Deputati, XIII Legislatura, *Atti Parlamentari – V Commissione Bilancio*, no.25, 25 May 1999, 22.

22. Legge 15, marzo 1997, no.59.

23. Camera dei Deputati, XIII Legislatura, *Atti Parlamentari – Resoconto Stenografico*, 7 October 1997, 14.

24. For instance, see Enzo Bianco, Mayor of Catania and President of the Associazione Nazionale Comuni d'Italia in: *Nuovo Mezzogiorno* XL, no.1, January 1998, 6.

25. Camera dei Deputati. XIII Legislatura, *Atti Parlamentari. V Commissione- Bilancio*, 15 April 1998, 356.

26. Ibid., 373.

27. A copy of the resolution may be found in: Camera dei Deputati. XIII Legislatura. Servizi Studi, *Dossier Provvedimento: Riordino enti e società di promozione e istituzione di 'Sviluppo Italia'*, November 1998, 5.

28. Article 2 of the *decreto legislativo* also allows local authorities or agencies to take a share, up to one-quarter of all shares, in any future offers of capital for Sviluppo Italia.

29. It is interesting to note that there is only one specific reference to the South in the *decreto legislativo*; but even in this instance, the South is included in a sentence in Article 1 that speaks of the 'Mezzogiorno and other depressed areas' eligible for EU funds.

30. Massimo D'Alema tried to allay these fears by saying that Sviluppo Italia would be 'una società snella' ('a slim company') and not a cumbersome, centralised bureaucracy more concerned with patronage than development. 'D'Alema: è il momento di investire sull'Italia,' *La Repubblica*, 4 December 1998.

31. On 11 February 2000, Bianchi resigned from the presidency, a decision that caused a minor crisis within Sviluppo Italia.

32. In fact, the number of agencies fused into Sviluppo Italia was seven. ENISUD did not enter into the agency as an agreement could not be reached with ENI on a fusion of the agency. See: 'Enisud non entrera' in Sviluppo Italia,' http://www.sviluppoitalia.it/search/notizia.asp?which = 57, 8 July 1999.

33. *http://www.sviluppoitalia.it/motoridellosviluppo*

34. 'Sviluppo Italia costituisce il gruppo di lavoro sui Patti territoriali,' http://www.sviluppo *italia.it/search/notizia.asp*, 27 July 1999.

35. 'Sviluppo Italia – Varato l'aumento di capitale,' http://www.sviluppoitalia.it/search/approfondimento, 17 September 1999.

36. 'Che cosa farà Sviluppo Italia,' *Nuovo Mezzogiorno* XLI, no.12 December 1998, 5–6.

Documentary Appendix

Compiled by Davide Martelli

As always, the documentary appendix is designed to give the economic, political and social background to the events presented by the rest of the book. The appendix is divided into three sections, each of which has a general theme.

In the first section (Tables A1 to A7), standard information on population, the workforce, social conflict, births and deaths, crime rates and key economic indicators is presented. Compared to past editions, the only major change is in the table illustrating the crime figures. This alteration was imposed by methodological changes in the calculation of crime figures on the part of Istat, the Italian statistical agency.

The second section is concerned with electoral results. Since a national referendum, elections to the European parliament, several parliamentary by-elections and local elections were all held in 1999, this section is necessarily very large. Tables B1 through B5 chart the provincial and municipal elections, B6 and B7 give a full picture of the European parliament results.Table B8 lists the by-elections and B9 gives the full result of the national referendum on electoral reform. In all the tables dealing with electoral results, the names of the different parties and civic lists has been left unchanged from the Italian edition. English-language readers should consult the list of acronyms at the beginning of this volume.

The last section is given over to institutional data. A full list of the ministers serving in the D'Alema government formed shortly before Christmas 1999 is included in Table C1.

Table A1 *Resident population by age-group and sex[a]*

	Age Group			
	0–14	15–64	65 and Over	Total Population
Men and Women				
1989	9,924	39,467	8,112	57,504
1990	9,620	39,620	8,335	57,576
1991	9,385	39,804	8,558	57,746
1992	8,846	39,164	8,950	56,960
1993	8,725	39,210	8,352	56,287
1994	8,620	39,247	9,401	57,268
1995	8,678	39,090	8,872	56,640
1996	8,517	39,171	9,645	57,333
1997	8,443	39,178	9,840	57,461
1998	8,355	39,068	10,190	57,613
Men				
1989	5,096	19,586	3,255	27,938
1990	4,941	19,678	3,349	27,968
1991	4,825	19,802	3,445	28,072
1992	4,547	19,472	3,635	27,654
1993	4,468	19,508	3,507	27,483
1994	4,415	19,528	3,848	27,791
1995	4,465	19,460	3,634	27,559
1996	4,364	19,498	3,956	27,818
1997	4,328	19,522	4,044	27,894
1998	4,292	19,534	4,141	27,968

[a] Numbers rounded to nearest thousand.

Source: Istat, *Annuario statistico italiano, Rome, 1990-1999.*

Table A2 Labour market distribution[a]

| | Workforce | | | | | | | |
| | Employed | | | Total | Unemployed | Jobless | | Total |
	Agriculture	Manufacturing	Services			First Job Seekers	Others	
			Men and Women					
1989	1,946	6,753	12,305	21,004	507	1,405	954	23,870
1990	1,863	6,940	12,593	21,396	483	1,357	912	24,148
1991	1,823	6,916	12,853	21,592	469	1,285	898	24,244
1992	1,749	6,851	12,859	21,459	551	1,370	878	24,258
1993[b]	1,669	6,725	12,073	20,427	846	1,031	483	22,787
1994	1,574	6,587	11,959	20,119	983	1,048	529	22,679
1995	1,490	6,494	12,025	20,009	1,005	1,150	570	22,734
1996	1,402	6,475	12,211	20,088	1,011	1,204	548	22,851
1997	1,370	6,449	12,268	20,087	1,031	1,225	548	22,891
1998	1,201	6,730	12,504	20,435	996	1,151	597	23,179
			Men					
1989	1,261	5,103	7,487	13,851	286	676	257	15,070
1990	1,197	5,233	7,586	14,015	264	667	246	15,192
1991	1,156	5,259	7,678	14,102	256	645	241	15,244
1992	1,105	5,214	7,626	13,945	297	692	238	15,172
1993[a]	1,045	5,145	7,141	13,246	493	533	90	14,363

continued overleaf

Table A2 *continued*

1994	999	5,022	7,036	13,057	593	552	105	14,307
1995	956	4,934	7,043	12,933	597	599	115	14,244
1996	915	4,912	7,073	12,900	594	630	112	14,236
1997	903	4,874	7,080	12,857	607	633	108	14,205
1998	810	5,106	7,174	13,090	588	607	118	14,403

[a] Numbers rounded to nearest thousand

[b] Since 1993, data have been revised to take into account the weighting mechanism introduced by the 1991 Census.

Source: Istat, *Compendio statistico italiano 1999*, Rome, 1999. The 1997 numbers are derived from Istat, *Forze di lavoro*, Rome, 1998.

Table A3 *Work disputes*

	Disputes	Participants[a]	Working Hours Lost
	Workplace disputes		
1989	1,295	2,108	21,001
1990	1,094	1,634	36,269
1991	784	750	11,573
1992	895	621	5,605
1993	1,047	848	8,796
1994	858	745	7,651
1995	545	445	6,365
1996	904	1,689	13,510
1997	923	737	8,299
1998	1,097	386	3,807
	Political Disputes[b]		
1989	2	2,344	10,052
1990	–	–	–
1991	7	2,202	9,322
1992	8	2,557	13,905
1993	7	3,536	15,084
1994	3	1,868	15,967
1995	–	–	–
1996	–	–	–
1997	3	19	149
1998	6	49	256

[a] Numbers in thousands.
[b] Conflicts connected with matters of political economy or social reform, national and international events.

Source: Istat, *Compendio statistico italiano 1999*, Rome, 1999. The information for 1997 is taken from Istat, *Bollettino mensile di statistica*, Rome, March 1998.

Table A4 *Births and Marriages*

	Births		Marriages			
	Total Births	% difference on previous year	Total Marriages	% difference on previous year	Religious Marriages	% difference on previous year
1989	560,688	−1.58	321,272	0.93	267,617	0.41
1990	569,255	1.53	319,711	−0.48	266,084	−0.57
1991	562,787	−1.14	312,061	−2.39	257,555	−3.20
1992	575,216	2.21	312,348	0.09	255,355	−0.85
1993	549,484	−4.47	302,230	−3.24	248,111	−2.84
1994	533,050	−2.99	285,112	−5.66	230,573	−7.07
1995	521,345	−5.12	283,025	−0.73	227,209	−1.46
1996	525,640	0.82	272,049	−3.88	216,671	−4.64
1997	528,901	0.62	273,111	0.39	216,265	−0.19
1998	515,439	−2.55	276,570	1.27	217,492	0.57

Source: Istat, *Annuario statistico italiano*, Rome, 1990–1999.

Table A5 *Serious crimes under judicial investigation*

Nature of Crime	Reported Crimes					
	Total			Unsolved		
	1996	1997	1998	1996	1997	1998
Mass murder	9	4	6	1	1	4
Murder	943	863	876	526	429	416
Infanticide	10	10	13	1	1	3
Homicide	48	51	29	11	11	1
Attempted murder	1,688	1,708	1,653	558	519	468
Manslaughter	1,688	1,517	1,578	183	162	216
Serious bodily harm	23,716	25,184	26,732	4,827	5,122	5,456
Sexual assault	1,151	1,582	1,846	209	284	340
Theft and burglary	1,393,974	1,401,471	1,478,221	1,313,590	1,325,173	1,399,646
Robbery	31,244	32,896	37,782	25,397	26,642	30,566
Extortion	3,842	3,352	3,534	879	841	957
Kidnapping	962	1,007	963	333	347	348
Conspiracy to commit crimes	1,017	834	761	–	–	–
Mafia membership	182	144	187	–	–	–
Arson	8,138	8,661	9,552	7,324	7,792	8,482
Bomb and dynamite attacks	1,147	1,159	1,286	1,079	1,087	1,175
Fraud	53,043	62,952	56,952	29,714	39,334	34,436
Smuggling	49,565	55,855	54,903	1,561	1,485	1,409
Production and sale of drugs	38,954	41,420	43,014	1,379	1,691	1,772
Prostitution-related crimes	3,566	2,714	2,893	291	183	301
Other crimes	808,104	797,370	702,967	425,699	424,772	308,197
Total	2,422,991	2,440,754	2,425,748	1,813,562	1,835,876	1,794,193

Source: Istat, *Annuario statistico italiano*, Rome, 1999.

Table A6 Gross domestic product (at market prices) and general index of consumer prices

| | Gross Domestic Product | | | Index of prices (1995 = 100) |
	Value at current prices (in billions of lire)	% difference on previous year	Value in 1995 prices (in billions of lire)	% difference on previous year	% difference on previous year
1989	1,191,961	9.4	1,951,455	3.8	6.6
1990	1,310,659	10.0	2,015,903	3.3	6.1
1991	1,427,571	8.9	2,043,943	1.4	6.4
1992	1,502,493	5.3	2,073,151	1.4	5.3
1993	1,550,296	3.2	2,020,894	-2.5	4.3
1994	1,638,666	5.7	2,091,429	3.5	3.9
1995	1,771,018	8.1	2,179,291	4.2	5.4
1996	1,873,494	5.8	2,189,717	0.5	3.9
1997	1,974,618	5.4	2,255,219	3.0	2.0
1998	2,057,731	4.2	2,305,755	2.2	2.0

Source: Banca d'Italia, Relazione annuale, Rome, 1999.

Table A7 *Size of the national debt and the annual deficit*

	National Debt			Budget Deficit		
	Total value (in billions of Lire)	% difference on previous year	% of GDP	Total value (in billions of Lire)	% difference on previous year	% of GDP
1989	1,141,836	12.9	95.8	119,466	-4.4	10.4
1990	1,284,895	12.5	98.0	122,471	2.5	11.4
1991	1,449,980	12.8	101.6	118,620	-3.1	10.6
1992	1,634,371	12.7	108.8	107,189	-9.6	10.2
1993	1,815,840	11.1	117.1	133,684	24.7	9.9
1994	1,984,067	9.3	121.1	126,199	-5.6	9.0
1995	2,129,307	7.3	120.1	146,592	16.2	7.0
1996	2,267,368	6.5	121.1	119,896	-18.2	6.4
1997	2,316,016	2.1	118.7	14,714	-88.7	0.8
1998	2,361,910	1.9	114.8	81,469	553.7	4.0

a Budget of Authorisation used as base.

Source: Banca d'Italia, *Relazione annuale*, Rome, 1999.

Table B1a *Turnout in the 13 June 1999 municipal elections*

	Electors	Voters	Valid votes	Invalid votes	Votes for mayor alone	Votes for party list	Blank ballots	% abstention	% invalid votes	% votes for mayor alone (of valid votes)	% for lists (of valid votes)
Vercelli	41,292	33,128	30,475	2,653	3,797	26,678	1,129	19.8	8.0	12.5	87.5
Verbano-Cusio-Ossola	27,005	19,996	18,860	1,136	2,292	16,568	482	26.0	5.7	12.2	87.8
Bergamo	99,743	75,813	71,298	4,515	8,682	62,616	2,121	24.0	6.0	12.2	87.8
Cremona	62,395	49,521	46,393	3,128	7,197	39,196	1,505	20.6	6.3	15.5	84.5
Padova	181,623	136,380	128,734	14,291	23,147	105,587	3,674	24.9	10.5	18.0	82.0
Imperia	35,318	27,514	26,231	1,025	1,820	24,411	549	22.1	3.7	6.9	93.1
Bologna	337,064	265,816	251,780	14,295	26,449	225,331	6,702	21.1	5.4	10.5	89.5
Ferrara	119,566	97,908	91,892	5,936	10,016	81,876	2,992	18.1	6.1	10.9	89.1
Cesena	77,926	62,852	58,715	4,138	2,587	56,128	2,125	19.3	6.6	4.4	95.6
Forlì	94,128	74,183	70,487	3,696	3,246	67,241	1,728	21.2	5.0	4.6	95.4
Modena	148,304	117,354	111,062	6,292	6,575	104,487	3,848	20.9	5.4	5.9	94.1
Reggio Emilia	117,935	93,316	88,678	4,638	6,283	82,395	2,631	20.9	5.0	7.1	92.9
Rimini	111,728	85,639	80,952	4,687	4,716	76,236	2,524	23.4	5.5	5.8	94.2
Arezzo	77,282	56,738	53,203	2,739	4,581	48,622	1,905	26.6	4.8	8.6	91.4
Firenze	323,968	223,494	210,607	12,887	16,461	194,146	6,304	31.0	5.8	7.8	92.2
Livorno	141,705	99,445	92,622	6,881	5,382	87,240	2,992	29.8	6.9	5.8	94.2
Prato	141,461	102,665	95,106	7,559	7,046	88,060	3,876	27.4	7.4	7.4	92.6
Perugia	127,381	99,288	92,173	6,507	4,985	87,188	3,274	22.1	6.6	5.4	94.6
Terni	93,632	72,195	68,036	4,161	8,292	59,744	1,787	22.9	5.8	12.2	87.8
Ascoli Piceno	45,475	35,302	33,283	2,019	2,919	30,364	864	22.4	5.7	8.8	91.2

Pesaro	77,494	59,939	55,884	4,055	4,803	51,081	1,898	22.7	6.8	8.6	91.4
Viterbo	50,497	41,932	39,333	2,575	1,979	37,354	929	17.0	6.1	5.0	95.0
Teramo	47,206	37,869	36,086	1,785	1,623	34,463	662	19.8	4.7	4.5	95.5
Campobasso	44,234	33,702	31,783	1,919	2,462	29,321	603	23.8	5.7	7.7	92.3
Avellino	47,353	37,596	34,546	3,050	1,231	33,315	1,090	20.6	8.1	3.6	96.4
Bari	288,700	207,141	189,143	17,998	11,690	177,453	6,617	28.3	8.7	6.2	93.8
Foggia	127,448	96,710	89,641	7,796	5,914	83,727	3,991	24.1	8.1	6.6	93.4
Potenza	57,048	46,321	43,678	2,643	2,697	40,981	793	18.8	5.7	6.2	93.8

Source: Istituto Cattaneo re-eleboration of Ministry of the Interior figures.

Table B1b *Turnout in the run-off elections of 27 June 1999*

	votes	Valid votes	Invalid votes	Blank ballots	Abstentionism rate	% supplementary abstentionism	% Invalid second-round votes
Vercelli	26,460	25,392	1,068	423	35.9	16.1	4.0
Bergamo	53,828	51,459	2,369	1,049	46.0	22.0	4.4
Padova	116,231	112,853	3,378	1,342	36.0	11.1	2.9
Bologna	228,128	223,852	4,276	1,603	32.3	11.2	1.9
Rimini	62,017	60,951	1,066	431	44.5	21.2	1.7
Arezzo	45,222	44,283	939	348	41.5	14.9	2.1
Avellino	24,966	23,986	980	357	47.3	26.7	3.9
Potenza	38,660	37,534	1,126	295	32.2	13.4	2.9

Source: Istituto Cattaneo re-eleboration of Ministry of the Interior figures.

Table B2 *Municipal Elections of 13 June 1999 in provincial capitals. Percentage votes of party lists.*

	No. candidates for mayor	No. Lists	Party lists	Civic Lists	DS	PDCI	PRC	PPI	Verdi	I Democratici	RI	Socialists	Lega	FI	AN	CCD	UDEUR	Other Lists	Civic Lists
Vercelli	6	18	11	7	12.2	4.7	2.8	3.0	4.7	3.0	-	2.6	7.1	33.8	5.9	1.6	-	1.8	15.7
Verbano-Cusio-Ossola	9	15	11	4	19.7	7.0	3.5	6.8	2.6	-	-	4.9	3.6	21.3	14.1	1.9	-	5.0	9.6
Bergamo	7	20	13	7	14.6	1.5	3.8	6.7	2.5	5.8	-	1.7	16.0	23.9	10.2	2.6	-	2.9	4.8
Cremona	10	16	12	4	19.9	2.9	5.8	9.2	1.9	4.2	-	-	8.1	21.0	8.0	2.2	-	14.6	2.2
Padova	13	25	12	13	16.4	8.2	2.3	5.7	2.5	7.2	-	0.8	4.4	19.3	10.2	1.6	-	7.7	12.8
Imperia	4	12	11	1	18.4	1.9	2.6	7.1	-	3.2	2.5	1.5	3.5	40.9	6.3	9.0	-	-	3.1
Bologna	8	16	12	4	25.3	3.9	5.0	1.7	2.5	11.5	-	2.5	1.8	11.5	11.0	-	-	4.3	22.4
Ferrara	6	15	12	3	37.9	2.7	4.1	4.1	2.3	2.9	-	3.4	1.8	19.2	11.7	1.2	-	0.3	8.4
Cesena	9	13	11	2	34.4	2.6	5.0	7.4	4.1	-	-	3.3	1.6	17.8	6.4	-	-	9.3	8.1
Forlì	9	14	11	3	36.2	2.2	4.5	5.8	3.8	3.6	-	1.4	1.9	19.3	10.7	-	-	6.6	4.0
Modena	7	15	11	4	40.0	1.6	4.9	3.4	-	6.5	-	1.4	3.0	17.0	9.2	2.7	-	3.8	6.5
Reggio Emilia	6	12	11	1	39.1	2.7	4.3	6.7	2.4	8.1	-	3.4	4.1	13.7	11.9	3.1	-	-	0.5
Rimini	7	16	14	2	28.4	2.0	4.7	8.7	2.2	6.9	-	2.0	1.9	23.8	14.3	-	0.4	12.0	3.0
Arezzo	4	12	10	2	28.3	4.3	6.6	5.9	2.2	3.0	-	5.0	-	19.3	19.6	-	-	1.3	4.5
Firenze	12	24	20	4	31.5	5.8	5.6	3.7	2.2	4.5	1.8	3.2	0.6	15.4	13.0	2.7	-	6.6	4.6
Livorno	4	11	10	1	38.6	2.8	10.9	7.7	2.6	3.7	-	2.3	-	13.5	12.1	-	-	-	4.4
Prato	8	15	14	1	37.8	2.7	4.7	5.0	1.5	5.9	-	1.9	1.2	17.1	14.2	2.0	-	1.1	3.9
Perugia	8	15	14	1	32.7	4.9	6.2	6.1	1.7	4.3	-	7.0	0.5	13.5	16.1	2.6	-	2.1	2.3
Terni	6	18	15	3	30.5	5.1	4.2	6.6	0.9	2.6	1.6	4.2	0.9	11.1	11.3	4.2	-	4.5	14.0

Ascoli Piceno	6	15	13	2	13.7	3.5	2.2	6.6	1.2	7.7	1.1	2.0	-	17.1	23.1	*11.8*	-	2.8	7.2
Pesaro	6	13	12	1	36.2	3.2	4.0	5.4	4.1	5.9	2.6	4.2	-	19.0	9.4	2.5	-	1.9	1.6
Viterbo	9	17	17	-	11.4	1.2	3.8	13.7	1.0	3.5	**3.5**	3.4	-	21.3	24.8	4.6	2.6	6.2	-
Teramo	5	15	11	4	16.2	1.4	2.2	20.0	-	7.4	-	1.5	-	14.4	8.2	8.5	-	3.2	17.0
Campobasso	3	14	14	-	23.7	3.1	4.1	20.8	1.8	-	-	2.8	-	11.1	7.4	8.3	-	11.0	-
Avellino	9	16	14	2	13.6	1.0	1.9	26.4	-	3.2	1.5	3.4	-	10.2	9.8	5.8	7.5	4.3	11.4
Bari	9	21	18	3	14.4	1.2	2.4	5.4	1.9	3.6	2.4	8.0	-	17.0	15.7	7.8	2.3	15.2	2.7
Foggia	7	30	25	5	9.1	1.0	1.2	8.3	0.7	2.1	1.9	6.6	-	17.8	22.7	6.3	5.9	12.2	3.7
Potenza	5	14	13	1	13.5	-	2.2	17.7	2.8	7.5	6.6	5.1	-	12.7	7.2	3.3	18.1	1.8	1.5
12 Dicembre																			
Caltanissetta	4	15	12	3	12.5	2.4	3.3	7.7	-	2.7	3.5	4.5	-	16.7	10.7	6.4	10.7	7.8	11.1
Siracusa	8	18	13	5	7.0	1.1	1.0	14.3	-	6.0	3.1	3.7	-	19.1	10.3	2.2	**7.1**	9.5	15.6

Bold type indicates that the party presented itself with other minor parties; italics that the party presented itself with other national parties.

Source: Istituto Cattaneo re-eleboration of Ministry of the Interior figures.

Table B3 *Elections for the municipal councils of provincial capitals 13 June and Run-off results 27 June 1999*

Capital	Mayoral candidate[a]	First Round Votes (%)	Run-off Votes (%)	First Round Votes	Run-off Votes	Parties and civic lists expressing support[b]	Votes for supporting lists	First Round votes for supporting lists (%)	Votes for candidate alone
Vercelli	Piccioni, Lorenzo	40.0	47.7	12,187	12,116	AN, Lista civica, Verdi-Verdi, Pensionati Europa, FI, Piemonte Naz. Europa, (CCD, LN)	11,441	93.9	746
	Bagnasco, Gabriele	23.9	52.3	7,287	13,276	Vercelli 2003, PRC, Verdi, Democrats	5,121	70.3	2,166
	Valeri, Gilberto	23.2		7,062		SDI, PDCI, DS, Per Vercelli, PPI	6,402	90.7	660
	Borasio, Francesco Giuseppe Carlo	6.7		2,030		LN	1,897	93.4	133
	Robutti, Carlo Lorenzo	4.8		1,465		Unione civica	1,398	95.4	67
	Debianchi, Renzo	1.4		444		CCD	419	94.4	25
	Total	100.0	100.0	30,475	25,392		26,678	87.5	3,797
Verbania	**Reschigna, Aldo**	42.2		7,953		PPI, DS, SDI, Non solo centro, PDCI	6,463	81.3	1,490
	Cattaneo, Valerio	35.9		6,777		FI, AN, CCD	6,196	91.4	581
	Parachini, Marco	7.8		1,473		Cittadini Verbania	1,382	93.8	91
	De Magistris, Roberto	3.3		623		LN	588	94.4	35
	Tigano, Giorgio	3.2		599		MS-FT	552	92.2	47
	Di Gregorio, Vladimiro	3.1		587		PRC	581	99.0	6
	Caruso, Paolo	2.4		451		Verdi	424	94.0	27

District	Candidate	%		Votes		List		%	
	Turconi, Massimo	1.2		232		Lista autonomista	219	94.4	13
	Garzoli, Gabriele Gian Maria	0.9		165		Pensionati e giovani	163	98.8	2
	Total	100.0		18,860			16,568	87.8	2,292
Bergamo	**Veneziani, Cesare**	40.3	57.8	28,737	29,731	Bergamo per Bergamo, CCD-P.Segni, Liberal Sgarbi-altri, AN, DC, FI	26,015	90.5	2,722
	Vicentini, Guido	31.0	42.2	22,073	21,728	I Democratici, PPI , DS, PDCI, SDI, (*Verdi, Lista aperta*)	18,998	86.1	3,075
	Bordogna, Raffaella	18.4		13,128		LN, Catt. Padani-altri, Bergamo imprenditori, Bergamo sicura	11,021	84.0	2,107
	Tazzioli, Massimo	4.0		2,849		Verdi, Lista aperta	2,321	81.5	528
	Trussardi, Roberto	3.6		2,552		PRC	2,389	93.6	163
	Vivona, Vittorio Sirluigi	1.4		1,000		Bergamo liberale	942	94.2	58
	Benzoni, Giancarlo	1.3		959		MS-FT	930	97.0	29
	Total	100.0		71,298	51,459		62,616	87.8	8,682
Cremona	**Bodini, Paolo**	50.0		23,216		PDCI, I Democratici, PPI, Verdi, DS, Catt. dem. soc.	17,761	76.5	5,455
	Bonetti, Gian Paolo	27.0		12,551		FI, AN	11,353	90.5	1,198
	De Petris, Petrisso	7.1		3,273		LN	3,159	96.5	114
	Zampini in Rizzi, Cinzia Anna Teresa	5.0		2,311		PRC	2,268	98.1	43
	Melega, Agostino	2.8		1,304		Liberal Sgarbi-altri	1,170	89.7	134
	Colace, Gianfranco Mario	2.0		926		CCD	875	94.5	51
	Boldrini, Carmela	2.0		945		Part. pens.	914	96.7	31

continued

Table B3 *continued*

Capital	Mayoral candidate[a]	First Round Votes (%)	Run-off Votes (%)	First Round Votes	Run-off Votes	Parties and civic lists expressing support[b]	Votes for supporting lists	First Round votes for supporting lists (%)	Votes for candidate alone
	Foderaro, Giuseppe	2.0		930		Centro	836	89.9	94
	Bosio, Giuseppe	1.5		679		Vivere Cremona	620	91.3	59
	Di Pascale, Stanislao	0.6		258		Alternativa	240	93.0	18
	Total	100.0		46,393			39,196	84.5	7,197
Padova	**Mistrello in Destro, Giustina**	42.2	50.5	54,340	57,001	CCD, FI, Insieme per Padova, AN, Lista autonomista, (*Veneto nord-est, Buongoverno Padova, Socialista, Crist. dem., SDI, Comitati federati*)	45,366	83.5	8,974
	Zanonato, Flavio	41.6	49.5	53,552	55,852	Fed. Verdi-altri, DS, PDCI, I Democratici, PPI , (*PRC*)	42,203	78.8	11,349
	Gasperini, Luciano	4.9		6,259		18006 Padova, LN	5,056	80.8	1,203
	Scanagatta, Silvio	2.8		3,606		Veneto nord-est, Socialista, Crist. Dem., Comitati federati	2,997	83.1	609
	Ottolini, Cesare	2.1		2,725		PRC	2,444	89.7	281
	Casarin, Luca	1.4		1,807		Non solo Verdi	1,576	87.2	231
	Ronchitelli, Riccardo	1.2		1,490		SDI	1,406	94.4	84
	Mocavero, Paolo	1.1		1,451		Destra veneta	1,288	88.8	163
	Casertano, Nevio	1.0		1,303		Lg. veneta Repubblica	1,185	90.9	118
	Levante, Mario	0.6		724		Veneto libero	667	92.1	57

Province	Candidate	Lists	%	Votes	Total	Votes	%	Diff
	Celin, Sergio	Lista per Padova	0.6	713		677	95.0	36
	Berlese, Alessandro	Buongoverno Padova	0.4	573		514	89.7	59
	Pero, Alberto Antonio	Part. umanista	0.1	191		208	108.9	–17
	Total		100.0	128,734	112,853	105,587	82.0	23,147
Imperia	**Sappa, Luigi**	FI, CCD, RI-Dini, Cen-sin (Ls. Civiche), AN	59.6	15,646		15,081	96.4	565
	Berio, Davide	SDI, PDCI, PPI, F. Verdi-I Democratici, DS	34.1	8,936		7,848	87.8	1,088
	Guasco, Roberto	LN	3.7	963		855	88.8	108
	Grenci, Salvatore	PRC	2.6	686		627	91.4	59
	Total		100.0	26,231		24,411	93.1	1,820
Bologna	Bartolini, Silvia	I Democratici, Verdi, SDI, per Bologna, PPI, PDCI	46.6	117,371	110,389	104,749	89.2	12,622
	Guazzaloca, Giorgio	Lista civica, Governare Bologna, FI, AN	41.5	104,571	113,463	92,341	88.3	12,230
	Zamboni, Maurizio	PRC	4.6	11,461		11,194	97.7	267
	Ruocco, Anselmo	Destra	2.7	6,909		6,363	92.1	546
	Poli, Mauro	Lista civica	1.8	4,544		4,008	88.2	536
	Pasquini, Luigi	LN	1.7	4,224		4,100	97.1	124
	Dalle, Nogare Roberto	Socialisti Liberali	0.9	2,297		2,289	99.7	8
	Dinacci, Aldo	Mps-Genitori sempre	0.2	403		287	71.2	116
	Total		100.0	251,780	223,852	225,331	89.5	26,449
Ferrara	**Sateriale, Gaetano**	PRC, PRI, DS, SDI, Verdi, I Democratici, PPI, PDCI	54.8	50,333		47,250	93.9	3,083
	Sgarbi, Vittorio	FI, Lista per Ferrara	26.2	24,041		19,503	81.1	4,538

continued

Table B3 *continued*

Capital	Mayoral candidate[a]	First Round Votes (%)	Run-off Votes (%)	First Round Votes	Run-off Votes	Parties and civic lists expressing support[b]	Votes for supporting lists	First Round votes for supporting lists (%)	Votes for candidate alone
	Balboni, Alberto	13.6		12,469		AN, CCD,	10,589	84.9	1,880
	Fortini, Antonio	2.1		1,925		Lista civica	1,711	88.9	214
	Fantoni, Gianluca	1.7		1,602		Rinascita estense	1,349	84.2	253
	Teodori, Luca	1.6		1,522		LN	1,474	96.8	48
	Total	100.0		91,892			81,876	89.1	10,016
Cesena	**Conti, Giordano**	55.1		32,360		PPI , PRI, DS, PDCI, SDI	30,665	94.8	1,695
	Bianconi, Laura	17.6		10,346		FI-CCD	10,018	96.8	328
	Venturi, Carlo	6.3		3,703		AN	3,616	97.7	87
	Ugolini, Denis	5.0		2,914		Cen-sin. (Ls. civiche)	2,763	94.8	151
	Donini, Minica	4.9		2,866		PRC	2,790	97.3	76
	Fabbri, Davide	4.1		2,389		Verdi	2,297	96.1	92
	Magnani, Alberto	3.2		1,888		Lista civica	1,812	96.0	76
	Fantini, Maurizio	2.3		1,337		Centro	1,280	95.7	57
	Martino, Lorenzo	1.5		912		LN	887	97.3	25
	Total	100.0		58,715			56,128	95.6	2,587
Forlì	**Rusticali, Franco**	56.7		39,927		PPI , DS, PRI, I Democratici, SDI, PDCI	37,560	94.1	2,367
	Gagliardi, Stefano	18.9		13,317		FI-CCD	12,958	97.3	359

Place		%	Votes	Party	Votes	%	
	Fratesi, Luigi	10.4	7,324	AN	7,181	98.0	143
	Basini, Brian	4.4	3,088	PRC	3,014	97.6	74
	Morelli in Mordenti, Sandra	3.8	2,663	Verdi	2,544	95.5	119
	Pini, Gianluca	1.9	1,355	LN	1,306	96.4	49
	Grilanda, Ettore	1.4	1,014	Lista civica	931	91.8	83
	Gugnoni, Pier Paolo	1.3	941	L'intesa	921	97.9	20
	Cortini, Floriano	1.2	858	Unione Romagna	826	96.3	32
	Total	100.0	70,487		67,241	95.4	3,246
Modena	**Barbolini, Giuliano**	53.2	59,140	DS, PPI, PDCI, I Democratici, Verdi Lib. e solidali, SDI	56,826	96.1	2,314
	Ricci, Gianni	35.1	39,002	CCD, FI, AN, Modena a colori	35,387	90.7	3,615
	Frieri, Francesco Raphael	4.7	5,272	PRC	5,121	97.1	151
	Berti, Carlo	2.9	3,182	LN	3,092	97.2	90
	Galli, Gaetano	2.4	2,616	Verdi per Modena	2,372	90.7	244
	Greco, Teodosio	1.4	1,513	Lista civica	1,388	91.7	125
	Gandolfi, Michele	0.3	337	S.o.s. Italia	301	89.3	36
	Total	100.0	111,062		104,487	94.1	6,575
Reggio Emilia	**Spaggiari, Antonella**	62.3	55,237	PDCI, SDI, PPI, I Democratici, DS, Verdi	51,448	93.1	3,789
	Eboli, Marco	26.2	23,231	AN, FI	21,115	90.9	2,116
	Colzi in Tosi, Carla Maria	4.1	3,638	PRC	3,512	96.5	126
	Fossa, Gabriele	4.0	3,527	LN	3,411	96.7	116
	Zobbi, Tarcisio Costante	2.9	2,617	CCD-CDU	2,534	96.8	83
	Crotti in Gasparini, Emanuela	0.5	428	Lista civica	375	87.6	53
	Total	100.0	88,678		82,395	92.9	6,283

continued

Table B3 *continued*

Capital	Mayoral candidate[a]	First Round Votes (%)	Run-off Votes (%)	First Round Votes	Run-off Votes	Parties and civic lists expressing support[b]	Votes for supporting lists	First Round votes for supporting lists (%)	Votes for candidate alone
Rimini	**Ravaioli, Alberto**	49.3	51.4	39,885	31,304	DS, SDI, Crist. soc., PPI-RI-PRI-CDU, PDCI, I Democratici, Verdi	37,820	94.8	2,065
	Gentilini, Mario	41.0	48.6	33,162	29,647	FI, Lista ecologica, Socialista, AN	30,737	92.7	2,425
	Mangianti, Cesare	4.5		3,668		PRC	3,589	97.8	79
	Sensoli, Fausto	1.8		1,473		LN	1,437	97.6	36
	Stambazzi, Giancarlo	1.7		1,356		Noi per Rimini	1,302	96.0	54
	Balducci in Vandelli, Patrizia	1.3		1,060		Lista civica	1,017	95.9	43
	Di Spirito, Mario	0.4		348		U.D.Eur	334	96.0	14
	Total	100.0	100.0	80,952	60,951		76,236	94.2	4,716
Arezzo	Nepi, Paolo	46.5	48.6	24,726	21,507	DS, I Democratici, PPI-CDU-RI, PDCI, SDI, Verdi	23,673	95.7	1,053
	Lucherini, Luigi	43.9	51.4	23,390	22,776	Millenium, AN, FI-CCD, Liberal Sgarbi	20,259	86.6	3,131
	Nicotra, Alfio	6.5		3,455		PRC	3,212	93.0	243
	Aquilanti, Giuliana	3.1		1,632		Lista civica	1,478	90.6	154
	Total	100.0	100.0	53,203	44,283		48,622	91.4	4,581
Firenze	**Domenici, Leonardo**	51.7		108,839		DS, Verdi, PDCI, I Democratici, SDI, PPI , RI-altri	100,631	92.5	8,208

	Name	%	Votes	List	Votes	%	Votes
	Scaramuzzi, Franco	35.6	74,955	FI, Azione per FIrenze, AN, Lista pens., CCD, Liberal Sgarbi-altri	68,101	90.9	6,854
	Falqui, Enrico	5.4	11,279	PRC	10,936	97.0	343
	Pepi, Giangualberto	1.5	3,051	MS-FT	2,998	98.3	53
	Pallanti, Giovanni	1.3	2,830	Insieme per FIrenze, PRI-Lib-Eldr.	2,348	83.0	482
	Ferretti, Stefania	0.8	1,730	Lista indipendente	1,577	91.2	153
	Barlozzetti, Ugo	0.8	1,712	Lista civica	1,596	93.2	116
	Mazzerelli, Alessandro	0.7	1,385	Mov. aut. toscano	1,319	95.2	66
	Sottani, Giuliano	0.7	1,552	Socialista	1,500	96.6	52
	Farfoglia, Daniele	0.6	1,266	Partito DC	1,239	97.9	27
	Gnaga, Simone Enrico	0.5	1,130	LN	1,102	97.5	28
	Vecchi, Paolo	0.4	878	Part. umanista	799	91.0	79
	Total	100.0	210,607		194,146	92.2	16,461
Livorno	**Lamberti, Gianfranco**	58.8	54,422	SDI, Lib-PRI-RI, PDCI, I Democratici, Verdi, DS, PPI	51,584	94.8	2,838
	Sgherri, Maria Rosa	25.8	23,865	AN, FI-CCD	22,278	93.4	1,587
	Trotta, Alessandro	10.7	9,946	PRC	9,505	95.6	441
	Bianchi, Massimo	4.7	4,389	Livorno insieme	3,873	88.2	516
	Total	100.0	92,622		87,240	94.2	5,382
Prato	**Mattei, Fabrizio**	54.6	51,900	Verdi, PDCI, SDI, DS, I Democratici, PPI	48,186	92.8	3,714
	Pagnini, Andrea	33.5	31,850	AN, CCD-P. Segni, FI	29,310	92.0	2,540
	Neri, Gino	4.5	4,311	PRC	4,137	96.0	174
	Cecchi, Lamberto	4.1	3,871	Lista civica	3,462	89.4	409
	Lamberti, Marco	1.1	1,109	LN	1,033	93.1	76
	Mazzeo, Francesco	1.0	963	U.D.Eur	918	95.3	45

continued

Table B3 *continued*

Capital	Mayoral candidate[a]	First Round Votes (%)	Run-off Votes (%)	First Round Votes	Run-off Votes	Parties and civic lists expressing support[b]	Votes for supporting lists	First Round votes for supporting lists (%)	Votes for candidate alone
	Cupelli in Serroni, Teonilde	0.9		843		Liberal Sgarbi-altri	797	94.5	46
	Berti, Antonio	0.3		259		Part. umanista	217	83.8	42
	Total	100.0		95,106			88,060	92.6	7,046
Perugia	**Locchi, Renato**	58.4		54,249		PDCI, DS, PRC, SDI, Verdi, PPI	51,065	94.1	3,184
	Serra, Mario	32.6		30,267		CCD-Civica, FI, AN	28,050	92.7	2,217
	Ventura, Floriano	4.1		3,827		I Democratici	3,723	97.3	104
	Zuccaccia, Giancarlo	2.2		2,050		Risveglio	2,015	98.3	35
	Bertolini, Ettore	1.3		1,196		MS-FT	1,150	96.2	46
	Pitti, Claudio	0.6		578		Fronte nazionale	560	96.9	18
	Miroballo, Francesco	0.5		437		LN	428	97.9	9
	Di Mizio, Dora	0.3		224		Part. umanista	197	87.9	27
	Total	100.0		92,828			87,188	93.9	5,640
Terni	**Rafiaelli, Paolo**	53.9		36,675		PDCI, DS, RI-Dini, PRC, SDI, PPI, PRI, I Democratici	32,974	89.9	3,701
	Melasecche, Germini Enrico	42.5		28,903		CCD, AN-P. Segni, Socialista, FI, Terni insieme, Giovani	24,528	84.9	4,375
	Busi, Carlo	1.2		789		MS-FT	726	92.0	63
	Santaniello, Delfino	1.1		782		Liberal Sgarbi-altri	804	102.8	-22

Saco, Dulanto Rosalia	1.0	707	Verdi	553	78.2	154
Virili, Luigino	0.3	180	Dem. dir. Terni	159	88.3	21
Total	100.0	68,036		59,744	87.8	8,292
Ascoli Piceno						
Celani, Piero	52.7	17,550	FI, AN, CCD-CDU	15,796	90.0	1,754
Allevi, Roberto	29.1	9,693	SDI, DS, I Democratici, PDCI, Crist. soc.	8,691	89.7	1,002
Procaccini, Domenico	7.4	2,441	PPI , RI-Dini	2,335	95.7	106
Meloni, Sestilio	5.7	1,891	Verdi, PRC, Patto per Ascoli	1,920	101.5	-29
Aliberti, Davide Massimo	4.1	1,365	Crescita	1,310	96.0	55
Olimpi, Laura Maria	1.0	343	La via radicale	312	91.0	31
Total	100.0	33,283		30,364	91.2	2,919
Pesaro						
Giovanelli, Oriano	55.0	30,749	PRC, PDCI, DS, PPI , SDI, RI-Dini	28,423	92.4	2,326
Pantanelli, Roberto	18.0	10,033	FI	9,712	96.8	321
Moretti, Luciano	12.1	6,767	CCD, AN	6,034	89.2	733
Tornati, Giorgio	8.6	4,823	Lista civica, I Democratici	3,832	79.5	991
Milazzo, Alberto Maria	4.3	2,405	Verdi	2,087	86.8	318
Rinaldi, Giovanni Massimo	2.0	1,107	MS-FT	993	89.7	114
Total	100.0	55,884		51,081	91.4	4,803
Viterbo						
Gabbianelli, Giancarlo	53.1	20,890	FI, AN, CDL, CCD	19,850	95.0	1,040
Cordelli, Francesco Maria	30.2	11,876	PDCI, DS, Verdi, PPI , RI-altri	11,484	96.7	392
Emiliani, Emilio	4.6	1,811	PRC	1,426	78.7	385
Sementilli, De Luca Rita Anna Giuseppa	3.8	1,474	U.D.Eur, Socialista-Liberal Sgarbi	1,368	92.8	106
Bruni, Antonella	3.6	1,398	I Democratici	1,298	92.8	100
Arieti, Italo Leonello	2.0	778	SDI	890	114.4	-112

continued

Table B3 *continued*

Capital	Mayoral candidate[a]	First Round Votes (%)	Run-off Votes (%)	First Round Votes	Run-off Votes	Parties and civic lists expressing support[b]	Votes for supporting lists	First Round votes for supporting lists (%)	Votes for candidate alone
	Monteverdi, Enrico	1.0		406		MS-FT	386	95.1	20
	Grattarola, Agostino	0.9		370		PRI	335	90.5	35
	Occhini, Giuseppe	0.8		330		Fronte nazionale	317	96.1	13
	Total	100.0		39,333			37,354	95.0	1,979
Teramo	**Sperandio, Angelo**	53.8		19,413		I Democratici, DS, Per Teramo, PPI, PDCI, SDI	18,173	93.6	1,240
	Chiodi, Giovanni	41.0		14,781		Orizzonti nuovi, CCD, FI, DC, AN, MS-FT-altri	14,399	97.4	382
	Masci, Umberto	2.3		840		Lista interamnia	838	99.8	2
	Iacovoni, Antonio Giuseppe Silvio	2.0		730		PRC	771	105.6	-41
	Buongrazio, Filippo	0.9		322		Lista ecologica	282	87.6	40
	Total	100.0		36,086			34,463	95.5	1,623
Campobasso	**Massa, Augusto**	57.1		18,154		DS, PDCI, Verdi, PPI, PRC, SDI	16,495	90.9	1,659
	Cufari, Adalberto Bernardino	41.8		13,277		P. pop. progressista, CDU, Nuovo centro, FI, AN, CCD, Unione molisana	12,542	94.5	735
	Piciocco, Antonio	1.1		352		Fronte nazionale	284	80.7	68
	Total	100.0		31,783			29,321	92.3	2,462

Avellino	**Di Nunno, Antonio**	47.3	68.4	16,357	16,404	7,582	PPI, PDCI, PRC, RI-Dini, F: Verdi-I Democratici, DS	15,864	97.0	493
	Romano, Angelo	23.6		8,140			AN, FI, CDU, (*CCD*)	7,555	92.8	585
	Cucciniello, Gerardo	10.6		3,679			Insieme per Avellino	3,523	95.8	156
	Amatetti, Pierluigi	6.3		2,172			U.D.Eur	2,515	115.8	-343
	Iannaccone, Arturo	5.5		1,916			CCD	1,928	100.6	-12
	De Fazio, Antonio	3.4		1,167			SDI	1,129	96.7	38
	Cerullo, Gaetano	1.5		504			MS-FT	388	77.0	116
	Martone, Vincenzo	0.9		315			Lista civica	270	85.7	45
	Festa, Simona	0.9		296			Part. umanista	143	48.3	153
	Total	100.0	100.0	34,546	23,986			33,315	96.4	1,231
Bari	**Di Cagno, Abbrescia Simone**	54.1		102,288			FI, CDL, Liberal Sgarbi-altri, CCD, AN, MS-FT, Ambiente club	95,677	93.5	6,611
	Vacca, Giuseppe	33.8		63,915			Verdi, DS, I Democratici, PDCI, SDI, PPI, PRC	59,204	92.6	4,711
	Barattolo, Filippo	3.3		6,214			Socialista	6,346	102.1	-132
	Sorrentino, Francesco	2.3		4,304			RI-Dini	4,303	100.0	1
	Bonomo, Giovanni	2.0		3,889			U.D.Eur-PRI	3,999	102.8	-110
	Cipriani, Luigi	1.9		3,590			Gr. indip. libertà	3,613	100.6	-23
	Veronico, Nicola	1.2		2,221			CDU	2,086	93.9	135
	Signorile, Oronzo	0.8		1,579			Lista civica	1,563	99.0	16
	Sebastiano, Domenico	0.6		1,143			Lista civica	662	57.9	481
	Total	100.0		189,143				177,453	93.8	11,690
Foggia	**Agostinacchio, Paolo Antonio Mario**	52.5		47,105			AN, FI, CCD, Ambiente club	39,714	84.3	7,391

continued

Table B3 *continued*

Capital	Mayoral candidate[a]	First Round Votes (%)	Run-off Votes (%)	First Round Votes	Run-off Votes	Parties and civic lists expressing support[b]	Votes for supporting lists	First Round votes for supporting lists (%)	Votes for candidate alone
	Ciliberti, Orazio Francesco Michele	22.6		20,268		DS, PPI, Verdi, PRC, RI-Dini, I Democratici	19,579	96.6	689
	Salatto, Potito Francesco Pio	16.9		15,151		U.DEUR, CDL, Rinnovamento, SDI	17,577	116.0	-2,426
	Mongiello, Giovanni	3.1		2,772		Mov. dem. centro, CDU, Cattolici dem., Donne protagoniste, M. dem. giovani Foggia, Perif. abbandonata, Nuova DC, Verdi federalisti, I Conservatori, I Moderati, Commercianti uniti	2,984	107.6	-212
	Pontone, Italo	2.3		2,021		Lista civica	1,942	96.1	79
	Novelli, Anna Maria	2.1		1,887		Verdi per l'ambiente, PDCI, Donne per cambiare	1,522	80.7	365
	Lops, Giuseppe	0.5		437		All. meridionale aut.	409	93.6	28
	Total	100.0		89,641			83,727	93.4	5,914
Potenza	Bonito, Oliva Prospero	49.4	48.1	21,561	18,069	PRC, I Democratici, RI-Dini, PPI, Verdi, DS, SDI	22,670	105.1	-1,109
	Fierro, Gaetano	24.9	51.9	10,871	19,465	UDEUR	7,411	68.2	3,460
	Blasi, Gianfranco	24.1		10,544		AN, CCD, Patto Segni, FI	10,057	95.4	487
	Postiglione, Bonaventura	1.0		440		Nuovo progetto	632	143.6	-192

	%	Votes	Votes (2nd)	List	Index	Votes (2nd)	Diff.
Nardella, Gianfranco	0.6	262		MS-FT	80.5	211	51
Total	100.0	43,678	37,534		93.8	40,981	2,697
Caltanissetta **Messana, Salvatore Antonio Giuseppe**	53.2	14,483	15,879	DS, PPI, PRC, U.D.Eur, RI-Dini, I Democratici, PDCI, SDI	112.8	16,331	-1,848
Panepinto, Francesco Antonio	46.8	11,968	13,945	CDU, AN, FI, CCD, (*Lista Mancuso, P. Siciliano d'azione*)	120.1	14,372	-2,404
Mancuso, Giuseppe	25.2	9,261		Lista Mancuso, P. Siciliano d'azione	38.1	3,530	5,731
Aiello, Giuseppe	2.9	1,081		Aiello sindaco	29.2	316	765
Totale	100	36,793	29,824	Totale	93.9	34,549	2,244
Siracusa **Bufardeci, Gianbattista**	73.6	27,070	30,906	FI, AN, I liberal Sgarbi, CCD, CDU, Socialista, (*Fed. dei valori*)	90.9	24,618	2,452
Spagna, Fausto	26.4	13,311	11,097	PPI (Pop), DS, Noi siciliani-FNS, RI-Dini, SDI, (*U.D.Eur-Altri, Lista Franco Greco, Siracusa nuova, PRC, I Democratici*)	129.8	17,278	-3,967
Fatuzzo, Marco	13.6	8,248		PDCI, I Democratici	48.9	4,032	4,216
Greco, Franco	10.5	6,330		Lista Franco Greco	74.8	4,738	1,592
Vella, Antonino	3.7	2,264		UDEUR-Altri	179.9	4,072	-1,808
Midolo, Giuseppe	3.3	1,993		Siracusa nuova	92.3	1,839	154
Impelluso, Sebastiano	1.2	716		Fed. dei valori	119.0	852	-136
Aglieco, Gaspare	1.0	592		PRC	92.9	550	42
Totale	100.0	60524	42003	Totale	95.8	57,979	2,545

[a] Winning mayoral candidate in bold.

[b] Lists expressing support in second round only in brackets.

Source: Istituto Cattaneo reeleboration of Ministry of the Interior figures.

Table B4 *Turnout in the 13 June provincial elections*

	Electors	Voters	Valid votes	Invalid votes	Votes for mayor alone	Votes for party lists	Blank ballots	Abstentions (%)	Invalid Votes (%)	Votes for candidate alone (%)	% Votes for lists (of valid votes)
Alessandria	377,728	289,002	258,557	30,445	29,498	229,059	20,021	23.5	10.5	11.4	88.6
Asti	180,723	138,698	120,162	18,536	17,527	102,635	13,375	23.3	13.4	14.6	85.4
Cuneo	466,813	369,767	320,032	49,735	42,045	277,987	33,179	20.8	13.5	13.1	86.9
Novara	291,750	224,558	198,350	26,208	20,329	178,021	15,547	23.0	11.7	10.2	89.8
Torino	1,895,193	1,335,015	1,191,892	143,123	121,020	1,070,872	76,337	29.6	10.7	10.2	89.8
Vercelli	156,607	124,513	108,281	16,232	7,994	100,287	10,171	20.5	13.0	7.4	92.6
Biella	165,423	131,420	115,265	16,155	12,548	102,717	10,068	20.6	12.3	10.9	89.1
Verb.-Cus.Ossola	144,534	107,006	96,760	10,246	12,048	84,712	6,088	26.0	9.6	12.5	87.5
Bergamo	794,567	635,051	575,571	59,480	35,842	539,729	40,755	20.1	9.4	6.2	93.8
Brescia	897,347	710,806	642,996	67,810	44,396	598,600	47,335	20.8	9.5	6.9	93.1
Cremona	282,420	231,232	203,932	27,300	23,636	180,296	15,815	18.1	11.8	11.6	88.4
Milano	3,150,111	2,241,399	2,049,597	191,802	183,170	1,866,427	108,781	28.8	8.6	8.9	91.1
Sondrio	154,352	113,862	101,489	12,373	14,156	87,333	8,076	26.2	10.9	13.9	86.1
Lecco	254,685	198,316	179,555	18,761	11,468	168,087	11,774	22.1	9.5	6.4	93.6
Lodi	162,503	132,116	118,792	13,324	10,263	108,529	8,293	18.7	10.1	8.6	91.4
Belluno	198,988	125,805	114,137	11,668	19,712	94,425	6,892	36.8	9.3	17.3	82.7
Padova	716250	399223	369217	30006	80,979	288,238	14,873	44.3	7.5	21.9	78.1
Rovigo	211,690	170,558	149,253	21,305	9,189	140,064	14,171	19.4	12.5	6.2	93.8
Venezia	712,557	492,415	436,949	55,466	23,929	413,020	27,378	30.9	11.3	5.5	94.5
Verona	676,659	508,719	457,471	51,248	29,260	428,211	33,580	24.8	10.1	6.4	93.6

Imperia	191,141	133,267	120,445	12,822	10,831	109,614	7,270	30.3	9.6	9.0	91.0
Savona	249,227	189,409	167,796	21,613	12,905	154,891	13,130	24.0	11.4	7.7	92.3
Bologna	792,085	645,566	598,379	47,187	30,385	567,994	29,445	18.5	7.3	5.1	94.9
Ferrara	312,392	256,672	231,033	25,639	16,615	214,418	17,494	17.8	10.0	7.2	92.8
Forlì·-Cesena	306,393	246,213	226,495	19,718	8,449	218,046	12,156	19.6	8.0	3.7	96.3
Modena	526,199	423,188	392,355	30,833	14,891	377,464	22,620	19.6	7.3	3.8	96.2
Parma	349,582	261,771	237,129	24,642	26,248	210,881	16,074	25.1	9.4	11.1	88.9
Piacenza	235,379	182,869	164,869	18,000	21,086	143,783	10,819	22.3	9.8	12.8	87.2
Reggio Emilia	372,800	304,601	282,219	22,382	11,880	270,339	15,087	18.3	7.3	4.2	95.8
Rimini	230,696	181,089	166,839	14,250	6,494	160,345	9,638	21.5	7.9	3.9	96.1
Arezzo	271,466	209,795	186,858	22,937	8,037	178,821	16,714	22.7	10.9	4.3	95.7
Firenze	807,880	596,965	545,848	51,117	25,902	519,946	32,594	26.1	8.6	4.7	95.3
Grosseto	186,860	146,322	133,442	12,880	7,960	125,482	7,847	21.7	8.8	6.0	94.0
Livorno	290,268	216,333	196,290	20,043	7,456	188,834	12,907	25.5	9.3	3.8	96.2
Pisa	328,687	244,454	221,192	23,262	13,403	207,789	14,867	25.6	9.5	6.1	93.9
Pistoia	232,642	170,776	152,910	17,866	9,298	143,612	10,764	26.6	10.5	6.1	93.9
Siena	215,840	170,201	155,138	15,063	4,842	150,296	9,595	21.1	8.9	3.1	96.9
Prato	187,525	136,589	124,317	12,272	9,486	114,831	7,341	27.2	9.0	7.6	92.4
Perugia	519,971	399,209	356,895	42,314	12,441	344,454	27,094	23.2	10.6	3.5	96.5
Terni	192,128	151,625	136,505	15,120	13,374	123,131	9,294	21.1	10.0	9.8	90.2
Ascoli Piceno	315,212	236,851	209,658	27,193	13,088	196,570	18,445	24.9	11.5	6.2	93.8
Macerata	257,134	193,499	169,452	24,047	9,432	160,020	17,259	24.7	12.4	5.6	94.4
Pesaro E Urbino	302,888	235,183	210,200	24,983	9,553	200,647	16,543	22.4	10.6	4.5	95.5
Frosinone	445,785	320,992	286,727	34,265	4,935	281,792	19,950	28.0	10.7	1.7	98.3
Latina	432,436	309,090	280,241	28,849	4,658	275,583	15,402	28.5	9.3	1.7	98.3
Rieti	126,025	102,243	93,172	9,071	4,934	88,238	5,340	18.9	8.9	5.3	94.7

continued

Table B4 *Continued*

	Electors	Voters	Valid votes	Invalid votes	Votes for mayor alone	Votes for party lists	Blank ballots	Abstentions (%)	Invalid Votes (%)	Votes for candidate alone (%)	% Votes for lists (of valid votes)
Chieti	369,121	242,358	215,320	27,038	5,793	209,527	15,760	34.3	11.2	2.7	97.3
L'aquila	283,531	187,939	169,869	18,070	4,634	165,235	9,658	33.7	9.6	2.7	97.3
Pescara	273,273	184,388	167,883	16,505	17,210	150,673	8,900	32.5	9.0	10.3	89.7
Teramo	256,401	190,368	169,957	20,411	6,347	163,610	13,519	25.8	10.7	3.7	96.3
Campobasso	232,355	150,825	131,891	18,934	9,408	122,483	11,361	35.1	12.6	7.1	92.9
Isernia	92,319	59,373	52,186	7,187	1,775	50,411	4,299	35.7	12.1	3.4	96.6
Avellino	416,137	279,141	245,063	34,078	2,705	242,358	20,920	32.9	12.2	1.1	98.9
Napoli	2,460,845	1,426,490	1,277,321	149,169	43,253	1,234,068	78,802	42.0	10.5	3.4	96.6
Salerno	913,310	650,382	582,552	67,830	15,072	567,480	41,887	28.8	10.4	2.6	97.4
Bari	1,316,629	881,524	772,463	109,061	23,108	749,355	62,582	33.0	12.4	3.0	97.0
Brindisi	342,431	237,259	210,715	26,544	5,715	205,000	14,643	30.7	11.2	2.7	97.3
Lecce	703,952	484,169	436,584	47,585	20,058	416,526	26,279	31.2	9.8	4.6	95.4
Taranto	488,991	326,367	297,681	28,686	13,461	284,220	13,137	33.3	8.8	4.5	95.5
Matera	172,095	117,496	100,864	16,632	3,027	97,837	6,823	31.7	14.2	3.0	97.0
Potenza	359,380	258,819	222,650	36,169	6,129	216,521	21,800	28.0	14.0	2.8	97.2
Catanzaro	337,551	215,504	194,628	20,876	5,410	189,218	10,879	36.2	9.7	2.8	97.2
Cosenza	654,408	430,833	371,676	59,157	3,240	368,436	32,235	34.2	13.7	0.9	99.1
Crotone	147,709	94,262	86,264	7,998	2,076	84,188	4,484	36.2	8.5	2.4	97.6
Vibo Valentia	160,837	102,968	94,682	8,286	1,896	92,786	4,239	36.0	8.0	2.0	98.0

Run-off (data)

	Voters	Valid votes	Invalid votes	Blank ballot	2nd round absentionism (%)	Additional absentionism (%)	2nd round invalid votes (%)
Alessandria	178,667	170,815	7,852	3,612	52.7	29.2	4.4
Asti	83,101	79,930	3,171	1,279	54.0	30.7	3.8
Cuneo	215,047	205,976	9,071	4,059	53.9	33.1	4.2
Novara	108,840	103,145	5,695	2,115	62.7	39.7	5.2
Torino	684,232	659,392	24,840	7,938	63.9	34.3	3.6
Vercelli	74,954	70,589	4,365	2,194	52.1	31.6	5.8
Biella	83,268	79,593	3,675	1,433	49.7	29.1	4.4
Verb.-Cus.Ossola	66,201	64,267	1,934	808	54.2	28.2	2.9
Bergamo	331,055	306,425	24,630	13,282	58.3	38.2	7.4
Brescia	329,888	315,979	13,909	6,890	63.2	42.4	4.2
Cremona	141,461	135,881	5,580	2,439	49.9	31.8	3.9
Milano	1,172,287	1,138,351	33,936	12,877	62.8	34.0	2.9
Sondrio	62,562	60,757	1,805	778	59.5	33.3	2.9
Lecco	96,489	92,134	4,355	1,770	62.1	40.0	4.5
Lodi	77,128	74,093	3,035	1,089	52.5	33.8	3.9
Belluno	61,132	59,113	2,019	950	69.3	32.5	3.3
Padova	287,628	275,555	12,073	5,315	59.8	15.5	4.2
Rovigo	91,059	86,803	4,256	2,042	57.0	37.6	4.7
Venezia	235,727	224,938	10,789	4,965	66.9	36.0	4.6

continued

Table B4 *Continued*

	Voters	Valid votes	Invalid votes	Blank ballot	2nd round absentionism (%)	Additional absentionism (%)	2nd round invalid votes (%)
Verona	225,792	218,366	7,426	4,059	66.6	41.8	3.3
Savona	110,814	106,410	4,404	1,691	55.5	31.5	4.0
Parma	166,743	160,913	5,830	2,530	52.3	27.2	3.5
Piacenza	125,565	120,649	4,916	2,152	46.7	24.4	3.9
Ascoli Piceno	145,360	140,786	4,574	2,292	53.9	29.0	3.1
Rieti	67,410	65,219	2,191	769	46.5	27.6	3.3
Chieti	167,963	161,228	6,735	2,715	54.5	20.2	4.0
L'aquila	116,828	112,603	4,225	1,567	58.8	25.1	3.6
Isernia	43,762	42,106	1,656	693	52.6	16.9	3.8
Avellino	136,896	127,804	9,092	4,487	67.1	34.2	6.6
Bari	486,388	463,601	22,787	10,062	63.1	30.1	4.7
Catanzaro	135,734	130,344	5,390	2,076	59.8	23.6	4.0

Table B5 *Election of provincial presidents 13 June and run-offs of 27 June*

Capital	Candidate for president[a]	1st round votes	2nd round votes	1st round (%)	2nd round (%)	Parties and civic lists expressing support[b]	Votes for supporting lists	1st round votes for supporting lists (%)	Votes for candidate alone
Alessandria	**Palenzona, Fabrizio**	104,577	86,717	40.4	50.8	PDCI, PPI, I Democratici, SDI, DS	92,589	88.5	11,988
	Cavallera, Ugo	98,201	84,098	38.0	49.2	CCD-CDU, AN, FI, (*Part. pens.*, *Alessandria autonoma, Nuova proposta, LN*)	87,857	89.5	10,344
	Rossi, Oreste detto Tino	33,276		12.9		Lav. pens. padani, Alessandria autonoma, Nuova proposta, Catt. padani-altri, LN	27,988	84.1	5,288
	Priora, Domenico	13,325		5.2		PRC	12,353	92.7	972
	Cavaliere, Pasquale	5,515		2.1		Verdi	4,895	88.8	620
	Benvenuto, Quintilio	3,663		1.4		Part. pens	3,377	92.2	286
	Total	258,557	170,815	100.0	100.0	Total	229,059	88.6	29,498
Asti	**Marmo, Roberto**	57,169	46,226	47.6	57.8	AN-altri, Socialista-altri, FI, P. Segni	50,069	87.6	7,100
	Goria, Giuseppe	39,612	33,704	33.0	42.2	PDCI, PRC, SDI, Lista locale	31,545	79.6	8,067
	Fogliato, Sebastiano	16,116		13.4		LN, Obiettivo sviluppo	14,722	91.4	1,394
	Aizzi, Angelo	4,080		3.4		Part. Pens	3,857	94.5	223
	Longo, Renato	3,185		2.6		Antiproib. ref. Verde, Artigiani commer., PRC.	2,442	76.7	743
	Total	120,162	79,930	100.0	100.0	Total	102,635	85.4	17,527

continued

Table B5 *continued*

Capital	Candidate for president[a]	1st round votes	2nd round votes	1st round (%)	2nd round (%)	Parties and civic lists expressing support[b]	Votes for supporting lists	1st round votes for supporting lists (%)	Votes for candidate alone
Cuneo	**Quaglia, Giovanni**	141,130	112,606	44.1	54.7	Insieme a Quaglia, PPI-I Democratici-altri, SDI-altri, DS	118,391	83.9	22,739
	Crosetto, Guido	107,496	93,370	33.6	45.3	FI, AN-altri, CCD, Piemonte naz. Europa, (Granda che lavora, Granda autonoma, LN)	96,095	89.4	11,401
	Gazzola, Paolo	54,908		17.1		LN, Granda autonoma, Granda che lavora	48,830	88.9	6,078
	Baracco, Michele	11,779		3.7		PRC	10,735	91.1	1,044
	Bertone, Marco	4,719		1.5		Connubio giovanile	3,936	83.4	783
	Total	320,032	205,976	100.0	100.0	Total	277,987	86.9	42,045
Novara	**Pagani, Maurizio**	90,823	55,226	45.8	53.5	Socialista, CCD, FI, AN	82,255	90.6	8,568
	Cattaneo, Paolo	74,691	47,919	37.6	46.5	PDCI, SDI, I Democratici, Verdi, PPI, DS	65,017	87.0	9,674
	Zenoni, Emilio Maria	19,367		9.8		LN	18,329	94.6	1,038
	Lucini, Giovanni	11,030		5.6		PRC	10,230	92.7	800
	Ramazzotti, Danilo	2,439		1.2		U.D.Eur	2,190	89.8	249
	Total	198,350	103,145	100.0	100.0	Total	178,021	89.8	20,329
Torino	**Bresso, Mercedes**	510,889	364,370	42.9	55.3	RI-altri, PDCI, SDI, DS, PPI, I Democratici, Verdi	449,765	88.0	61,124

Ferrero, Alberto	452,586	295,022	38.0	44.7	AN-altri, Socialista, Piemonte naz. Europa, CCD, FI, (*Pensionati Europa, Lav. pens. padani, LN*)	421,457	93.1	31,129
Borghezio, Mario		80,554	6.8		LN, Lav. pens. padani	68,341	84.8	12,213
Marchiaro, Elio		62,009	5.2		PRC	58,382	94.2	3,627
Lupi, Alessandro		23,665	2.0		Verdi-Verdi, Liberal Sgarbi	19,880	84.0	3,785
Cavallo, Liliana		19,487	1.6		Pens. Europa	17,903	91.9	1,584
Costa, Rosa Anna		17,309	1.4		U.D.Eur-CDU	15,997	92.4	1,312
Bonino, Bruna		16,844	1.4		Mov. fed. it.	11,571	68.7	5,273
Meluzzi, Alessandro		5,851	0.5		Centro liberaldem.	5,110	87.3	741
Tevere, Antonio		2,698	0.2		Part. umanista	2,466	91.4	232
Total	659,392	291,892	100.0	100.0	Total	1,070,872	89.8	121,020
Vercelli Baltaro, Giulio	46,803	40,557	43.2	57.5	AN, MS-FT, FI, Pens. Europa, Piemonte naz.Europa, (*Part. DC, LN, CCD*)	43,699	93.4	3,104
Julini, Norberto	28,961	30,032	26.8	42.5	PPI , DS, SDI, (*I Democratici, PRC-Fed. Verdi-altri*)	26,540	91.6	2,421
Fossale, Ercole Mario Giuseppe		9,868	9.1		LN	9,576	97.0	292
Scheda, Roberto		8,542	7.9		Un. prov. di centro	7,786	91.1	756
Ferraro, Domenico		5,440	5.0		I Democratici	5,143	94.5	297
Poy, Bruno		4,593	4.2		CCD, Part. DC	4,128	89.9	465
Fecchio, Claudio		4,074	3.8		PRC-F. Verdi-altri	3,415	83.8	659
Total	70,589	108,281	100.0	100.0	Total	100,287	92.6	7,994
Biella Scanzio, Orazio	52,195	41,627	45.3	52.3	FI, CCD, AN, (*LN*)	46,727	89.5	5,468
Marsoni in Mori Ubaldini, Silvia	43,721	37,966	37.9	47.7	DS, SDI, Verdi-PDCI, Lista locale	37,849	86.6	5,872

continued

Table B5 *continued*

Capital	Candidate for president[a]	1st round votes	2nd round votes	1st round (%)	2nd round (%)	Parties and civic lists expressing support[b]	Votes for supporting lists	1st round votes for supporting lists (%)	Votes for candidate alone
	Simonetti, Roberto	9,753		8.5		LN	9,109	93.4	644
	Nuccio, Renato	7,872		6.8		PRC	7,464	94.8	408
	Ferrari, Giancarlo	1,724		1.5		Mov. ind. biellese	1,568	91.0	156
	Total	115,265	79,593	100.0	100.0	Total	102,717	89.1	12,548
Verb.-Cus.-Ossola	**Guarducci, Ivan**	42,118	32,945	43.5	51.3	FI, CCD-CDU-altri, AN-altri, (LN)	36,554	86.8	5,564
	Borghi, Enrico	33,532	31,322	34.6	48.7	DS, PPI , Verdi, PDCI, SDI	28,224	84.2	5,308
	Paracchini, Pierangelo	8,379		8.7		LN	8,039	95.9	340
	Cottini, Claudio	5,703		5.9		Rin. socialista	5,194	91.1	509
	Alberganti, Carluccio	4,923		5.1		PRC	4,726	96.0	197
	Rebecchi, Adriano	2,105		2.2		MS-FT	1,975	93.8	130
	Total	96,760	64,267	100.0	100.0	Total	84,712	87.5	12,048
Bergamo	**Bettoni, Valerio**	193,136	153,969	33.6	50.2	CCD, AN, Unione cacciatori, Dem. crist., FI, (*Provincia comunità*)	181,926	94.2	11,210
	Cappelluzzo, Giovanni	170,821	153,456	29.7	49.8	LN	164,874	96.5	5,947
	Minuti, Luigi	169,568		29.5		PDCI, DS, PPI , I Democratici, SDI, Verdi	152,687	90.0	16,881
	Armanni, Vittorio	19,441		3.4		PRC	18,707	96.2	734
	Donadoni, Silvano	12,951		2.2		Provincia comunità	12,521	96.7	430
	Lamura, Roberto	6,647		1.1		MS-FT	6,286	94.6	361

Province	Candidate	Votes	Votes	%	%	List	Votes	%	
Brescia	Goisis, Piergiorgio	3,007		0.5		Mov. fed. it.	2,728	90.7	279
	Total	575,571	306,425	100.0	100.0	Total	539,729	93.8	35,842
	Cavalli, Alberto	236,514	158,976	36.8	50.3	CCD, Unione cacciatori, FI, AN, Socialista, P. Segni	222,009	93.9	14,505
	Galperti, Guido	220,942	157,003	34.4	49.7	DS, SDI, I Democratici, PDCI, PPI-RI, Verdi	201,104	91.0	19,838
	Molgora, Daniele	107,590		16.7		LN	102,875	95.6	4,715
	De Paoli, Elidio	37,696		5.9		Lega pens., All.lomb. aut.	34,529	91.6	3,167
	Lorenzi, Roberto Andrea	22,971		3.6		PRC	22,067	96.1	904
	Comensoli in Garatti, Maria Anna	8,744		1.3		Italia unita	8,274	94.6	470
	Bosio, Adriano	8,539		1.3		MS-FT	7,742	90.7	797
	Total	642,996	315,979	100.0	100.0	Total	598,600	93.1	44,396
Cremona	**Corada, Gian Carlo**	78,749	75,354	38.6	55.5	Verdi, DS, PPI , SDI, I Democratici, PDCI	66,433	84.4	12,316
	Jacini, Giovanni	77,017	60,527	37.8	44.5	CCD, Centro, AN, FI, (Part.pens., Liberal Sgarbi-altri)	69,405	90.1	7,612
	Robusti, Giovanni	26,717		13.1		LN, A.p.c.a.terra	23,439	87.7	3,278
	Bettenzoli, Piergiuseppe	10,776		5.3		PRC	10,538	97.8	238
	Ranzenigo, Franco	6,583		3.2		Part. pens	6,583	100.0	0
	Sciacca, Elia Paolo	3,215		1.6		Liberal Sgarbi-altri	3,078	95.7	137
	Compagnini, Domenico	875		0.4		Alternativa	820	93.7	55
	Total	203,932	135,881	100.0	100.0	Total	180,296	88.4	23,636
Milano	**Colli, Ombretta**	914,313	573,135	44.6	50.3	FI, P. Segni, AN, CCD, Liberal Sgarbi, (CDU)	836,487	91.5	77,826

continued

Table B5 *continued*

Capital	Candidate for president[a]	1st round votes	2nd round votes	1st round (%)	2nd round (%)	Parties and civic lists expressing support[b]	Votes for supporting lists	1st round votes for supporting lists (%)	Votes for candidate alone
	Tamberi, Livio	811,827	565,216	39.6	49.7	SDI, DS, PRI, I Democratici, Verdi, PRC, PDCI, PPI, RI-altri	725,820	89.4	86,007
	Formentini, Marco	226,786		11.1		LN	212,370	93.6	14,416
	Jonghi, Lavarini Roberto	38,085		1.9		Lg. naz.l. f. d., Ls. Cito Lg. az. merid., MS-FT	36,245	95.2	1,840
	Maggis, Aldo	33,352		1.6		CDU	32,391	97.1	961
	Brocchi, Stefania Cristina	9,975		0.5		Part. umanista	8,931	89.5	1,044
	Filograna, Eugenio	8,356		0.4		U.D.Eur	7,816	93.5	540
	Tinazzi, Cristiano	6,903		0.3		Fronte nazionale	6,367	92.2	536
	Total	2049597	1138351	100.0	100.0	Total	1,866,427	91.1	183,170
Sondrio	**Tarabini, Eugenio**	44,139	32,070	43.5	52.8	FI, AN-CCD, Popolari retici	38,879	88.1	5,260
	Dioli, Enrico	37,563	28,687	37.0	47.2	SDI, Prog. dem., PPI-altri, PRC	30,615	81.5	6,948
	Zeli, Pierluigi	19,787		19.5		LN, Lista autonomista	17,839	90.2	1,948
	Total	101,489	60,757	100.0	100.0	Total	87,333	86.1	14,156
Lecco	**Anghileri, Mario**	70,557	53,380	39.3	57.9	DS, PPI, SDI, Verdi, I Democratici, RI, PRI-Lib-Eldr., UDEUR	64,969	92.1	5,588
	Puccio, Guido	58,686	38,754	32.7	42.1	CCD, AN-P. Segni, FI	55,101	93.9	3,585
	Invernizzi, Carlo	38,811		21.6		LN	37,016	95.4	1,795
	Valsecchi, Claudia	9,336		5.2		PRC	8,973	96.1	363

	Candidate	Votes	Votes	%	%	List	Votes	%	Votes
	Bussola, Paolo	2,165		1.2		MS-FT	2,028	93.7	137
	Total	179,555		100.0	100.0	Total	168,087	93.6	11,468
Lodi	**Guerini, Lorenzo**	92,134	48,32 3	40.7	56.1	Cento paesi, SDI, PDCI, PPI, I Democratici, DS	42,273	87.5	6,050
	Peviani, Mariano	41,591	32,502	39.5	43.9	FI, AN-P. Segni, CCD, Amministratori	43,989	93.6	2,995
	Rossi, Mauro	14,461		12.2		LN	13,601	94.1	860
	Malabarba, Giovanni	7,142		6.0		PRC	6,936	97.1	206
	Invernizzi, Gianmario	1,882		1.6		Forza nuova	1,730	91.9	152
	Total	118,792		100.0	100.0	Total	108,529	91.4	10,263
Belluno	**De Bona, Oscar**	43,850	38,706	38.4	65.5	Lg. veneta Repubblica, Lista autonomista, PPI-altri, SDI	31,950	72.9	11,900
	Costola, Angelo Giuseppe	26,849	20,407	23.5	34.5	AN, FI	24,073	89.7	2,776
	Viel, Livio	16,171		14.2		DS, Verdi, PDCI	13,552	83.8	2,619
	Dall'o, Andrea	12,813		11.2		LN	11,798	92.1	1,015
	Fascina, Giuseppe	8,373		7.3		I Democratici	7,680	91.7	693
	Dalla Gasperina, Marisa	3,042		2.7		Autonomia veneta	2,593	85.2	449
	Sperandio, Gino	3,039		2.7		PRC	2,779	91.4	260
	Total	114,137	59,113	100.0	100.0	Total	94,425	82.7	19,712
Padova	**Casarin, Vittorio**	159,342	152,604	43.1	55.4	CCD, FI, AN, Insieme provincia, (CDU-altri, Veneto nord est, Socialista, Veneto libero)	121,825	76.5	37,517
	Ziglio, Antonino	146,420	122,951	39.7	44.6	PDCI, I Democratici, DS, PPI, Fed. Verdi, PRC.	113,597	77.6	32,823
	Manzolini, Flavio	26,860		7.3		LN, Lista autonomista, Cat. Pad.-Lav. Pad.	21,472	79.9	5,388

continued

Table B5 *continued*

Capital	Candidate for president[a]	1st round votes	2nd round votes	1st round (%)	2nd round (%)	Parties and civic lists expressing support[b]	Votes for supporting lists	1st round votes for supporting lists (%)	Votes for candidate alone
	Sidoti, Ignazio	14,198		3.8		Veneto nord est, Socialista, CDU-altri	11,984	84.4	2,214
	Pellegatti, Francesco	9,479		2.6		Lg. veneta repubblica	8,157	86.1	1,322
	Zanon, Domenico	4,321		1.2		SDI	3,895	90.1	426
	Nicolussi, Luca Maria	3,585		1.0		Non solo Verdi	2,920	81.5	665
	Agostini, Ruggero	3,508		0.9		Centro	3,191	91.0	317
	Ramundo, Nicola	1,504		0.4		Veneto libero	1,197	79.6	307
	Total	369,217	275,555	100.0	100.0	Total	288,238	78.1	80,979
Rovigo	**Saccardin, Federico**	72,242	50,564	48.4	58.3	SDI, PRC, Verdi, PDCI, DS, I Democratici, PPI, Nord-est	66,175	91.6	6,067
	Brigo, Alberto	40,066	36,239	26.9	41.7	FI, Lista locale, (AN, CCD)	38,019	94.9	2,047
	Previati, Andrea	17,103		11.5		AN	16,522	96.6	581
	Astolfi, Andrea	7,911		5.3		LN	7,692	97.2	219
	Donzelli, Onofrio	4,969		3.3		Crist. dem.	4,909	98.8	60
	Ghezzo, Ermenegildo	4,229		2.8		CCD	4,091	96.7	138
	Furlan, Wander	2,733		1.8		Lg. veneta Republica	2,656	97.2	77
	Total	149,253	86,803	100.0	100.0	Total	140,064	93.8	9,189
Venezia	**Busatto, Luigino**	173,007	126,672	39.6	56.3	PPI, PRC, SDI, DS, Verdi, PDCI, RI, (*I Democratici*)	163,843	94.7	9,164

Falcier, Luciano	156,533	98,266	35.8	43.7	AN, CCD-altri, FI, (*Lg. veneta Repubblica*)	146,553	93.6	9,980
Semi, Maria Luisa	35,831		8.2		I Democratici	33,849	94.5	1,982
Mazzonetto, Alberto	33,923		7.8		LN	32,685	96.4	1,238
Bazzi, Giorgio	15,997		3.7		Lg. veneta Repubblica	15,409	96.3	588
Laroni, Nereo	7,493		1.7		Socialista	7,126	95.1	367
Fontanin, Piero	7,150		1.6		MS-FT	6,984	97.7	166
Bonaventura, Mario	7,015		1.6		Veneto nord-est	6,571	93.7	444
Total	436,949	224,938	100.0	100.0	Total	413,020	94.5	23,929
Verona Merlin, Aleardo	189,893	115,760	41.5	53.0	AN, CCD, Veneto nord-est, FI	180,111	94.8	9,782
Bonfante, Franco	136,199	102,606	29.8	47.0	PPI, DS, Lista locale, SDI, Verdi, I Democratici	124,714	91.6	11,485
Zaninelli, Stefano	68,476		15.0		LN, Lega veneta, A.p.c.a..terra, Lista Autonomista, Rinnov. di centro, Cattolici federal.	64,092	93.6	4,384
Borghesi, Antonio	25,254		5.5		Lg. veneta Repubblica	23,445	92.8	1,809
Venturi, Luciano	15,047		3.3		PRC	14,553	96.7	494
Arduini, Carlo	10,087		2.2		Progetto Verona	9,613	95.3	474
Bussinello, Roberto	7,252		1.6		MS-FT	6,799	93.8	453
Testini, Alessandro	4,195		0.9		Socialista	3,877	92.4	318
Attrezzi, Elideo	1,068		0.2		Liberalitalia	1,007	94.3	61
Total	457,471	218,366	100.0	100.0	Total	428,211	93.6	29,260
Imperia Boscetto, Gabriele	69,656		57.8		FI, AN, CCD, RI	63,274	90.8	6,382
Crespi, Eraldo	31,042		25.8		SDI, PDCI, PPI, Verdi, DS	28,047	90.4	2,995
Porro, Mariano	7,208		6.0		LN, Lista autonomista	6,334	87.9	874

continued

Table B5 *continued*

Capital	Candidate for president[a]	1st round votes	2nd round votes	1st round (%)	2nd round (%)	Parties and civic lists expressing support[b]	Votes for supporting lists	1st round votes for supporting lists (%)	Votes for candidate alone
	Gandolfo, Giovanni	7,167		5.9		I Democratici	6,818	95.1	349
	Ardissone, Zefferino	5,372		4.5		PRC	5,141	95.7	231
	Total	120,445	0	100.0	0.0	Total	109,614	91.0	10,831
Savona	**Garassini, Alessandro**	74,636	56,083	44.5	52.7	DS, Verdi, SDI, RI, PPI, PDCI, I Democratici	68,160	91.3	6,476
	Piccardo, Sandro	64,741	50,327	38.6	47.3	AN, CCD-CDU, FI, Part. pens, Socialista, (LN)	59,866	92.5	4,875
	Melgrati, Marco	11,300		6.7		LN	10,614	93.9	686
	Marengo, Bruno	9,568		5.7		PRC	9,021	94.3	547
	Crepaldi, Graziano	3,383		2.0		Part. DC	3,311	97.9	72
	Porta Valenti, Gabriella	2,505		1.5		PRI-altri	2,339	93.4	166
	Raiteri, Erminio	1,663		1.0		Alpazur	1,580	95.0	83
	Total	167,796	106,410	100.0	100.0	Total	154,891	92.3	12,905
Bologna	**Prodi, Vittorio**	338,878		56.6		PDCI, PPI, SDI, DS, RI, Verdi, I Democratici	319,732	94.4	19,146
	Davoli, Fabrizio	192,327		32.1		CCD, AN, FI	183,258	95.3	9,069
	Tedde in Mazzetti, Giuseppina	30,339		5.1		PRC	29,809	98.3	530
	Mignardi, Marco	16,495		2.8		LN	15,686	95.1	809
	Nanni, Giuseppe	8,287		1.4		Socialista liberali	7,744	93.4	543

Province	Candidate	Votes	%		Coalition/Party	%	Votes	Votes
	Gherardi, Marco	7,227	1.2		Dem. crist.	97.6	7,052	175
	Musghi, Pier Luigi	4,826	0.8		CDU	97.7	4,713	113
	Total	598,379	100.0	0	Total	94.9	567,994	30,385
Ferrara	**Dall'acqua, Pier Giorgio**	133,704	57.9		PPI, DS, Verdi, PDCI, PRC, SDI, I Democratici	97.0	129,682	4,022
	Fava, Paolo	47,830	20.7		Alleanza Ferrara	82.6	39,528	8,302
	Scanavini, Rossano	42,402	18.3		AN, CCD	91.0	38,602	3,800
	Bottoni, Sergio	7,097	3.1		LN	93.1	6,606	491
	Total	231,033	100.0	0	Total	92.8	214,418	16,615
Forlì-Cesena	**Gallina, Piero**	126,109	55.7		I Democratici, SDI, DS, PDCI, PRI, PPI	95.2	120,006	6,103
	Nervegna, Antonio	43,532	19.2		FI-CCD	98.2	42,732	800
	Fontana, Elliot Giovanni	26,053	11.5		AN	97.6	25,433	620
	Poeta, Pier Giorgio	13,045	5.8		PRC	97.8	12,757	288
	Riguzzi, Roberto	7,925	3.5		Verdi	96.7	7,666	259
	Zanoni, Gianluca	5,058	2.2		LN	97.0	4,906	152
	Metri, Corrado	2,701	1.2		Unione Romagna	94.2	2,544	157
	Biserna, Rotilio	2,072	0.9		L'intesa	96.6	2,002	70
	Total	226,495	100.0	0	Total	96.3	218,046	8,449
Modena	**Pattuzzi, Graziano**	223,110	56.9		SDI, I Democratici, PDCI, PPI, Verdi lib. e solidali, DS	96.2	214,558	8,552
	Bertacchi, Massimo	119,897	30.5		AN, CCD, FI	95.9	114,967	4,930
	Silvestri, Alfredo	21,820	5.6		PRC	97.8	21,348	472
	Barbieri, Giorgio	17,737	4.5		LN	96.7	17,156	581
	Battaglia, Francesco	7,327	1.9		Verdi per Modena	96.7	7,088	239

continued

Table B5 *continued*

Capital	Candidate for president[a]	1st round votes	2nd round votes	1st round (%)	2nd round (%)	Parties and civic lists expressing support[b]	Votes for supporting lists	1st round votes for supporting lists (%)	Votes for candidate alone
	Bruini, Francesco	2,464		0.6		PRI	2,347	95.3	117
	Total	392,355	0	100.0	0.0	Total	377,464	96.2	14,891
Parma	**Borri, Andrea**	105,503	90,698	44.5	56.4	Verdi, DS, PPI, PDCI, I Democratici	94,274	89.4	11,229
	Paglia, Paolo	81,579	70,215	34.4	43.6	AN, FI, Nuove idee, Part. federal., (CCD, A.p.c.a. terra, Socialista)	71,606	87.8	9,973
	Cavitelli, Giorgio	15,417		6.5		LN, Lista autonomista	14,026	91.0	1,391
	Novari, Pier Paolo	14,905		6.3		PRC	14,429	96.8	476
	Berni, Italo	4,824		2.0		SDI	4,607	95.5	217
	Vignali, Salvatore	4,672		2.0		CCD	4,623	99.0	49
	Cinquetti, Bernardo	3,323		1.4		Lista civica	865	26.0	2,458
	Menozzi, Dario	2,980		1.2		A.p.c.a. terra	2,736	91.8	244
	Somenzi, Pietro	2,596		1.1		Socialista	2,476	95.4	120
	Balzani, Antonio	1,330		0.6		U.D.Eur	1,239	93.2	91
	Total	237,129	160,913	100.0	100.0	Total	210,881	88.9	26,248
Piacenza	**Squeri, Dario**	62,677	63,336	38.0	52.5	PDCI, DS, Con Squeri, (Pensionati, A.p.c.a. terra, LN)	53,342	85.1	9,335
	Maccagni, Luciano	68,519	57,313	41.6	47.5	CCD, FI-altri, AN, (Part. pens.)	59,672	87.1	8,847
	Siboni, Enrico	18,397		11.1		LN, Pens., A.p.c.a. terra	16,312	88.7	2,085
	Tribi, Fernando	10,002		6.1		PRC	9,439	94.4	563

Location	Name					Part. pens			
	Spinelli, Pietro	5,274		3.2			5,018	95.1	256
	Total	164,869	120,649	100.0	100.0	Total	143,783	87.2	21,086
Reggio Emilia	**Ruini, Roberto**	178,590		63.3		PDCI, I Democratici, PPI, Verdi, DS, SDI	170,859	95.7	7,731
	Cataliotti, Liborio	70,422		25.0		CCD-CDU, AN, FI	66,943	95.1	3,479
	Camellini, Maurizio	16,982		6.0		PRC	16,666	98.1	316
	Alessandri, Angelo	16,225		5.7		LN	15,871	97.8	354
	Total	282,219	0	100.0	0.0	Total	270,339	95.8	11,880
Rimini	**Fabbri, Ferdinando**	86,298		51.7		DS, I Democratici, PDCI, PPI-RI-PRI-CDU, SDI, Verdi	82,292	95.4	4,006
	Fabbri, Maria Flora	39,938		24.0		FI	38,833	97.2	1,105
	Barletta, Domenico	22,387		13.4		AN	21,715	97.0	672
	Rossi, Giancarlo	9,355		5.6		PRC	9,100	97.3	255
	Diotalevi, Giancarlo	4,533		2.7		LN	4,366	96.3	167
	Amedei, Giorgio	1,719		1.0		Lista ecologica	1,580	91.9	139
	Frigiola, Savino	1,410		0.9		Unione Romagna	1,348	95.6	62
	Abbati, Giorgio	1,199		0.7		UDEUR	1,111	92.7	88
	Total	166,839	0	100.0	0.0	Total	160,345	96.1	6,494
Arezzo	**Ceccarelli, Vincenzo**	100,151		53.6		Verdi, PDCI, PPI-CDU-RI, DS, SDI	96,399	96.3	3,752
	Petri, Danilo	66,883		35.8		FI-CCD, AN, I Liberal Sgarbi	63,512	95.0	3,371
	Bottai, Laura	15,015		8.0		PRC	14,383	95.8	632
	Rossi De Vermandois, Carlo	3,024		1.6		Lista locale	2,806	92.8	218
	Andreani, Egiziano	1,785		1.0		LN	1,721	96.4	64
	Total	186,858	0	100.0	0.0	Total	178,821	95.7	8,037

continued

Table B5 *continued*

Capital	Candidate for president[a]	1st round votes	2nd round votes	1st round (%)	2nd round (%)	Parties and civic lists expressing support[b]	Votes for supporting lists	1st round votes for supporting lists (%)	Votes for candidate alone
Firenze	**Gesualdi, Michele**	319,724		58.6		DS, SDI, Verdi, PDCI, RI, PPI, I Democratici	304,433	95.2	15,291
	Corsinovi, Alessandro	164,440		30.1		FI, AN, Liberal Sgarbi-altri, CCD	156,092	94.9	8,348
	D'amico, Eugenio Carmelo	42,607		7.8		PRC	41,393	97.2	1,214
	Paolinelli, Romolo	6,839		1.3		MS-FT	6,615	96.7	224
	Mansani, Leonello	4,601		0.8		Socialista	4,430	96.3	171
	Lelli, Antonio	3,993		0.7		LN	3,672	92.0	321
	Fedi, Franco	3,644		0.7		Mov. aut. toscano	3,311	90.9	333
	Total	545,848	0	100.0	0.0	Total	519,946	95.3	25,902
Grosseto	**Scheggi, Lio**	70,196		52.6		PDCI, I Democratici, PRI, PPI, DS, SDI, PRC	66,337	94.5	3,859
	Carlotti, Alessandro	53,826		40.3		CDU, FI, M.a.t.-altri, AN	50,330	93.5	3,496
	Corsi, Hubert	5,847		4.4		CCD	5,443	93.1	404
	Bausani, Emilia	2,115		1.6		Verdi	1,993	94.2	122
	Benassi, Antonio	809		0.6		Ls civiche federate	761	94.1	48
	Menconi, Moreno	649		0.5		LN	618	95.2	31
	Total	133,442	0	100.0	0.0	Total	125,482	94.0	7,960
Livorno	**Frontera, Claudio**	116,677		59.5		PPI, DS, SDI, Verdi, Lib-PRI-RI, I Democratici, PDCI	113,292	97.1	3,385
	Zingoni, Maurizio	59,945		30.5		AN, FI-CCD	56,522	94.3	3,423

City	Candidate	Votes	%		Party	Votes	%	
	Giannoni, Luciano	19,668	10.0		PRC	19,020	96.7	648
	Total	196,290	100.0	0	Total	188,834	96.2	7,456
Pisa	Nunes, Gino	120,668	54.6		PDCI, I Democratici, SDI, Verdi, DS, PPI-RI.	114,326	94.7	6,342
	Rossi, Alberto	77,858	35.2		CCD, AN, FI	71,581	91.9	6,277
	Frosini, Alessandro	19,980	9.0		PRC	19,420	97.2	560
	Valleggi, Claudio	2,686	1.2		LN	2,462	91.7	224
	Total	221,192	100.0	0	Total	207,789	93.9	13,403
Pistoia	Venturi, Gianfranco	80,459	52.6		Soc. rep. dem., DS, I Democratici, PPI, Verdi, PDCI, RI	76,913	95.6	3,546
	Gorbi, Federico	55,337	36.2		AN, FI-CCD, I Liberal Sgarbi	50,812	91.8	4,525
	Berti, Francesco	14,792	9.7		PRC	13,862	93.7	930
	Gai, Vezio	2,322	1.5		LN	2,025	87.2	297
	Total	152,910	100.0	0	Total	143,612	93.9	9,298
Siena	Ceccherini, Fabio	99,785	64.3		Verdi, SDI, I Democratici, PPI, DS, PDCI	97,196	97.4	2,589
	Battistini, Loretana	42,502	27.4		AN, FI-CCD	40,498	95.3	2,004
	Lenzi, Mauro	12,851	8.3		PRC	12,602	98.1	249
	Total	155,138	100.0	0	Total	150,296	96.9	4,842
Prato	Mannocci, Daniele	63,215	50.8		DS, SDI, Verdi-PDCI, PPI, I Democratici	59,041	93.4	4,174
	Mencattini, Enrico Giovanni	45,369	36.5		AN, FI-CCD	41,103	90.6	4,266
	Benvenuti, Gino	9,598	7.7		PRC	9,188	95.7	410
	Vaiani, Mauro	2,282	1.8		Insieme per Prato	2,006	87.9	276

continued

Table B5 *continued*

Capital	Candidate for president[a]	1st round votes	2nd round votes	1st round (%)	2nd round (%)	Parties and civic lists expressing support[b]	Votes for supporting lists	1st round votes for supporting lists (%)	Votes for candidate alone
	Paradiso, Emilio	1,590		1.3		LN	1,463	92.0	127
	Pezzoli, Andrea	1,329		1.1		Liberal Sgarbi-altri	1,190	89.5	139
	Bonaccorsi, Patrizia	934		0.8		UDEUR	840	89.9	94
	Total	124,317	0	100.0	0.0	Total	114,831	92.4	9,486
Perugia	**Cozzari, Giulio**	205,851		57.7		PDCI, SDI, DS, PRC, Verdi, PPI, RI	199,719	97.0	6,132
	Biagiotti, Bruno	121,921		34.1		FI, AN, CCD	116,763	95.8	5,158
	Libori, Fausto	18,506		5.2		I Democratici	17,355	93.8	1,151
	Grilli, Francesco	8,819		2.5		MS-FT	8,819	100.0	0
	Dionigi, Giuseppe	1,798		0.5		LN	1,798	100.0	0
	Total	356,895	0	100.0	0.0	Total	344,454	96.5	12,441
Terni	**Cavicchioli, Andrea**	79,386		58.1		SDI, DS, PRC, PDCI, PRI, PPI, I Democratici	74,727	94.1	4,659
	Ciaurro, Gian Franco	51,877		38.0		CCD, AN - P. Segni, FI	43,466	83.8	8,411
	Fani, Sandro	2,953		2.2		MS-FT	2,808	95.1	145
	Moretti, Stefano	2,289		1.7		Socialista	2,130	93.1	159
	Total	136,505	0	100.0	0.0	Total	123,131	90.2	13,374
Ascoli Piceno	**Colonnella, Pietro**	104,559	73,950	49.9	52.5	I Democratici, PPI , DS, PRI, SDI, PDCI, Verdi, RI-U.D.Eur	97,745	93.5	6,814
	Castelli, Guido	84,905	66,836	40.5	47.5	CCD-CDU, AN, FI	79,385	93.5	5,520

Region	Candidate	Votes	%	Parties	Votes	%	Votes
	Volponi, Alessandro	12,732	6.1	PRC	12,268	96.4	464
	Orsini, Alberto	4,818	2.3	MS-FT	4,801	99.6	17
	Forlì, Paolo	2,644	1.2	La via radicale	2,371	89.7	273
	Total	209,658	100.0	Total	196,570	93.8	13,088
		140,786					
Macerata	**Pigliapoco, Sauro**	85,444	50.4	PDCI, DS, PRC, PPI, SDI, PRI-RI, I Democratici	80,629	94.4	4,815
	Torresetti, Giorgio	72,010	42.5	FI, AN, CCD-CDU	68,285	94.8	3,725
	Leopardi, Vanni	5,102	3.0	Verdi	4,474	87.7	628
	Turchi, Pierpaolo	4,751	2.8	MS-FT	4,584	96.5	167
	Farabolini, Valerio	1,242	0.8	Alternativa	1,208	97.3	34
	Rossetti, Pierino	903	0.5	LN	840	93.0	63
	Total	169,452	100.0	Total	160,020	94.4	9,432
		0	0.0				
Pesaro e Urbino	**Ucchielli, Palmiro**	110,243	52.5	PPI-PRI, PDCI, SDI, Verdi, RI, DS	105,102	95.3	5,141
	Cicoli, Claudio	42,648	20.3	FI	40,877	95.8	1,771
	Colucci, Gianfranco	28,633	13.6	AN, CCD	27,046	94.5	1,587
	Adanti, Valter	14,443	6.9	PRC	14,022	97.1	421
	Olivieri, Graziano	12,070	5.7	I Democratici	11,555	95.7	515
	Cancellieri, Giorgio	2,163	1.0	LN	2,045	94.5	118
	Total	210,200	100.0	Total	200,647	95.5	9,553
		0	0.0				
Frosinone	**Scalia, Francesco**	159,992	55.8	PRI, PPI, U.D.Eur, I Democratici, SDI, PDCI, CDU, DS, RI, Verdi	157,108	98.2	2,884
	Turchetta, Attilio	114,751	40.0	AN, CCD, Lista locale, FI, I Liberal Sgarbi, MS-FT	112,822	98.3	1,929
	Giorgi, Francesco	11,984	4.2	PRC	11,862	99.0	122
	Total	286,727	100.0	Total	281,792	98.3	4,935
		0	0.0				

continued

Table B5 *continued*

Capital	Candidate for president[a]	1st round votes	2nd round votes	1st round (%)	2nd round (%)	Parties and civic lists expressing support[b]	Votes for supporting lists	1st round votes for supporting lists (%)	Votes for candidate alone
Latina	**Martella, Paride**	144,039		51.4		Il Polo democratico, CDU, AN, P. Segni-altri, CCD, FI	142,175	98.7	1,864
	Fiumara, Erasmo	108,592		38.7		SDI, Verdi, I Democratici, PPI, DS, RI-altri, PDCI	106,324	97.9	2,268
	D'acunto, Pasquale	8,895		3.2		PRC	8,661	97.4	234
	Solli, Franco	8,833		3.2		U.D.Eur	8,747	99.0	86
	Baldi, Gianfranco	6,472		2.3		MS-FT	6,363	98.3	109
	Domizi, Loreto	3,410		1.2		Fronte nazionale	3,313	97.2	97
	Total	280,241	0	100.0	0.0	Total	275,583	98.3	4,658
Rieti	**Calabrese, Giosuè**	44,960	40,050	48.2	61.4	DS, RI, SDI, PPI , PDCI, Verdi, PRI, Per Calabrese	42,226	93.9	2,734
	Belloni, Antonio	37,044	25,169	39.8	38.6	Socialista, CCD, Lista civica, AN, I Liberal Sgarbi, FI, (MS-FT)	35,401	95.6	1,643
	Pompei, Giovanni	4,802		5.1		PRC	4,626	96.3	176
	Giuli, Eraldo	3,334		3.6		I Democratici	3,175	95.2	159
	Pirri, Alberto	2,042		2.2		MS-FT	1,873	91.7	169
	Barba, Giuseppe	990		1.1		Fronte nazionale	937	94.6	53
	Total	93,172	65,219	100.0	100.0	Total	88,238	94.7	4,934

Province	Candidate					Coalition			
Chieti	**Febbo, Mauro**	105,917	49.2	84,228	52.2	AN, DC, FI, Liberal Sgarbi-CDU, CCD, MS-FT	102,800	97.1	3,117
	Pulsinelli Manfredi, Giovanni	92,728	43.1	77,000	47.8	PDCI, PPI, SDI, DS, I Democratici, Verdi, (PRC)	90,369	97.5	2,359
	Mascioli, Cesare	9,997	4.6			PRC	9,784	97.9	213
	Marchione, Florindo Raffaele	4,991	2.3			RI-UDEUR	4,918	98.5	73
	De Virgiliis in D'alò, Clementina	1,687	0.8			Fronte Naz-altri	1,656	98.2	31
	Total	215,320	100.0	161,228	100.0	Total	209,527	97.3	5,793
L'aquila	Verderosa, Marcello	79,115	46.6	54,360	48.3	DS, U.D.Eur, PPI, PDCI, Lib., I Democratici, SDI, Verdi	76,887	97.2	2,228
	Susi, Palmiero	77,270	45.5	58,243	51.7	FI, Liberal Sgarbi-altri, CCD, MS-FT, AN, (RI)	75,276	97.4	1,994
	Mancini, Laura	6,166	3.6			PRC	6,043	98.0	123
	Verini, Antonio	5,420	3.2			RI	5,234	96.6	186
	Vecchioli, Paolo	1,898	1.1			Fronte nazionale	1,795	94.6	103
	Total	169,869	100.0	112,603	100.0	Total	165,235	97.3	4,634
Pescara	**De Dominicis, Giuseppe**	91,272	54.4			PPI, DS, SDI, Verdi, PDCI, PRC, I Democratici, Lib. lib. lib	78,779	86.3	12,493
	Di Biase, Licio	75,082	44.7			AN, CCD, Pescara futura, Liberal Sgarbi-altri, FI, DC, MS-FT	70,554	94.0	4,528
	Pichiecchio, Massimo	1,529	0.9			Fronte nazionale	1,340	87.6	189
	Total	167,883	100.0	0	0.0	Total	150,673	89.7	17,210
Teramo	**Rufini, Claudio**	102,328	60.2			DS, PPI, PDCI, PRC, Verdi, I Democratici, SDI, PRI	98,687	96.4	3,641

continued

Table B5 *continued*

Capital	Candidate for president[a]	1st round votes	2nd round votes	1st round (%)	2nd round (%)	Parties and civic lists expressing support[b]	Votes for supporting lists	1st round votes for supporting lists (%)	Votes for candidate alone
	Albi, Paolo	65,739		38.7		AN, FI, DC, CCD, MS-FT, Social-CDU-Sgarbi	63,171	96.1	2,568
	Montebello, Antonio	1,890		1.1		Fronte nazionale	1,752	92.7	138
	Total	169,957	0	100.0	0.0	Total	163,610	96.3	6,347
Campobasso	**Chieffo, Antonio**	70,651		53.6		PRC, SDI, PDCI, Verdi, DS, PPI, I Democratici	64,138	90.8	6,513
	Picciano, Michele	57,862		43.9		FI, Socialista, P. pop. Progressista, Liberal Sgarbi, AN, Nuovo Centro, CCD, CDU	55,197	95.4	2,665
	D'aloisio, Roberto	1,789		1.3		MS-FT	1,662	92.9	127
	Carrozzelli, Saturnino	1,589		1.2		Fronte nazionale	1,486	93.5	103
	Total	131,891	0	100.0	0.0	Total	122,483	92.9	9,408
Isernia	**Mauro, Raffaele**	22,858	25,027	43.8	59.4	FI, CCD, AN, (MS-FT, Liberal Sgarbi)	22,122	96.8	736
	Pellegrino, Domenico	16,665	17,079	31.9	40.6	PDCI, PRC, DS, I Democratici, Verdi, (SDI)	16,035	96.2	630
	Barbaro, Domenico	6,894		13.2		PPI	6,647	96.4	247
	Di Domenico, Ettore	2,945		5.7		SDI	2,881	97.8	64

Province	Name	Votes	%	Votes	%	Coalition / Party	Votes	%	
	Mancini, Giovancarmine	2,824	5.4			Liberal Sgarbi, MS-FT	2,726	96.5	98
	Total	52,186	100.0	42,106	100.0	Total	50,411	96.6	1,775
Avellino	**Maselli, Francesco**	64,885	26.5	75,571	59.1	PPI, PDCI, RI, (CDU, U.D.Eur, SDI, Verdi)	64,509	99.4	376
	Aurisicchio, Raffaele	55,789	22.8			DS, PRC, I Democratici	54,898	98.4	891
	Fioretti, Felice	51,070	20.8			FI, AN	49,975	97.9	1,095
	Venezia, Lorenzo	19,529	8.0			U.D.Eur	19,523	100.0	6
	Mainolfi, Luigi	17,261	7.0			SDI	17,261	100.0	0
	Di Cecilia, Franco	14,834	6.1			CCD	14,742	99.4	92
	Sorvino, Luigi Stefano	11,335	4.6			CDU	11,165	98.5	170
	Pacilio, Massimo	4,505	1.8			MS-FT	4,457	98.9	48
	Napolitano, Vincenzo	3,647	1.5			Verdi	3,647	100.0	0
	Ariniello, Consolino	1,656	0.7			Mov. pop. dem. sud	1,642	99.2	14
	Russomanno, Aleandro Igor	552	0.2			Part. umanista	539	97.6	13
	Total	245,063	100.0	52,233	40.9	Total	242,358	98.9	2,705
	Total			127,804	100.0				
Napoli	**Lamberti, Amato**	650,078	50.9			Verdi, PRI, SDI, PDCI, PRC, PPI, DS, I Democratici, RI	626,603	96.4	23,475
	Caldoro, Stefano	494,051	38.7			AN, Libertas, CCD, FI, Per Napoli, Socialista	480,613	97.3	13,438
	Di Nardo, Aniello	56,747	4.5			U.D.Eur	56,020	98.7	727
	Monaco, Ciro	32,319	2.5			Verdi Federalisti, PPE, Lista donne, Libertasport, Vesuvio, Cattolici liberali	29,674	91.8	2,645
	Bruno, Raffaele	18,298	1.4			MS-FT	17,793	97.2	505
	Albano, Giovanni	11,946	0.9			Liberal Sgarbi	11,291	94.5	655

continued

Table B5 *continued*

Capital	Candidate for president[a]	1st round votes	2nd round votes	1st round (%)	2nd round (%)	Parties and civic lists expressing support[b]	Votes for supporting lists	1st round votes for supporting lists (%)	Votes for candidate alone
	Di Costanzo, Giuseppe	6,587		0.5		Fronte nazionale	6,334	96.2	253
	Torre, Antonio	4,296		0.4		All. meridionale, Forza nuova	2,977	69.3	1,319
	Vestuto, Gianfranco	2,999		0.2		Lega Sud	2,763	92.1	236
	Total	1,277,321	0	100.0	0.0	Total	1,234,068	96.6	43,253
Salerno	**Andria, Alfonso**	309,939		53.2		DS, PPI, RI, PRI, PDCI, SDI, Verdi	299,376	96.6	10,563
	Cardiello, Franco	177,758		30.5		AN, CCD, FI	174,864	98.4	2,894
	Lubritto, Antonio	46,272		7.9		UDEUR	45,559	98.5	713
	Avagliano, Lucio	19,995		3.4		I Democratici	19,610	98.1	385
	Mari, Francesco	14,259		2.5		PRC	14,059	98.6	200
	Celentano, Nicolina	9,770		1.7		MS-FT	9,564	97.9	206
	Festa, Nicola	4,559		0.8		Fronte nazionale	4,448	97.6	111
	Total	582,552	0	100.0	0.0	Total	567,480	97.4	15,072
Bari	**Matarrese, Antonio**	355,623	224,575	46.0	48.4	CCD, Liberal Sgarbi-altri, Ambiente club, Ls. Cito Lg. az. merid., FI, AN, CDL, (*CDU, Socialista*)	345,246	97.1	10,377
	Vernola, Marcello	317,747	239,026	41.1	51.6	Verdi, PRC, DS, PPI, I Democratici, SDI, PDCI, (*Gr. indip. libertà, RI*)	307,868	96.9	9,879

Province	Candidate	Votes		%		List	Votes	%	Votes
	Pisicchio, Alfonsino	37,140		4.8		RI	35,923	96.7	1,217
	Belardi, Raffaele	16,771		2.2		Socialista	16,137	96.2	634
	Pantaleo, Domenico	13,721		1.8		UDEUR-PRI	13,468	98.2	253
	Magarelli, Pantaleo detto Leo	13,393		1.7		CDU	13,081	97.7	312
	Incardona, Giuseppe Maria, Renato	12,902		1.7		MS-FT	12,711	98.5	191
	Ladisa, Michele	5,166		0.7		Gr. indip. libertà	4,921	95.3	245
	Total	772,463	463,601	100.0	0	Total	749,355	97.0	23,108
Brindisi	Frugis, Nicola	117,494		55.8		CCD, CDL, FI, AN, PRI, Centro democratico	114,467	97.4	3,027
	Panzuti, Carlo	79,536		37.7		PDCI, PPI, SDI, I Democratici, PRC, DS, Verdi	77,397	97.3	2,139
	Notarpietro, Attilio	4,332		2.1		MS-FT	4,236	97.8	96
	Mola, Beniamino	3,942		1.9		Sud libero, CDU	3,786	96.0	156
	Perrino, Angelo	1,978		0.9		Liberal Sgarbi	1,864	94.2	114
	Pede, Filafelfio	1,995		0.9		Socialista-altri	1,895	95.0	100
	Aprile, Carlo	1,438		0.7		Ls. Cito Lg. az. merid.	1,355	94.2	83
	Total	210,715	0	100.0	0.0	Total	205,000	97.3	5,715
Lecce	Ria, Lorenzo	221,290		50.7		SDI, I Democratici, PPI, DS, PRC, RI, PDCI, Verdi	208,948	94.4	12,342
	Madaro, Carlo	198,381		45.4		CDL, unità repubblicana, Liberal Sgarbi, CCD, AN, Socialista, Ambiente club, FI	191,207	96.4	7,174
	Quarta, Nicola	9,960		2.3		U.D.Eur	9,764	98.0	196
	Mongiò, Benito Vittorio	5,636		1.3		MS-FT	5,504	97.7	132
	Chirizzi, Mauro	1,317		0.3		Forza nuova	1,103	83.8	214
	Total	436,584	0	100.0	0.0	Total	416,526	95.4	20,058

continued

Table B5 *continued*

Capital	Candidate for president[a]	1st round votes	2nd round votes	1st round (%)	2nd round (%)	Parties and civic lists expressing support[b]	Votes for supporting lists	1st round votes for supporting lists (%)	Votes for candidate alone
Taranto	**Rana, Domenico**	159,276		53.5		Ls. Cito Lg. az. merid., FI, AN, CCD, CDL, Socialista	154,114	96.8	5,162
	Carrozzo, Gaetano	109,003		36.6		I Democratici, PRC, DS, PDCI, Verdi, PPI	103,144	94.6	5,859
	Carducci, Alfengo	11,410		3.8		UDEUR, CDU	9,946	87.2	1,464
	Graniglia, Salvatore	9,684		3.3		SDI	9,248	95.5	436
	Infesta, Nicola	8,308		2.8		Prospettive	7,768	93.5	540
	Total	297,681	0	100.0	0.0	Total	284,220	95.5	13,461
Matera	**Carelli, Giovanni**	54,731		54.3		SDI, PPI, RI-U.D.Eur, PDCI, Verdi, PRC, DS	53,459	97.7	1,272
	Carmentano, Cesare Nicola	32,989		32.7		AN, CCD, FI	31,731	96.2	1,258
	Cancellaro, Filomena Patrizia	10,889		10.8		I Democratici	10,443	95.9	446
	Venezia, Nunzio Paolo	2,255		2.2		MS-FT	2,204	97.7	51
	Total	100,864	0	100.0	0.0	Total	97,837	97.0	3,027
Potenza	**Santarsiero, Vito**	142,848		64.2		I Democratici, PDCI, DS, RI, PRC, PPI, SDI, Verdi	138,892	97.2	3,956
	Naborre, Camillo	57,257		25.7		AN, CCD, FI, P. Segni	55,863	97.6	1,394
	Bongiovanni, Pietro	14,070		6.3		UDEUR	13,608	96.7	462

	Adamo, Francesco	4,251		1.9		Socialista	4,127	97.1	124
	Porfidio, Romeo	3,069		1.4		MS-FT	2,970	96.8	99
	Cafaro in Baldassarre, Carmela	1,155		0.5		Nuovo progetto	1,061	91.9	94
	Total	222,650	0	100.0	0.0	Total	216,521	97.2	6,129
Catanzaro	Traversa, Michele	90,066	66,701	46.3	51.2	Per il sud, Lista locale, CDU, Donne insieme, Liberal Sgarbi, AN, P. Segni, CCD, FI, (Liberalitalia)	87,218	96.8	2,848
	Ciconte, Vincenzo Antonio	89,885	63,643	46.2	48.8	PPI, I Democratici, Verdi, SDI, DS, UDEUR, PDCI, RI	87,635	97.5	2,250
	Serrao, Domenico	7,416		3.8		PRC	7,310	98.6	106
	Frisini, Michelangelo	3,883		2.0		Socialista	3,823	98.5	60
	Siracusa, Massimo	2,028		1.0		Liberalitalia	1,923	94.8	105
	Vono, Giovambattista	1,350		0.7		Fronte nazionale	1,309	97.0	41
	Total	194,628	130,344	100.0	100.0	Total	189,218	97.2	5,410
Cosenza	Acri, Antonio	196,767		52.9		UDEUR, PPI, Verdi, SDI, I Democratici, PDCI, DS	195,424	99.3	1,343
	Acciardi, Maria Rita	47,494		12.8		FI	47,494	100.0	0
	Caputo, Giuseppe	40,394		10.9		AN, P. Segni	38,951	96.4	1,443
	Bisogno, Francesco	20,813		5.6		CCD	20,813	100.0	0
	Veneziano, Francesco	19,932		5.4		PRC	19,932	100.0	0
	Gemelli, Vitaliano	17,263		4.6		CDU	17,241	99.9	22
	Aquino, Fausto	13,704		3.7		RI	13,687	99.9	17
	Savastano, Francesco	7,476		2.0		Socialista-altri	7,456	99.7	20
	Serra, Stanisla	6,994		1.9		MS-FT	6,599	94.4	395
	Rosito, Carmine	839		0.2		Fascismo e libertà	839	100.0	0
	Total	371,676	0	100.0	0.0	Total	368,436	99.1	3,240

continued

Table B5 *continued*

Capital	Candidate for president[a]	1st round votes	2nd round votes	1st round (%)	2nd round (%)	Parties and civic lists expressing support[b]	Votes for supporting lists	1st round votes for supporting lists (%)	Votes for candidate alone
Crotone	**Talarico, Carmine Giuseppe**	54,092	0	62.7		UDEUR, DS, RI, I Democratici, Fed. laburista, SDI, PDCI, PPI, Verdi	53,341	98.6	751
	Rizzuto, Ottavio	26,769		31.0		AN, CCD, FI, CDU	25,515	95.3	1,254
	Falbo, Rosario	3,555		4.1		PRC	3,511	98.8	44
	Elia, Antonio	1,848		2.2		P. Segni	1,821	98.5	27
	Total	86,264	0	100.0	0.0	Total	84,188	97.6	2,076
Vibo Valentia	**Bruni, Ottavio Gaetano**	58,669		62.0		PPI, Verdi-PDCI, CDU, U.D.Eur, DS, SDI, RI	58,122	99.1	547
	Vallone, Gaetano	19,467		20.6		Socialista, FI, AN	18,667	95.9	800
	Salerno, Nazzareno	7,276		7.7		CCD	7,002	96.2	274
	Sirgiovanni, Filippo	4,139		4.4		I Democratici	3,976	96.1	163
	Malerba, Matteo	2,892		3.0		PRC	2,854	98.7	38
	Tassone, Francesco	1,256		1.3		Mov. meridionale	1,205	95.9	51
	La Torre, Michelangelo	983		1.0		MS-FT	960	97.7	23
	Total	94,682	0	100.0	0.0	Total	92,786	98.0	1,896

[a] Winning candidate in bold.

[b] Lists expressing support in second round only in brackets.

Source: Istituto Cattaneo re-eleboration of Ministry of the Interior figures.

Table B6 *Turnout for the European elections of 13 June 1999.*

Region	Total Electorate	Total Voters	Valid Votes	Blank Votes (% of Invalid votes)	% voting
Piedmont	3,643,356	2,723,226	2,447,085	5.5	74.7
Valle d'Aosta	101,533	65,558	60,558	3.4	64.6
Lombardy	7,533,149	5,688,438	5,301,556	3.7	75.5
Liguria	1,424,897	979,624	904,288	3.6	68.8
Trentino-Alto Adige	750,472	510,946	474,414	3.2	68.1
Venetia	3,766,251	2,839,594	2,616,395	4.0	75.4
Friuli-Venezia Giulia	1,049,248	721,254	663,361	4.0	68.7
Emilia Romagna	3,399,537	2,751,621	2,582,923	3.5	80.9
Tuscany	3,007,206	2,232,725	2,060,458	4.1	74.2
Umbria	697,539	551,707	495,874	5.8	79.1
Marches	1,241,210	943,935	845,462	6.5	76.0
Lazio	4,432,667	2,969,884	2,744,314	3.0	67.0
Abruzzi	1,138,725	805,689	696,874	7.7	70.8
Molise	304,758	210,233	174,671	10.5	69.0
Campania	4,648,191	2,975,798	2,628,169	6.2	64.0
Apulia	3,308,669	2,289,755	1,987,890	6.8	69.2
Basilicata	510,188	376,418	306,591	8.7	73.8
Calabria	1,744,725	1,109,235	938,618	8.6	63.6
Sicily	4,208,827	2,490,603	2,244,722	3.0	59.2
Sardinia	1,363,808	945,610	783,272	9.2	69.3

Source: Istituto Cattaneo re-eleboration of Ministry of the Interior figures.

Table B7 *European Elections 13 June 1999. Performance of party lists.*

		Piedmont	Valle d'Aosta	Lombardy	Liguria	Trentino-Alto Adige	Venetia	Friuli-V. Giulia	Emilia Romagna	Tuscany	Umbria
DS	Valid votes	335,942	4,516	681,815	199,029	34,255	290,392	84,394	847,100	657,364	147,067
	%	13.7	7.5	12.9	22.0	7.2	11.1	12.7	32.8	31.9	29.6
PPI	Valid votes	51,844	751	143,343	20,093	15,515	90,092	19,141	67,228	61,018	17,420
	%	2.1	1.2	2.7	2.2	3.3	3.5	2.9	2.6	3.0	3.5
RI	Valid votes	22,418	164	30,494	5,846	2,020	14,956	3,150	9,079	20,889	3,302
	%	0.9	0.3	0.6	0.7	0.4	0.6	0.5	0.3	1.0	0.7
Fed. dei Verdi	Valid votes	47,065	1,585	94,295	15,773	23,894	50,560	11,941	47,762	32,040	5,424
	%	1.9	2.6	1.8	1.7	5.0	1.9	1.8	1.8	1.6	1.1
PRI-Lib-Eldr	Valid votes	9027	94	17565	4608	1588	4700	1648	21737	12514	2778
	%	0.4	0.2	0.3	0.5	0.3	0.2	0.3	0.8	0.6	0.6
SDI	Valid votes	33,080	190	65,954	12,026	3,621	31,181	9,299	32,435	43,182	18,256
	%	1.3	0.3	1.2	1.3	0.8	1.2	1.4	1.3	2.1	3.7
PDCI	Valid votes	62,511	656	100,139	24,225	2,746	32,207	10,552	51,793	67,348	19,523
	%	2.6	1.1	1.9	2.7	0.6	1.2	1.6	2.0	3.3	3.9
I Democratici	Valid votes	203,907	1,902	357,705	67,016	33,018	225,499	48,449	203,966	106,037	25,588
	%	8.3	3.1	6.8	7.4	7.0	8.6	7.3	7.9	5.1	5.2
UV	Valid votes	6,505	27,811	5,623	1,203	–	–	–	–	–	–
	%	0.3	45.9	0.1	0.1						
SVP	Valid votes	–	–	–	–	146,459	2,659	4,008	2,002	–	–
	%					30.9	0.1	0.6	0.1		
U.D.Eur	Valid votes	12,521	189	18,258	4,772	615	10,821	1,725	3,625	2,783	2,058
	%	0.5	0.3	0.3	0.5	0.1	0.4	0.3	0.1	0.1	0.4
CDU	Valid votes	50,103	502	126,435	15,114	7,026	94,715	18,022	37,035	27,725	8,382
	%	2.0	0.8	2.4	1.7	1.5	3.6	2.7	1.4	1.3	1.7
PRC	Valid votes	111,923	1,670	211,278	50,741	8,318	72,607	24,297	128,749	153,237	31,340

%	4.6	2.8	4.0	5.6	1.7	2.8	3.7	5.0	7.4	6.3
LN Valid votes	190,909	1,178	694,681	33,415	11,539	280,328	67,157	76,702	12,845	1,532
%	7.8	1.9	13.1	3.7	2.4	10.7	10.1	3.0	0.6	0.3
FI Valid votes	706,656	10,650	1,618,404	240,242	80,190	679,418	177,057	527,516	402,349	92,906
%	28.9	17.6	30.5	26.6	16.9	26.0	26.7	20.4	19.5	18.7
AN-P, Segni Valid votes	182,638	2,271	319,307	76,921	27,843	216,857	63,010	221,528	224,581	65,610
%	7.5	3.8	6.0	8.5	5.9	8.3	9.5	8.6	10.9	13.2
CCD Valid votes	28,397	258	59,282	12,543	7,996	46,820	9,236	32,747	38,744	8,406
%	1.2	0.4	1.1	1.4	1.7	1.8	1.4	1.3	1.9	1.7
Lista Bonino Valid votes	322,289	5,365	616,609	97,211	40,097	312,355	86,439	211,225	148,924	30,844
%	13.2	8.9	11.6	10.8	8.4	11.9	13.0	8.2	7.2	6.2
MS-FT Voti validi	33,248	317	60,841	12,005	4,134	30,149	10,720	31,080	30,879	11,583
%	1.4	0.5	1.2	1.3	0.9	1.2	1.6	1.2	1.5	2.3
Cito Valid votes	3,188	49	5,743	922	301	2,786	635	2,432	1,483	403
%	0.1	0.1	0.1	0.1	0.1	0.1	0.1	0.1	0.1	0.1
P. pensionati Valid votes	26,876	245	60,983	8,872	3,950	26,981	7,346	20,942	11,531	2,322
%	1.1	0.4	1.2	1.0	0.8	1.0	1.1	0.8	0.6	0.5
LDR Valid votes	3,408	61	6,225	1,017	1,681	8,113	871	1,991	1,595	403
%	0.1	0.1	0.1	0.1	0.4	0.3	0.1	0.1	0.1	0.1
P. Umanista Valid votes	2,630	134	6,577	694	–	–	–	–	1,969	399
%	0.1	0.2	0.1	0.1	–	–	–	–	0.1	0.1
Liga rep. ven. Valid votes	–	–	–	–	17,608	92,199	3,724	4,195	–	–
%	–	–	–	–	3.7	3.5	0.6	0.2	–	–
Cobas Valid votes	–	–	–	–	–	–	–	–	1,421	328
%	–	–	–	–	–	–	–	–	0.1	0.1
Socialista Valid votes	–	–	–	–	–	–	–	–	–	–
%	–	–	–	–	–	–	–	–	–	–
Total Valid votes	2,447,085	60,558	5,301,556	904,288	474,414	2,616,395	662,821	2,582,869	2,060,458	495,874
%	100.0	100.0	100.0	100.0	100.0	100.0	100.0	100.0	100.0	100.0

Table B7 European Elections 13 June 1999. Performance of party lists.

		Marches	Lazio	Abruzzi	Molise	Campania	Apulia	Basilicata	Calabria	Sicily	Sardinia	Total
DS	Valid votes	200,875	504,924	121,732	20,034	362,569	281,502	60,361	154,025	268,398	123,538	5,379,832
	%	23.8	18.4	17.5	11.5	13.8	14.2	19.7	16.4	12.0	15.8	17.4
PPI	Valid votes	35,847	120,829	34,578	10,682	210,360	105,230	28,602	70,529	163,354	50,174	1,316,630
	%	4.2	4.4	5.0	6.1	8.0	5.3	9.3	7.5	7.3	6.4	4.3
RI	Valid votes	6,050	21,747	7,862	1,270	70,242	29,954	5,743	23,461	65,125	6,533	350,305
	%	0.7	0.8	1.1	0.7	2.7	1.5	1.9	2.5	2.9	0.8	1.1
Fed. dei Verdi	Valid votes	16,637	46,117	9,226	2,436	56,583	28,017	9,547	10,968	20,642	10,142	540,654
	%	2.0	1.7	1.3	1.4	2.1	1.4	3.1	1.2	0.9	1.3	1.7
PRI-Lib-Eldr	Valid votes	11949	20199	1890	1056	24704	7991	1040	5917	13719	1955	166679
	%	1.4	0.7	0.3	0.6	0.9	0.4	0.3	0.6	0.6	0.3	0.5
SDI	Valid votes	15,321	60,981	18,835	4,681	122,615	78,359	11,755	45,078	46,229	11,096	664,174
	%	1.8	2.2	2.7	2.7	4.7	4.0	3.8	4.8	2.1	1.4	2.1
PDCI	Valid votes	26,633	56,058	16,060	2,339	40,988	29,629	5,521	25,628	22,353	19,066	615,975
	%	3.2	2.0	2.3	1.3	1.6	1.5	1.8	2.7	1.0	2.4	2.0
I Democratici	Valid votes	61,959	185,261	72,221	42,927	190,009	197,026	36,853	75,414	212,122	34,052	2,380,931
	%	7.3	6.7	10.4	24.6	7.2	9.9	12.0	8.0	9.4	4.3	7.7
UV	Valid votes	–	–	–	–	–	–	–	–	–	–	41,142
	%											0.1
SVP	Valid votes	–	–	–	–	–	–	–	–	–	–	155,128
	%											0.5
U.D.Eur	Valid votes	3,619	27,272	9,799	1,312	134,637	34,374	10,316	41,144	158,855	18,231	496,926
	%	0.4	1.0	1.4	0.7	5.1	1.7	3.4	4.4	7.1	2.3	1.6
CDU	Valid votes	24,222	35,470	20,877	6,836	61,987	38,052	9,018	35,237	30,662	16,481	663,901
	%	2.9	1.3	3.0	3.9	2.4	1.9	2.9	3.8	1.4	2.1	2.1
PRC	Valid votes	46,858	133,219	31,763	5,961	104,469	65,894	11,815	40,096	50,172	37,436	1,321,843
	%	5.5	4.9	4.6	3.4	4.0	3.3	3.9	4.3	2.2	4.8	4.3

LN	Valid votes	3,697	3,903	1,186	441	4,932	2,577	1,082	2,267	2,375	756	1,393,502
	%	0.4	0.1	0.2	0.3	0.2	0.1	0.4	0.3	0.1	0.1	4.5
FI	Valid votes	179,789	565,211	170,898	36,314	663,937	556,954	55,449	200,766	603,120	231,502	7,799,328
	%	21.3	20.6	24.5	20.8	25.3	28.0	18.1	21.4	26.9	29.6	25.2
AN-P. Segni	Valid votes	104,654	558,581	85,983	16,962	281,695	252,371	26,867	95,983	271,783	99,735	3,195,180
	%	12.4	20.4	12.3	9.7	10.7	12.7	8.8	10.2	12.1	12.7	10.3
CCD	Valid votes	17,305	94,888	22,563	5,904	114,261	82,155	10,394	52,877	146,879	12,160	803,815
	%	2.0	3.5	3.2	3.4	4.3	4.1	3.4	5.6	6.5	1.6	2.6
Lista Bonino	Valid votes	64,112	219,588	49,355	9,653	115,553	94,448	12,055	33,137	85,855	66,658	2,621,772
	%	7.6	8.0	7.1	5.5	4.4	4.8	3.9	3.5	3.8	8.5	8.5
MS-FT	Valid votes	18,130	64,915	16,290	4,122	47,961	46,553	5,455	16,683	35,182	11,776	492,023
	%	2.1	2.4	2.3	2.4	1.8	2.3	1.8	1.8	1.6	1.5	1.6
Cito	Valid votes	1,008	3,728	1,732	719	7,267	47,199	3,003	4,449	4,408	880	92,335
	%	0.1	0.1	0.2	0.4	0.3	2.4	1.0	0.5	0.2	0.1	0.3
P. pensionati	Valid votes	5,064	13,828	3,306	797	11,190	7,236	1,246	3,800	7,710	4,843	229,068
	%	0.6	0.5	0.5	0.5	0.4	0.4	0.4	0.4	0.3	0.6	0.7
LDR	Valid votes	605	3,627	718	225	2,210	2,369	469	1,159	2,030	20,009	58,786
	%	0.1	0.1	0.1	0.1	0.1	0.1	0.1	0.1	0.1	2.6	0.2
P. Umanista	Valid votes	587	1,972	–	–	–	–	–	–	–	–	14,962
	%	0.1	0.1									0.0
Liga rep. ven.	Valid votes	–	–	–	–	–	–	–	–	–	–	117,726
	%											0.4
Cobas	Valid votes	541	1,996	–	–	–	–	–	–	–	–	4,286
	%	0.1	0.1									0.0
Socialista	Valid votes	–	–	–	–	–	–	–	–	33,749	6,249	39,998
	%									1.5	0.8	0.1
Totale	Valid votes	845,462	2,744,314	696,874	174,671	2,628,169	1,987,890	306,591	938,618	2,244,722	783,272	30,956,901
	%	100.0	100.0	100.0	100.0	100.0	100.0	100.0	100.0	100.0	100.0	100.0

Source: Istituto Cattaneo re-eleboration of Ministry of the Interior figures.

Table B8 *By-elections held on 9 May 1999*

No.	Region	Candidates	Votes	%	Party support	Electorate	Voters	Invalid votes	Blank Ballots	% voting	Invalid votes (%)
1	Emilia-R.	**Manzella Andrea**	69,824	62.9	Ulivo	218,923	117,505	6,515	2,896	53.7	5.5
		Ridolfi Rodolfo	34,380	31.0	FI, AN, CCD						
		Monti Mauro	6,786	6.1	LN						
5	Veneto	**Stifoni Piergiorgio**	27,964	33.0	LN	196,271	89,265	4,434	2,036	45.5	5.0
		Pasqualetto Lucio	23,510	27.7	Polo						
		Casotto Sergio	21,230	25.0	Ulivo						
		Dogà Pietro	4,806	5.7	Lega delle regioni						
20	Puglia	**Tatarella Salvatore**	24,505	57.5	FI, CCD, Dem. di centro, Cdl	107,525	46,050	3,050	693 M.	42.8	6.6 pugliese/
					Amb. club, AN	Puglia,					
		Tedesco Alberto	15,956	37.4	Ulivo						
		Diomede Michele	2,192	5.1	Grande sud						
7	Puglia	**Maritati Alberto**	47,929	53.8	Ulivo	189,390	94,891	5,755	2,389	50.1	6.1
		Camilli Fabrizio	41,207	46.2	Polo						
24	Lombardia	**Rebecchi Aldo**	18,266	43.1	Ulivo	97,862	45,059	4,779	1,433	46.0	10.6
		Bontempi Giacomo	15,406	36.3	Polo						
		Orizio Battista	7,580	17.9	LN, Pens. padani, Impr. padani, Cobas terra, Cattolici padani						
		Manzoni Sandro	1,127	2.7	Italia unita						

Table B8 *By-elections held on 28 November 1999*

No.	Region	Candidates	Votes	%	Party support	Electorate	Voters	Invalid votes	Blank Ballots	% voting	Invalid votes (%)
6	**Marche**	**Mascioni Giuseppe**	41.178	49,1	Ulivo	184.718	88.760	4.915	2.049	48,1	5,5
		Cicoli Claudio	30.708	36,6	Polo						
		Cecchini M. Cristina	11.959	14,3	PRC						
6	**Umbria**	**Micheli Enrico Luigi**	27.572	54,8	Ulivo	102.579	53.186	2.902	779	51,8	5,5
		Melasecche Germini Enrico	18.507	36,8	CCD, FI, AN						
		Botondi Guido	4.205	8,4	PRC						
8	**Toscana**	**Ventura Michele**	27.109	56,8	Ulivo	103.141	50.920	3.180	1.231	49,4	6,2
		Bosi Enrico	14.113	29,6	FI, AN, CCD						
		Barbagli Giovanni	5.728	12,0	PRC						
		Vennarini Franca	771	1,6	LN						
12	**Emilia-R.**	**Parisi Arturo**	31.011	48,9	Ulivo	100.703	65.118	1.633	473	64,7	2,5
		Tura Sante	28.625	45,1	FI, AN, CCD, CDU, Governare Bologna						
		Loreti Tiziano	2.852	4,5	PRC						
		Banasiak Anna	731	1,2	LN						
		Busin Marc	187	0,3	Italia u. lib. dem.						
5	**Basilicata**	**Luongo Antonio**	25.732	65,5	Ulivo	103.655	44.395	5.113	1.902	42,8	11,5
		Sissinni Francesco	13.542	34,5	FI, AN, CCD						

Source: Istituto Cattaneo re-elaboration of Ministry of the Interior figures.

Table B9 *Referendum on the abolition of the proportional quota in the electoral law, 18 April, 1999.*

	Electors	Voters	Valid votes	Votes for	% for	Votes against	% against	Invalid votes	Blank ballots	% voting	% invalid votes
Piedmont	3,669,338	1,917,111	1,804,198	1,614,726	89.5	189,472	10.5	112,913	44,583	52.1	5.8
Valle D'aosta	102,670	43,804	40,609	36,960	91.0	3,649	9.0	3,195	1,656	42.7	7.3
Lombardy	7,584,837	3,990,836	3,798,242	3,398,792	89.5	399,450	10.5	192,594	86,254	52.7	4.8
Trentino-Alto Adige	767,182	354,885	333,466	250,991	75.2	82,475	24.8	21,419	12,090	46.3	6.0
Venetia	3,831,075	2,156,498	2,046,877	1,875,347	91.6	171,530	8.4	109,621	41,647	56.3	5.1
Friuli-Venezia Giulia	1,085,745	517,704	493,964	451,429	91.4	42,535	8.6	23,740	9,637	47.7	4.6
Liguria	1,442,737	714,591	680,487	622,720	91.5	57,767	8.5	34,104	14,502	49.5	5.2
Emilia-Romagna	3,430,677	2,130,291	2,038,008	1,889,353	92.7	148,655	7.3	92,283	45,700	62.1	4.3
Tuscany	3,033,632	1,684,084	1,608,695	1,484,993	92.3	123,702	7.7	75,389	33,379	55.5	4.5
Umbria	712,453	398,673	383,325	354,775	92.6	28,550	7.4	15,348	6,541	56.0	3.8
Marches	1,257,596	714,781	671,294	623,241	92.8	48,053	7.2	43,487	19,316	56.9	6.1
Lazio	4,469,308	2,318,642	2,219,766	2,068,962	93.2	150,804	6.8	98,876	34,302	51.9	4.3
Abruzzi	1,179,323	607,206	573,800	535,737	93.4	38,063	6.6	33,406	14,697	51.5	5.5
Molise	324,547	147,357	136,075	127,245	93.5	8,830	6.5	11,282	4,597	45.4	7.6
Campania	4,746,741	1,938,930	1,829,283	1,694,396	92.6	134,887	7.4	109,647	46,186	40.8	5.7
Apulia	3,431,754	1,591,390	1,486,401	1,382,486	93.0	103,915	7.0	104,989	42,729	46.4	6.6
Basilicata	530,900	222,573	202,717	186,023	91.8	16,694	8.2	19,856	7,626	41.9	8.9
Calabria	1,814,576	632,010	577,753	533,320	92.3	44,433	7.7	54,257	22,041	34.8	8.6
Sicily	4,465,188	1,757,102	1,605,636	1,482,679	92.3	122,957	7.7	151,466	60,921	39.4	8.6
Sardinia	1,418,870	613,886	587,700	546,538	93.0	41,162	7.0	26,186	9,157	43.3	4.3
Total	49,299,149	24,452,354	23,118,296	21,160,713	91.5	1,957,583	8.5	1,334,058	557,561	49.6	5.5

Source: Istituto Cattaneo re-elaboration of Ministry of the Interior figures.

Table C1 *Composition of the second D'Alema government (21 December 1999)*

Minister	Party	Ministry	Junior ministers
Massimo D'Alema	DS	Prime Minister	8
Antonio Maccanico	RI	Institutional Reform	
Laura Balbo	DS	Equal Opportunities	
Katia Bellillo	PDCI	Regional Affairs	
Agazio Loiero	UDEUR	Relations with Parliament	
Franco Bassanini	DS	Public Administration	
Livia Turco	DS	Social Affairs	
Patrizia Toia	PPI	European Union	
Lamberto Dini	RI	Foreign Affairs	4
Oliviero Diliberto	PDCI	Justice	4
Enzo Bianco	Democrats	Interior	5
Vincenzo Visco	DS	Finance	3
Giuliano Amato	Non-party	Treasury	4
Sergio Mattarella	PPI	Defence	3
Luigi Berlinguer	DS	Education	4
Willer Bordon	Democrats	Public Works	4
Salvatore Cardinale	UDEUR	Telecommunications	2
Enrico Letta	PPI	Trade and Industry	3
Cesare Salvi	DS	Labour and Pensions	4
Piero Fassino	DS	Foreign Trade	1
Rosy Bindi	PPI	Health	3
Giovanna Melandri	DS	Cultural Affairs	2
Edo Ronchi	Verdi	Environment	2
Ortensio Zecchino	PPI	Universities and Technology	3
Paolo de Castro	Non-party	Agriculture and Forestry	2
Pierluigi Bersani	DS	Transport	3

About the Editors and Contributors

Gianfranco Baldini is temporary lecturer in the department of Politics, History and Institutions of the University of Bologna and contract lecturer in Political Science at the University of Calabria.

Jean Louis Briquet is a lecturer at the CNRS, *Centre d'études et de recherches internationales*, in Paris.

Michael Contarino is "Class of 1940 University Professor" at the University of New Hampshire.

Osvaldo Croci is Associate professor in the department of Political Science at Memorial University of Newfoundland.

Philip Daniels is Senior lecturer in European politics at the University of Newcastle upon Tyne.

Vincent Della Sala is Associate professor in the department of Political Science at Carleton University, Ottowa.

Mark Donovan is Director of Politics in the School of European studies at the Cardiff college of the University of Wales.

Mark Gilbert is lecturer in Italian History and Politics in the department of European Studies at the University of Bath. In 1999–2000, he was Professorial lecturer at the Johns Hopkins School of Advanced International Studies and Visiting professor in both the department of Sociology at the University of Trento and the Dickinson College Center for European Studies in Bologna.

Guido Legnante is a doctoral candidate at the European University Institute and also works at the University of Pavia.

Davide Martelli is a researcher at the Istituto Cattaneo.

Gianfranco Pasquino is Professor of Political Science at the University of Bologna and Adjunct professor at the Johns Hopkins School of Advanced International Studies in Bologna.

Véronique Pujas teaches Political Science and Political Sociology at the *Institut d'études politiques* at Grenoble.

Dwayne Woods is Associate professor of Political science in the department of Political Science at Purdue University, West Lafayette, Indiana.

INDEX

Abete, Luigi, 57
ACLI 60, 62
Agnelli, Giovanni, 14
Agnes, Biagio, 161, 162
Albright, Madeleine, 44
Alleanza Nazionale (AN), 2, 3, 7, 10,
    14, 23, 24, 30, 57, 58, 59, 62, 63,
    90, 93, 98, 102, 103, 104, 109, 112,
    143, 144, 145, 151
Almirante, Giorgio, 20
Amato, Giuliano, 1, 2, 3, 4, 8, 9, 10,
    11, 12, 15, 16, 17, 32, 59, 113,
    115, 119, 177
AN, *see Alleanza Nazionale*
Andreatta, Beniamino, 9, 19,
Andreotti Giulio, 6, 7, 8, 14, 15, 16,
    25, 26, 29, 108, 111, 118, 123, 124,
    125, 126, 127, 128, 129, 130, 131,
    132, 133, 134, 135
Angius, Gavino, 18
Anti-Mafia Commission, 10, 17, 126
Associazione 14 giugno, 5
Aznar, Josè Maria, 4, 102
Audit Court, 13

Bank of Italy, 9, 18, 26, 108, 191,
    102, 118
Baraldini, Silvia, 14
Barca, Fabrizio, 191
Bartolini, Silvia, 77, 78, 79
Bassanini, Franco, 8, 31, 194
Bassolino, Antonio, 8, 10, 170
Berger, Samuel, 42

Berlinguer, Luigi, 17
Berlusconi, Silvio, 3, 4, 6, 7, 9, 10,
    11, 13, 14, 15, 16, 17, 18, 19, 24,
    26, 27, 29, 30, 52, 54, 55, 57, 59,
    60, 62, 63, 64, 90, 93, 96, 98, 100,
    101, 102, 104, 112, 113, 115, 117,
    127, 133, 139, 140, 145, 147, 148,
    150, 151, 179
Bernabè, Franco, 4, 155, 156, 157,
    158, 159, 161, 162
Bersani, Pier Luigi, 28, 195, 196
Bertinotti, Fausto, 6, 8, 29
Bianchi, Patrizio, 198, 199
Bianco, Enzo, 28
Bicamerale (Joint Committee on
    Constitutional Reform), 52, 53,
    55, 57, 68, 109, 140, 149
Blair, Tony, 5, 95
Bocca, Giorgio, 124
Bompressi, Ovidio, 14, 16
Bonino, Emma, 5, 10, 11, 13, 23, 63,
    90, 95, 100, 113, 114, 115, 117
Bonino List, see Lista Bonino
Bordon, Willer, 28
Borrelli, Francesco Saverio, 6, 13, 17
Boselli, Enrico, 4, 9, 19, 20, 28, 102
Bossi, Umberto, 7, 10, 19, 94, 110,
    113
Brigate Rosse, 8
Buscetta, Tommaso, 130
Buttiglione, Rocco, 4, 12

Cacciari, Massimo, 17

CAF (Craxi-Andreotti-Forlani), 111, 148

Carnevale, Corrado, 130, 131

Caselli, Gian Carlo, 6, 125

Casini, Pierferdinando, 3, 26

Cassa per il Mezzogiorno (Southern Italy Development Found), 31, 186

Castagnetti, Pierluigi, 16, 17, 26, 27, 102

CCD, *see Centro Cristiano Democratico*

CDU, *see Cristiano Democratici Uniti*

Celentano, Rino, 13, 14

Cento Città, 2, 3, 58, 89

Centro Cristiano Democratico (CCD), 26, 102, 144, 145

Cermis, 5, 33, 34

CGIL, 12, 13, 172, 174, 177, 178, 179, 180, 182

Ciampi, Carlo Azeglio, 5, 8, 9, 11, 12, 15, 18, 19, 23, 26, 32, 93, 107, 108, 109, 115, 117, 118, 119, 170, 177, 191

CIPE, 185, 190, 193, 197

Cipolletta, Innocenzo, 11

Cirami, Melchiorre, 144

CISL, 11, 12, 13, 15, 172, 174, 177, 178, 179, 180, 182

Cofferati, Sergio, 2, 11, 12, 14

Colaninno, Roberto, 155, 156, 157, 158, 159, 160, 164, 165, 166

Colombo, Gherardo, 13

Comino, Domenico, 12, 13

Comunione e Liberazione, 14

Confindustria, 4, 11, 14, 57, 60, 62, 172, 174, 178, 179, 182, 199

Consob (Financial market-place watchdog), 4, 156, 159, 165

Constitutional Court, 1, 2, 13, 17, 53, 55, 148

Cosa Nostra, 123, 125, 126, 128, 129, 130, 131, 132, 134

Cossiga, Francesco, 1, 2, 3, 4, 8, 13, 15, 16, 17, 19, 23, 26, 28, 29, 30, 53, 58, 59, 60, 107, 108, 110, 111, 144

Cossutta, Armando, 6, 7, 44

Court of Account, 142

Court of Cassation, 8, 19, 130

Craxi, Bettino, 4, 13, 17, 18, 19, 26, 29, 110, 177

Cristiano Democratici Uniti (CDU), 12, 95, 102

Cuccia, Enrico, 165

D'Alema, Massimo, 1, 2, 3, 4, 5, 6, 7, 8, 9, 10, 11, 12, 13, 14, 15, 16, 17, 18, 19, 20, 21, 22, 23, 25, 27, 28, 29, 30, 31, 32, 37, 38, 41, 42, 43, 44, 45, 46, 47, 48, 52, 53, 57, 58, 59, 64, 68, 87, 88, 89, 90, 94, 95, 96, 99, 100, 103, 104, 112, 117, 119, 149, 166, 170, 179, 192

D'Amato, Antonio, 199

D'Ambrosio Gerardo, 13, 17, 18

D'Antona, Massimo, 8

D'Antoni, Sergio, 13, 14, 15, 26

Dalla Chiesa, Carlo Alberto, 124, 126

DC, *see Democrazia Cristiana*

De Benedetti, Carlo, 154, 155

De Gasperi, Alcide, 112

Delbono, Flavio, 77

Del Turco, Ottaviano, 10

Dell'Utri, Marcello, 5, 7, 12, 26

De Nicola, Enrico, 107

De Mita, Ciriaco, 107

Democratici di Sinistra (DS), 1, 2, 3, 6, 7, 8, 11, 13, 15, 16, 18, 19, 23, 24, 25, 27, 34, 40, 41, 52, 56, 57, 58, 59, 60, 62, 65, 68, 72, 74, 75, 79, 89, 90, 94, 96, 99, 103, 104, 112, 113, 115, 117, 118, 133, 145, 148, 180, 182

Democratici per l'Ulivo, 3, 4, 6, 10, 12, 13, 15, 16, 19, 21, 24, 25, 27, 28, 58, 59, 63, 64, 72, 77, 88, 89, 90, 91, 93, 94, 95, 96, 98, 99, 102, 103, 144, 146

Democrats, see Democratici per l'Ulivo

Democrats of the Left, see Democratici di Sinistra

Democrazia Cristiana (DC), 12, 18, 23, 25, 30, 53, 54, 75, 95, 101, 107, 110, 111, 113, 114, 123, 124, 125, 126, 129, 132, 133, 141, 161, 177

Diliberto, Oliviero, 14, 19

Dini, Lamberto, 7, 13, 17, 26, 32, 34, 39, 41, 43, 44, 52, 64, 113, 175, 177, 179

Di Pietro, Antonio, 2, 3, 4, 7, 14, 15, 19, 27, 56, 57, 58, 59, 72, 89, 144, 145

DPEF (Economic and Financial Plan-
  ning, Document), 11
DPSC, 191, 192, 193, 197, 199
Draghi, Mario, 159, 160
DS, *see Democratici di Sinistra*

ECOFIN, 9
Einaudi, Luigi, 114
ENEL (National Electric Company),
  17
ENI, 161, 162, 196
EU (European Union), 1, 30, 39, 47,
  48, 76, 91, 95, 149, 172, 190, 191,
  192, 193, 196, 197, 198
European Commission, 1, 3, 4, 5, 6,
  10, 11, 21, 59, 89, 90, 91, 118, 187,
  192, 193
European Parliament, 7, 8, 10, 24,
  26, 63, 68, 71, 87, 91, 96, 98, 100,
  102, 103, 104

Falcone, Giovanni, 111
Fanfani, Amintore, 129
Fazio, Antonio, 5, 11, 17, 18, 26, 108
FIAT, 11, 164, 189
FMI, *see International Monetary
  Found*
Fini, Gianfranco, 7, 9, 15, 18, 19, 23,
  59, 63, 64, 93, 98, 109, 110, 112,
  113, 117, 144, 145
First and Second Republic, 4, 25, 51,
  52, 53, 54, 57, 88, 110, 123, 124,
  133, 140, 151, 176, 180, 187
Folena, Pietro, 126
Folloni, Gianguido, 12
Forlani, Arnaldo, 111
Formigoni, Roberto, 15
Forza Italia (FI), 3, 5, 9, 13, 19, 22,
  24, 30, 56, 57, 58, 60, 62, 65, 72,
  90, 91, 93, 95, 100, 101, 102, 104,
  112, 113, 140, 143, 144, 145, 147,
  148, 149, 150
Fossa, Giorgio, 9, 14
Francescato, Grazia, 12, 17
Franceschini, Dario, 14

Garzòn, Baltazar, 26
Gasperini, Luciano, 108
Giarda, Piero, 5
Giordano, Michele, 18
Giovanardi, Carlo, 144
Gnutti, Vito, 13
Grasso, Pietro, 125

Greens, see Verdi
Gronchi, Giovanni, 107, 110, 111
Guazzaloca, Giorgio, 10, 25, 74, 75,
  76, 79, 81, 82

Holbrooke, Richard, 36, 38, 39
Hundred Cities, see Cento città

Illy, Riccardo, 82
Ingrao, Pietro, 108
International Monetary Found, 12
Iotti, Nilde, 18, 19
IRI, 161, 163, 195, 197
Italia dei Valori (l'), 2, 4, 57, 89, 143
*Italian Communists, see Partito dei
  Comunisti Italiani*
*Italian Renewal, see Rinnovamento
  Italiano*
*Italy of Values, see Italia dei Valori
  (l')*

Jervolino, Rosa Russo, 8, 12, 15, 28,
  108, 117

Kohl, Helmut, 102

La Forgia, Antonio, 3
La Malfa, Giorgio, 19, 28
Larizza, Pietro, 13, 14
Lega, see Lega Nord
Lega Nord (LN), 10, 12, 13, 19, 28,
  54, 60, 70, 94, 98, 108, 110, 113,
  144, 145, 187
Leone, Giovanni, 108, 111
Le Pen, Jean-Marie, 13
Liberty Pole, see Polo delle Libertà
Libonati, Bernardino, 156
Lima, Salvo, 126, 129, 132, 134
Lista Bonino, 10, 24, 25, 63, 72, 91,
  93, 94, 99, 100, 103, 104, 147
LN, *see Lega Nord*
Luccherini, Luigi, 82

Maccanico, Antonio, 10, 148
Mafia, 25, 124, 125, 126, 127, 129,
  130, 131, 134
Mancino, Nicola, 7, 16, 17, 108, 116
Manconi, Luigi, 5, 10, 11, 96
Mani Pulite, 6, 13
Marini, Franco, 1, 2, 4, 6, 7, 8, 9, 10,
  11, 15, 22, 24, 96, 108, 109, 110,
  111, 112, 114, 115, 116, 117
Martinazzoli, Mino, 11, 18, 108

Martino, Antonio, 102
Martone, 17
Mastella, Clemente, 4, 13, 28
Mattarella, Sergio, 117
Mediaset, 147, 148, 149, 164
Mediobanca, 158, 164, 165, 166
Milosevic, Slobodan, 7, 36, 38, 39, 46
Misserville, Romano, 20, 29
Missione Arcobaleno, 45
Mitrokhin (dossier), 16, 18, 26
Monti, Mario, 11, 12,
Moro, Aldo, 107, 124, 126
Movimento Sociale Italiano (MSI), 20
MSI, *see Movimento Sociale Italiano*
Mussi, Fabio, 18

National Association of Magistrates, 17
NATO, 6, 8, 22, 33, 34, 35, 36, 37, 38, 39, 40, 41, 42, 43, 44, 45, 46, 48, 90, 95

Ocalan, Abdullah, 2, 33
Occhetto, Achille, 5, 57
Olive Tree, see Ulivo
Olive Tree Coalition, see Ulivo
Olivetti (Private phone company), 4, 7, 30, 153, 154, 155, 156, 157, 158, 159, 160, 163, 165
Omnitel, 16, 154, 158
Operation Allied Force, 33, 34, 36, 42, 44, 45, 47
Operazione Alba, 37, 44

Pact, *see Patto Sociale*
Padre Pio, 8
Pannella, Marco, 10, 11, 13, 55, 56, 57, 63, 100, 111
Parisi, Arturo, 12, 14, 16, 17, 18, 27, 81, 99
Partito Comunista Italiano (PCI), 57, 75, 78, 79, 100, 126, 177
Partito dei Comunisti Italiani (PDCI), 3, 6, 7, 14, 19, 41, 44, 58, 59, 95, 144
Partito Democratico della Sinistra (PDS), 57, 75, 78, 79, 177
Partito della Rifondazione Comunista (PRC), 5, 6, 44, 54, 57, 58, 59, 70, 72, 89, 95, 108, 145, 195
Partito Popolare Italiano (PPI), 1, 2, 3, 4, 5, 6, 7, 8, 11, 13, 15, 16, 19,

22, 23, 24, 26, 28, 41, 54, 57, 59, 72, 89, 94, 95, 96, 101, 102, 108, 109, 110, 111, 112, 115, 116, 117, 145, 148
Partito radicale, 5, 7, 12, 13, 19, 23, 55, 57, 90, 94, 100, 111, 113, 141, 144, 147, 151
Partito Repubblicano Italiano (PRI), 41
Partito Socialista Italiano (PSI), 18, 25, 53, 110, 141, 161, 177
Pascale, Ernesto, 161, 162
Passigli, Stefano, 20, 56
Patto di Natale, 31, 171
Patto Segni, *93*
Patto sociale, 5, 169, 170, 171, 172, 173, 174, 175, 176, 178, 179, 180, 181, 182
PCI, *see Partito Comunista Italiano*
PDCI, *see Partito dei Comunisti Italiani*
PDS, *see Partito Democratico della Sinistra*
Pecorelli, Mino, 8, 15, 123
Pennacchi, Laura, 11
Pertini, Sandro, 111, 114
Piazza, Angelo, 8
Pietrostefani, Giorgio, 14, 16
Pili, Mauro, 15
Pivetti, Irene, 8, 17, 28
Polo, see Polo delle Libertà
Polo delle Libertà, 1, 2, 3, 7, 8, 9, 10, 11, 12, 13, 16, 23, 24, 25, 26, 27, 29, 44, 53, 59, 60, 72, 93, 96, 98, 108, 109, 112, 114, 115, 117, 118, 149
Pontone, Francesco, 143
Pope, 1, 8, 17
PPI, *see Partito Popolare Italiano*
PRC, *see Partito della Rifondazione Comunista*
Previti, Cesare, 15, 18
PRI, *see Partito Repubblicano Italiano*
Prodi, Romano, 1, 2, 3, 4, 5, 6, 7, 8, 9, 10, 11, 12, 15, 19, 21, 22, 23, 24, 25, 26, 27, 28, 44, 52, 58, 59, 60, 63, 64, 75, 81, 89, 90, 91, 94, 99, 100, 102, 112, 118, 144, 145, 170, 174, 177, 179, 189, 191, 192, 195
Progressives, see Progressisti (i)
Progressisti (i), 54

PSI, see *Partito Socialista Italiano*

Radicals, see *Partito radicale*
Ramazza, Alessandro, 75, 76
Ranieri, Umberto, 40, 47
Red Brigades, see *Brigate Rosse*
RI, see *Rinnovamento Italianoù*
Rinnovamento Italiano (RI), 19, 41, 102
Romiti, Cesare, 14
Rossi, Guido, 162
Rossignolo, Gian Mario, 162
Rugova, Ibrahim, 35, 38, 44

Sabbatini, Sergio, 145
Salvati, Michele, 31, 40
Salvi, Cesare, 10, 12, 18
Salvo, Ignazio, 130, 131
Santer, Jaques, 89, 90, 118
Sartori, Giovanni, 55, 56, 64
Sbacchi, Gioacchino, 131, 132
Scalfaro, Oscar Luigi, 1, 4, 5, 6, 7, 8, 14, 23, 45, 108, 109, 110, 111, 112, 116, 119
Schroeder, Gerard, 95
Scieri, Emanuele, 13
Scognamiglio, Carlo, 46
SDI, see *Socialisti Democratici Italiani*
Segni, Antonio, 110
Segni, Mario, 7, 9, 15, 55, 56, 59, 62, 63, 98, 141
Sindona, Michele, 124, 126
Social Pact, see *Patto sociale*
Socialisti Democratici Italiani (SDI), 19, 26, 28, 41, 103
Sofri, Adriano, 14, 16
Solana, Javier, 37, 48
Spaventa, Luigi, 4, 165
Sviluppo Italia (Development Italy), 31, 173, 185, 186, 194, 195, 196, 197, 198, 199, 200
Sudtiroler Volkspartei (SVP), 102
SVP, see *Sudtiroler Volkspartei*

Tangentopoli, 15, 26, 29, 57, 133, 140, 151
Tecnost, 155, 156, 158, 159, 163, 165, 166
Telecom, see Telecom Italia
Telecom Italia (National phone company), 4, 7, 8, 9, 16, 30, 153, 154, 155, 156, 157, 158, 159, 160, 161, 162, 163, 164, 165, 166
TIM, 16, 156, 157, 165, 166
Toghe sporche, 18
Tommasi di Vignano, Tommaso, 162
Treu, Tiziano, 11, 28
Trifoglio, 19, 20, 28, 29, 30
Tua Bologna (la), 25, 79
Tura, Sante, 81

UDEUR, see *Unione dei Democratici Europei*
UDR, see *Unione Democratica per la Repubblica*
UIL, 11, 12, 13, 172, 174, 177, 178, 179, 182
Ulivo, 1, 2, 3, 5, 7, 9, 12, 15, 16, 17, 18, 26, 27, 28, 52, 54, 58, 59, 72, 73, 81, 89, 99, 104, 108
UN (United Nations), 39
Unione dei Democratici Europei (UDEUR), 8, 17, 19, 20, 28, 29, 72, 102
Unione Democratica per la Repubblica (UDR), 2, 3, 4, 41, 53, 58, 59, 60, 144
UNSC (United Nations Security Council), 34, 38, 39, 43, 44, 46
Urbani, Giuliano, 60

Valiani, Leo, 15,
Vassalli, Giuliano, 17
Vatican, 1, 45
Veltri, Elio, 143
Veltroni, Walter, 2, 3, 5, 7, 8, 9, 10, 11, 12, 13, 15, 16, 17, 18, 23, 27, 58, 94, 112, 114, 115
Verdi, 1, 5, 6, 7, 8, 11, 12, 19, 41, 44, 57, 59, 95, 96, 141
Violante, Luciano, 15, 16, 17
Visco, Vincenzo, 11
Vitali, Walter, 75, 76, 79
Vitalone, Claudio, 15

Your Bologna, see *Tua Bologna (la)*

Zani, Mauro, 11, 76
Zevi, Bruno, 13